37/-

ECONOMICS and the
PUBLIC INTEREST

ECONOMICS and

Goodyear Publishing Company

RICHARD T. GILL
Harvard University

the PUBLIC INTEREST

PACIFIC PALISADES, CALIFORNIA

ECONOMICS AND THE PUBLIC INTEREST
Richard T. Gill

© Copyright 1968 by

Goodyear Publishing Company
Pacific Palisades, California

Library of Congress Catalog Card Number: 68-15758

Current printing (last number):
10 9 8 7 6 5 4 3 2 1

Designed by Maurine Lewis

Printed in the United States of America

Preface

This book has been written for students taking a one-semester course in economics and for interested citizens who wish a general introduction to modern economic analysis. It attempts to fill the gap that has long existed between the comprehensive textbook that treats every conceivable aspect of the field and the occasional popular article that describes (without analyzing) what modern economics is about. In an age when economic issues affect every individual in the nation, the need for a concise but still authoritative account of economic analysis is particularly pressing.

In a book of this length, selection is all important. The key, in this instance, is suggested by the title, *Economics and the Public Interest*. In choosing what to include and what to exclude, I have constantly asked the following question: what are the issues of public concern on which economic analysis has the most direct and immediate bearing? The theoretical structure of the book is dominated by this objective. The tools of analysis are developed not in isolation, but as useful tools to be applied to matters of pressing national concern. After studying this book, the reader should be able to make informed and intelligent judgments on those areas of our common life in which the forces of economics and the interest of the public as a whole are intertwined.

Given this objective, the balance of the book is somewhat different from that of the comprehensive textbook on economic principles. The treatment of formal price theory is relatively brief. By contrast, the discussion of macroeconomics—national income, unemployment, inflation, the balance of payments, modern economic growth—is more extensive. By picking and choosing in this way, I hoped to avoid the major danger of such a study: presenting a merely descriptive account of the work in the field. The analytic arguments presented in these pages will require the full and serious attention of the reader. Economics is ultimately a systematic subject; and unless that systematic structure is carefully studied, fundamentals of the discipline will be misunderstood.

In preparing my manuscript, I drew heavily on eight years' experience as director of the Principles of Economics course at Harvard College. I have also drawn on the experience of offering a fifteen-week television course on economics, on the New England Educational Television channel. In the television course, I was obliged to observe a principle of selection similar to that which has guided the writing of this book. The experience made me aware of some of the difficulties of conveying the fundamental principles of economics in a brief compass, but it also made me aware of the possibility and desirability of doing so.

One's indebtedness to other people in preparing a book of this nature is always very large. I have a special debt to Dr. Kenneth Deitch who has utilized his rich background as the head of the section staff of the Harvard Economics I course, to give me detailed criticisms of every chapter in the text. Dr. Deitch has also prepared the *Instructor's Manual* and *Student Guide*. Mr. Robert Edelstein helped in the preparation of many of the statistical tables. Professor Charles Frodigh, Hudson Valley Community College; Professor James B. Herendeen, The Pennsylvania State University; Professor John M. Kuhlman, The University of Missouri; and Professor John E. Sayre, Boston University, read rough drafts of the text and made numerous helpful comments. More generally, I am indebted to all my colleagues and students, who have collectively taught me whatever I have learned about communicating the fundamentals of economics, and to my wife, whose patience and enthusiasm have made this undertaking possible.

RICHARD T. GILL

Contents

part **III** PROBLEMS OF GROWTH,
DEVELOPMENT, AND AFFLUENCE

14

Modern
economic growth 219

15

The
underdeveloped
countries 243

16

The problems
of affluence 265

I

THE MODERN ECONOMY
Problems and Institutions

The economic problem

1

We all know something about economics because we are everyday participants in the economic life of our society. "Getting and spending, we lay waste our powers," complained Wordsworth, and the complaint has decided relevance for a modern industrial economy. We do pass a great many of our waking hours "getting and spending." If we are clever, we even try to economize during the process. We try to economize on the things we buy; we try to economize on the time and effort we put into producing the products or services we are offering for sale.

In these respects, we are taking part in the economic system of the country, and we daily gain certain insights into how that system functions.

At other times, however, economics seems

to be dealing with matters that are far removed from our personal knowledge and experience and, indeed, that seem far outside our personal control. The stock market rises or falls. Millions of people in India are starving. The general cost of living is going up. At such moments we feel we are being managed by external forces and we are inclined to say, as Mark Twain did about the weather: "Everybody talks about it, but nobody does anything about it." At such moments, the study of economics seems interesting, but also obscure and difficult.

Economic Breakdowns~
Past and Present

The remarkable thing about a modern industrial economy is that it functions so smoothly. We become *aware* of this remarkable fact, however, mainly when the system breaks down. And let no one mistake the fact: economic systems do break down, and, when they do, the costs and consequences are incalculable.

Take Germany after World War I. A general rise in prices during and after a major war is not very unusual, but in Germany the forces of inflation went so wild that they virtually destroyed the fabric of the society. Figure 1-1 shows· what happened to the wholesale price level in Germany in the 1920's, but only up to a point. By 1922, the numbers would push the curve off the top of the page of this book and, indeed, up through the ceiling of any ordinary-sized room. By 1923, the curve would be out of sight in the clouds. In September, 1923, German wholesale prices, in terms of marks, had risen *24 million times* above the level of a decade earlier. Two months later, the figure was close to a trillion! No wonder that people used wheelbarrows to bring home their weekly pay, or found marks cheaper than wallpaper for the walls of their homes!

Or take the United States in the year 1933. This was the worst year of the Great Depression when anywhere from 12 to 14 million Americans were out of work—25 per cent or more of our entire labor force. The personal suffering involved in this social catastrophe is hard to imagine. The Mayor of Youngstown, Ohio recorded this not untypical newspaper item of the period:

FATHER OF TEN DROWNS SELF

*Jumps from Bridge, Starts to Swim
Gives Up, Out of Work Two Years*

Out of work two years, Charles Wayne, aged 57, father of ten children,

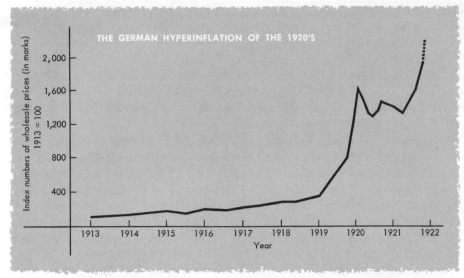

FIG. 1-1

This is an example of an inflation that got completely out of hand. By November, 1923 in Germany, the index of wholesale prices that had stood at 100 in 1913 reached the level of 73 trillion!

stood on the Spring Common bridge this morning, watching hundreds of other persons moving by on their way to work. Then he took off his coat, folded it carefully, and jumped into the swirling Mahoning River. Wayne was born in Youngstown and was employed by the Republic Iron and Steel Company for twenty-seven years as a hot mill worker.

"We were about to lose our home," sobbed Mrs. Wayne. "And the gas and electric companies had threatened to shut off the service." [1]

Such an item may seem melodramatic to the citizens of the affluent society of the 1960's, but in point of fact the burdens of unemployment were felt in every nook and cranny of American society in the 1930's. Even the educated and well-to-do were in deep trouble as this item from *The New York Times* attests: [2]

Organization of the Association of Unemployed College Alumni was announced yesterday after a meeting of graduates of nine eastern colleges at the offices of the League for Industrial Democracy. Estimating the number of unemployed alumni in this city alone at more than 10,000, the association made public a plan of action designed to enlist members throughout the country.

. . . . .

[1] Joseph L. Heffernan, "The Hungry City: A Mayor's Experience with Unemployment," *The Atlantic Monthly*, May, 1932.
[2] *The New York Times*, July 27, 1932.

Colleges represented at the meeting included Columbia, Harvard, New York University, Vassar, Hunter, City College, Swarthmore, Columbia Law School, and New York Dental School.

The Great Depression played few favorites—it struck at rich and poor alike!

These are historic episodes, but they could easily be duplicated in various parts of the world today. We have already mentioned starvation in India. Two successive droughts in 1965 and 1966 have brought a famine condition to that underdeveloped country in which, despite considerable assistance from abroad, the suffering is exceeding anything we knew in the Great Depression or perhaps in the entire course of American history. Latin-American countries are somewhat better off than are the desperately poverty-stricken countries of Asia, but even in Latin America we find many major cities ringed by slums in which living conditions are indescribably bad. The *favelas* of Rio de Janeiro, on the hillsides above the city, sometimes have a beautiful view, but

The shacks are often perched most precariously on steep slopes, supported by fragile wooden piles; sometimes, in a heavy tropical rainstorm, several come tumbling down, killing the inhabitants. The alleyways between the shacks are, of course, unpaved, and the houses follow no regular order. Sewers are totally lacking, and the only way to dispose of human waste and garbage is a copious rainfall. These *favelas*, of course, emit an overpowering stench, especially during the dry periods, which plagues not only the *favelados* (residents of the *favelas*), but also those who live nearby in what are often fashionable neighborhoods. *Favelas* also lack a public water supply, except at a few points where the city may have set up a public fountain or where the *favelados* may have opened up a fire plug of their own accord. In Rio, a common sight is that of women and children carrying water up the steep hillside in kerosene tins, an onerous task that keeps them busy several hours a day.[3]

For that matter, we do not really have to go abroad to find evidences of breakdowns in modern economic life. One of the curious facts about present-day economics is that the discovery of American affluence went hand in hand with the discovery of American poverty. Numerous writers have noticed that although our society in general is strikingly rich—on the average richer than any major society in the

[3] Charles Wagley, *An Introduction to Brazil* (New York: Columbia University Press, 1963), p. 117.

history of the world—nevertheless, there are important groups in our society where *relative* poverty is intense, and also surprisingly difficult to remedy. Sometimes the poverty is regional, as in Appalachia, which attracted the late President Kennedy's great concern. Sometimes it is a by-product of our urban-industrial way of life, as in the problem of our "inner cities" whose deterioration is now a major social and economic threat. Sometimes, poverty is a problem of special groups in the society, the Negro, the elderly, the uneducated, the physically or mentally handicapped.

Poverty of this sort does not represent a breakdown of our economic system comparable to the Great Depression. But it does indicate that the economic mechanisms of even the most strikingly successful national economies do have their flaws. And this causes us to wonder why such flaws should occur. Or—what comes to the same thing—it causes us to wonder how the modern economic system functions in the first place.

Character of Economic Problems

If we were to try to link together the various problems we have been discussing, we should find, I believe, that they had certain common characteristics.

One such characteristic is that they usually have a *quantitative* side to them. If we look deeply enough at almost any economic problem we will sooner or later find some quantities—numbers—involved. We spoke of "getting and spending," and what we get and spend is, among other things, money; and money is measured numerically: so many dollars, so many marks, so many pesos. Furthermore, we typically get money by producing certain goods that we sell for certain prices. How much money we get depends on what quantities of goods we produce and how many dollars per unit the goods will sell for—both numbers.

Indeed, whenever we consider what we loosely think of as "economic" problems, we invariably seem to meet with these numbers. We may be concerned about the price level (a number); or the percentage of the labor force unemployed (a number); or the poverty level of income (a number, currently around $3,000 per year); or the Russian rate of growth (a number) and whether it is greater than our rate of growth (it was, in the 1950's, but in the 1960's our performance improved greatly). And so on. Mind you, some of these numbers are hard to come by. Some are even philosophically complicated. But there is hardly any major economic problem into which a number does not enter somewhere.

And this fact is important because it helps explain certain aspects of the approach of modern economists to their subject. This approach is slightly different from that of the historian or of many other students of society. It is more statistical, more mathematical, more like the approach one might find in the natural sciences. Economists actually like to think of their subject as a science; and if one takes a look at a typical professional economics journal of today, its pages covered with differential equations and matrix algebra, one might think that he had wandered into physics or biochemistry by mistake!

But if this quantitative side is the first common characteristic of economic problems, the second—their *institutional* side—is almost the reverse. Economic problems are not generally reducible to simple scientific formulae. They deal with society, they deal with people, they deal with institutions, history, culture, ideology. The field may be a science, but it is a social (not a natural) science. Behind the numbers, behind the hard facts of resources and technological capabilities, we ultimately come face to face with human beings and the psychology of their behavior, whether individual or collective. Since this behavior is, in turn, conditioned by the past history of their society and its relationships to other societies, there is really no aspect of history, political science, or sociology that does not have some relevance to most major economic problems. Without knowing the history of twentieth century wars, who could follow the movements of price levels in our century? Without knowing the differences of history and culture that separate the continents, who could explain why people eat well in Europe and North America and starve in Asia? Without knowing the whole complex sociology of urban-rural life in the country, who could explain what is happening to American cities in the 1960's? Suburbia, exurbia, megalopolis—how complex these terms are, and yet they clearly have deep economic implications which the economist must try to comprehend.

Furthermore, and largely in consequence of the above, there is a third and final characteristic of most economic problems: they are usually *controversial*. This, by the way, is not unfortunate. Indeed, most economists have been drawn to the field at one time or another because of its controversial side. Economic problems are full of zest and spice, and economic discussions are quite capable of turning friends into distant acquaintances and vice versa. The controversial side does, however, demand a special kind of self-awareness when one is pursuing the analysis of an economic problem. We have to know whether what we are saying is true because we have carefully and objectively verified it or whether we are mainly expressing our own opinions—our own value judgments—that may conflict sharply with someone else's. Is my friend (or former friend) John wrong about the national debt because of logical error, empirical misinformation (he simply doesn't know the facts), or flaws in his moral character? Since John may also be asking the same questions about me, it is worthwhile to try to get the matter straight. Since economic problems characteristically weave these different threads together, it takes a particular effort of mental discipline to disentangle them.

Scarcity and Choice

So much for general characteristics. Now let us probe a bit more deeply. Can we define the nature of economic problems in a more fundamental way?

The answer will vary somewhat from economist to economist, but a fairly central definition would go something like this:

Economic problems in general arise because of the fact that the means society has for satisfying the material wants of its citizens are limited relative to those wants. Human desires for material goods—for survival, for luxury, for ostentation, whatever—generally exceed the volume of goods that can be made available for satisfying these desires.

Another way of putting this is to say that there is, in most economic matters, a fundamental problem of *scarcity* involved. Our desires are relatively unlimited. Our resources are relatively limited. The tension between desire and means of satisfying that desire is a reflection of the degree of scarcity involved.

Now this way of looking at the matter brings out immediately some important points about most economic problems. For one thing, it helps explain why many people when they talk about economics sometimes say, "It's all a matter of supply and demand!" Actually, this is one of those interesting statements that are true in some interpretations and quite false in others. In the technical sense in which economists use the terms *supply* and *demand*,[4] the statement isn't true at all. In fact, there is relatively little in real-world economics

_____

[4] See Chapter 2, pp. 23-31; also pp. 68-70, where the applicability of the technical terms *supply* and *demand* is discussed.

that can be analyzed by these terms. In the very general sense of our present discussion, however, the statement does have some validity. What it says is that there is this fundamentally two-sided nature of economic problems—human desires and scarce resources—and that economics is deeply concerned with the relationship of these two different sides.

Another point that this way of looking at the economic problem brings out very clearly is that economic problems are frequently concerned with *choice*. We want all these various goods. But we cannot produce them all at once. We must therefore choose. Either this or that. But not both. Scarcity forces choice on us, and a great many economic problems are concerned with the choices a society must make: what particular goods shall we produce? What scarce resources should we use in producing this or that good? And so on. Scarcity forces choice upon society, and the mechanisms a society employs to make its economic choices are quite as significant facts about that society as are its political system or the way it organizes its family life. Indeed, these economic, political, and social matters are, as we have said, usually very much interrelated.

Economic Possibilities: a Diagram

It will be useful now for us to illustrate this choice problem with the aid of a diagram. Economists often find simple diagrams useful both in explaining their subject to others and in understanding it themselves. The diagram we turn to now is a good example of the help such drawings can give, for it enables us to show quite straightforwardly some of the fundamental economic problems with which all societies must cope.

The diagram is called a production-possibility curve or, sometimes, a transformation curve.[5] In order to draw it, let us imagine a very simple, hypothetical society that is capable of producing only two products: food and steel. The technologists in the society have given us the information contained in Table 1-1. They have told us what is the maximum amount of steel we can produce for each possible amount of food that we are producing. We begin by producing 0 units of food; i.e., all our resources are going into steel production.

[5] The word *transformation* is sometimes used because the diagram is designed to show how a society, using all its resources, can produce different combinations of goods; i.e., how it can transform (by different resource use) one good into another.

We then begin diverting our resources from steel to food production, until finally, when we are producing 175 million bushels of food, there are no resources left over, and steel production is zero. The table, in theory, describes all the possible combinations of food and steel that the society can produce—its *production possibilities*—when all its resources of land, labor, and machines are fully employed.

TABLE
1 — 1

When food production is (million bushels)	Then the maximum possible steel production is (thousand tons)
0	1,050
20	1,035
40	990
60	930
80	840
100	720
120	595
140	410
160	190
175	0

The figures from Table 1-1 have been displayed graphically in Fig. 1-2. If we had a piece of graph paper, we could plot on it all the

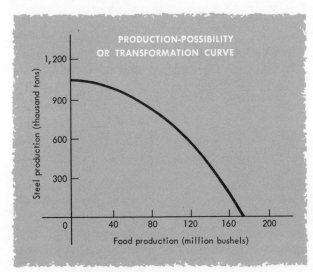

This curve graphically presents the hypothetical data from the table above. It shows the characteristic bowed-out shape of the production-possibility curve.

PRODUCTION-POSSIBILITY OR TRANSFORMATION CURVE

Steel production (thousand tons)

Food production (million bushels)

FIG. 1-2

points shown in Table 1-1. Then if we joined them together in a smooth curve, we would have the diagram shown in Fig. 1-2.

Now this diagram is nothing but a representation of the material presented in Table 1-1—i.e., basically, it gives us no new information —but it does show us something that is not obviously read off the table: the *shape* of the production-possibility curve. We notice, in particular, that the curve is bowed out, or, technically, "concave to the origin"; it is not simply a straight line from the *x*-axis to the *y*-axis.

What does this bowed-out shape mean? And why is it a fairly characteristic shape for the production-possibility curve?

The *meaning* of shape of the curve is fairly easy to see. It states that as we increase our production of one commodity it will be harder and harder to get still further units of that commodity. Harder in what sense? Harder in the sense that we will have to give up more units of the other commodity to add another unit of the first commodity. In other words, as we increase food production, we shall have to give up more and more units of steel to increase our food production by one unit.

The meaning of this last statement is illustrated in Fig. 1-3. In the portion of the curve indicated by the roman numeral I, we are producing relatively little food and a great deal of steel. To increase food production by a given amount a is relatively easy—we have to give up only b_I steel to do so. Now contrast this with the situation in Area II. Food production is much higher here. To increase food production by the same amount as before (a), we must now give up much more steel; i.e., b_{II} is much greater than b_I. And the same of

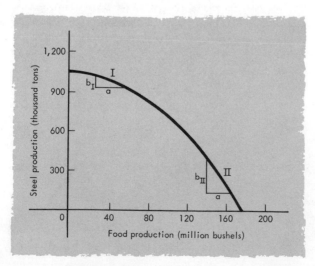

FIG. 1-3

The shape of the production-possibility curve illustrates this important generalization: as we produce more of one good, we must usually give up more of other commodities, to increase production of that good still further.

course would be true if we were speaking of increasing steel production as opposed to increasing food production.

This, then, is what the shape of the curve *means*, but now we ask: *why* does it have this particular shape? The fundamental answer to this question derives from the fact that not all productive agents and resources—*factors of production* as economists usually call them—are equally well suited to the production of different commodities. If *all* commodities were the product of *one* factor of production—say, homogeneous labor—then there would be no need for the curve to bow out as it does. But this is obviously not so. In our particular case, steel production requires iron ore while food production requires fertile, cultivable soils. Now there is no reason to expect that the best farming land will also be the land containing the richest iron deposits, quite the contrary in fact. What happens then as we keep increasing our food production?

In the beginning, when we are producing a great deal of steel and almost no food we are using excellent cultivable soil in our search for whatever bit of iron ore it may yield. By giving up just a bit of steel production, we release this rich land to the farmer and consequently gain a great deal of food production for a relatively small loss (b_I) of steel. As we keep increasing our food production, however, the situation changes. Now all the really good farming lands have been used. If we wish to increase food production any more, we must take over the land rich in iron ore but relatively poor for crops. This means that to get the same increase in food production we must make major sacrifices (to the amount of b_{II}) in our steel production.

Thus, it is empirically (though not universally or necessarily) true that it usually costs us more to produce more of a particular good, the more of it we have. The *opportunity cost*—the steel we have to give up to get more food—generally goes up as we proceed further and further in any one line of production.

Application to Major Economic Problems

We can now use this diagram to illustrate specifically and meaningfully some of the fundamental economic problems all societies face.

Figure 1-4 illustrates the choice problem that we have emphasized so much in our earlier discussion. Should the society locate itself at point *A* (lots of steel; little food) or at point *B* (little steel; lots of food) on its production-possibility curve? This is not the only kind of choice a society must make; but since economic problems tend to be interrelated, this choice is reflective of the solutions to many other choice problems as well.

How can or should this choice be made between A and B? Clearly, the choice the society will want to make will depend on a whole host

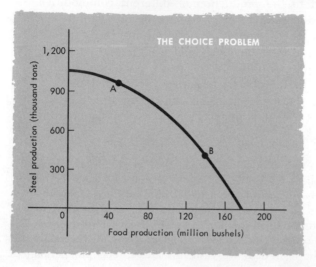

THE CHOICE PROBLEM

Steel production (thousand tons)

Food production (million bushels)

Among the fundamental choices a society must make is the choice of the composition of its output (A or B or some other point). This choice will reflect not only the stage of development of the economy, but also its economic *system*. Is choice decentralized, centralized, mixed, or what?

FIG. 1-4

of different factors. For example: if it has a very large population, then presumably it will need a fairly large production of food. If it is a very rich country, then it will presumably consume a higher proportion of industrial products (steel) as opposed to agricultural products (food). Even if it is a poor country, it may decide to sacrifice food production today, to make machines (steel), so that it can produce *both* more food and more steel in the future.

These are simply a few of the many considerations that will influence a society's choice between A and B on its production-possibility curve. *How* these factors influence that choice, moreover, is dependent upon a still further variable: the kind of economic *system* operating in that particular society. Does it have a traditional economy? A market economy? A planned or command economy? A mixed economy? The way in which these different possible economic *systems* work to influence economic choices will be a major concern for us in our remaining chapters of Part I.

Before carrying these matters further, however, let us use our diagram to illustrate two additional major economic problems. Until about 30 years ago, these two additional problems received very little attention among economists, but now they are at the very center of the field, and we shall devote most of parts II and III to them.

The first of these two problems lies in the field of what we might call *short-run aggregative* economics. It asks: what factors determine the state of health of the economy as a whole in the short-run? One

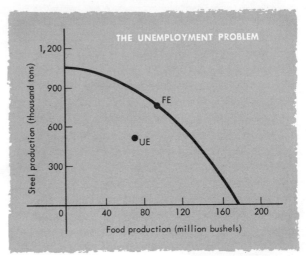

Will total output be at its full employment potential level (on the production-possibility curve) or will it be at a point *inside* the curve, signifying unemployment? Note that at *UE* we can have more of both food and steel if we can only get our laborers and machinery back into full operation.

FIG. 1-5

of the most important aspects of this question has to do with the employment problem. Are we utilizing all our available labor and other resources in production, or do we have men and factories standing idle and, consequently, a national income that is less than it might be? In terms of Fig. 1-5, the two situations are contrasted at points *FE* (full-employment production) and *UE* (unemployment or under-capacity production). The production-possibility curve does not tell us where the society *will* be, but where, technologically, it *can* be. It will take us a good bit of analysis to show the forces that determine where the economy in the aggregate will, in fact, be located at any given moment of time.

The other problem that can be illustrated by our diagram is that of *long-run economic growth*. Here, as Fig. 1-6 indicates, we are concerned with the shifting outward of the production-possibility curve over time. What these curves tell us is that in 1960 we were able to produce *both* more food and more steel than in 1950 and that, in 1970, we had advanced still further.

Now this growth-process—this shifting out of the production-possibility curve—does not happen automatically with the passage of time. Indeed, it is not too much of an exaggeration to say that economic growth, in its modern sense, was really unknown to the world until the British industrial revolution of the late eighteenth and early nineteenth centuries. Even today there are vast areas of the world, especially in Asia and Africa, where this process has not yet taken root. In

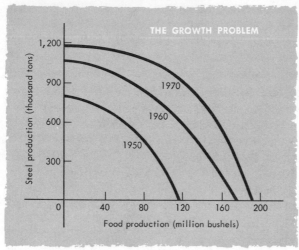

FIG. 1-6

A modern economy does not remain static but grows, as suggested by these outward shifts of the production-possibility curve. How to stimulate long-run growth is a major concern of many nations today.

the advanced industrial countries, however, growth is now a characteristic feature of economic life. Through a continuing process that involves population growth, the accumulation of machines and other capital goods, and, above all, a constant attention to invention and innovation—new products, new discoveries, new technologies of production—these modern economies are shifting out their production possibilities at a rate unknown in the early history of mankind.

Economic growth is not the cure-all for the social and moral ills of humanity. But it is an economic fact of the first magnitude; and like the other economic problems we have mentioned, it, too, will require our most serious attention.

Summary

We become aware of the workings of our economic system when there is some dramatic malfunction in one of its parts. Such malfunctions have occurred historically, as in the German hyperinflation of the 1920's or the worldwide Great Depression of the 1930's. But they also occur today, most obviously in the underdeveloped countries of Asia, Africa, and Latin America, but even in the affluent United States where poverty still exists.

The character of these various economic problems is similar in that (1) they usually involve a *quantitative* element—numbers appear in most economic problems; (2) they also involve an *institutional* element—they require a knowledge of the institutions, culture and ideology of a particular society; and (3) they are often *controversial* problems—one must be careful to isolate value-judgments from questions of fact or logic.

More deeply, these various economic problems ultimately arise from the problem of scarcity: the fact that human desires for material goods and services generally exceed the volume of those goods and services the economy is capable of providing. The problems of scarcity, and consequently of choice among alternatives, are illustrated in a production-possibility or transformation curve. This curve enables us to show hypothetically how a society might choose between this or that different combination of goods.

The production-possibility diagram is also useful in allowing us to illustrate important aggregative problems such as (1) short-run unemployment and undercapacity-production and (2) modern long-run economic growth.

Questions for Discussion

1 • List a few of the major economic problems facing the United States at the present time. What features of these problems lead you to characterize them as *economic* problems?

2 • Economists of a century or two ago worried about the so-called *paradox of value:* water is very useful but cheap, while diamonds are much less useful but expensive. How does the fundamental role of scarcity in economic problems help you understand this paradox?

3 • Under what special circumstances might the production-possibility curve have a shape such as the following:

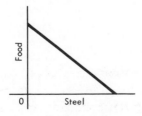

Could you imagine any circumstances in which it might have a shape such as this:

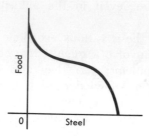

4 • At the height of World War II, the United States was devoting some 50 per cent of its total production to the war effort, yet private consumption, except for a few commodities, remained high. Use the production-possibility analysis to illustrate how these facts might be reconciled.

Suggested Reading

HEILBRONER, ROBERT L., *The Making of Economic Society*. Englewood Cliffs, N.J.: Prentice-Hall, Inc., 1962.

MULCAHY, RICHARD E., *Readings in Economics from Fortune,* 3rd ed. New York: Holt, Rinehart and Winston, Inc., 1967, Chaps. 1-5, 16-17.

SHANNON, DAVID, *The Great Depression*. Englewood Cliffs, N.J.: Prentice-Hall, Inc., 1960.

SLESINGER, REUBEN E., MARK PERLMAN, and ASHER ISAACS (eds.), *Contemporary Economics,* 2nd ed. Boston: Allyn and Bacon, Inc., 1967, pp. 1-51.

The market economy

2

The hard fact of scarcity can force many choices upon a society; and these choices, as we have indicated, will be deeply influenced by the kind of economic *system* operating in that society. In the next four chapters we shall be examining some of the different systems by which fundamental economic choices can be made. In this chapter, we shall focus on what economists sometimes call a *market economy*. We shall try to show how, through the operation of prices and markets, without any central planning or guidance, a society can solve its economic problems in a coherent way.

Choice through the Market

Since everyone brought up in the United States is familiar with the workings of prices and markets of various kinds, the subject of a market economy may seem one of the easier topics in economics.

But this view is misleading for two reasons. The first is that the successful functioning of a market economy is intrinsically complicated. Indeed, it is something of a social miracle. For the essence of such an economy is that nobody guides or even thinks about the economy as a whole. Everything is decentralized into the thousands and, indeed, millions of private, individual decisions being made by consumers, producers, and laborers, here, there, and everywhere. That such apparently haphazard means should produce anything like an orderly result is not something to be taken for granted—in fact, it should be regarded as rather astonishing.

The second reason for caution is that a pure market economy does not really exist in the modern world. Although we have all seen various markets—from the supermarket to the stock market—operating in the United States, it would be quite wrong to believe that this country makes all its crucial choices through the market mechanism. The government plays a considerable role in the present-day American economy, as, indeed, it does in all economies in the modern world. Furthermore, even in the private sector, the roles of business and labor in real life are often quite different from those described by standard economic theory. We shall return to these matters later on. For the moment, the important point to keep in mind is that the pure market economy is something of an abstraction. Its great importance for the student of economics is not as a description of reality but as a tremendously useful point of departure from which the complexities of modern industrial organization can be approached.

The tasks that our market economy must perform are numerous. For one thing, it must determine in one way or another how the income of a society is distributed. One man earns $4,000 a year; another $2,000; another $75,000. Whether one applauds or objects to any particular arrangement, it is clear that every economic system must have *some* determinate way of distributing its goods and services among its members. Anything less would bring social chaos.

Similarly, every economic system must provide some determinate way of deciding how the goods and services of the society are to be produced. One might think that this question of how to produce potatoes or automobiles or tablelamps is a purely technological—not an economic—question. But this is not so. For there are many different ways of producing any given product. All of these ways are feasible in a physical or engineering sense, but some may be better than others in an *economic* sense. Automation may be excellent for a society with a great deal of machinery and a shortage of labor, but it would hardly make sense for a society that is overflowing with unskilled labor and can barely afford the most rudimentary tools and machines. The question of how to produce different goods is vitally affected by the relative scarcities of the different factors of production. Thus, it falls squarely in the province of the economist; and like the question of the distribution of income, it is another problem for the market economy to solve.

Finally, there is the problem we have already spent some time on: what goods to produce? In terms of our earlier diagram (repeated here in Fig. 2-1), shall we produce at point A (lots of steel; little food) or at point B (little steel; lots of food)? In this chapter, we shall put particular emphasis on this aspect of the choice problem, for it will allow us to bring out quite clearly the essential features of the market economy in its over-all operations.

The Solution
of the Classical Economists

Now the notion that a good way to handle these choice problems— in fact, the notion that the *best* way to handle them—is through a price-and-market mechanism was really born sometime during the eighteenth century. Around the 1750's and 1760's, a number of French economists (sometimes called physiocrats) began to stress the view that there was a natural harmony between the decisions individuals made privately and the general social welfare. *Physiocracy* means "rule of Nature." Private self-interest and the social welfare were seen not as in conflict but as in a fundamental union more or less as a matter of "natural law."

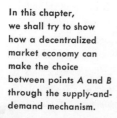

In this chapter, we shall try to show how a decentralized market economy can make the choice between points A and B through the supply-and-demand mechanism.

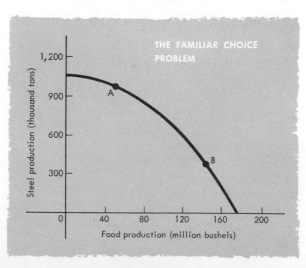

THE FAMILIAR *CHOICE* PROBLEM

Steel production (thousand tons)

Food production (million bushels)

FIG. 2-1

The most important development of this concept, however, came in Great Britain. Early British economists were interested in analyzing the implications of a market economy and in trying to demonstrate that if the government stayed in the background, the price-and-market mechanism could handle things quite satisfactorily. Since these early British economists did much to establish the field of economics as we know it today, it is worthwhile to say a word about them.

The key date is probably the year 1776. This year saw not only the beginning of the American Revolution—it saw also the publication of one of the most important economic treatises of all times: *The Wealth of Nations* by Adam Smith. Smith was a quite remarkable man, although his life was notably without incident. He never married. Except for a Grand Tour of the Continent—when, incidentally, he met some of the leading French physiocrats—he never traveled extensively. But he was a philosopher, a historian of science, and, above all, the greatest economist of his day. *The Wealth of Nations* is a spacious book that can be read for pleasure even now. It is filled with rolling eighteenth century sentences but also with sharp phrases that catch whole pages of argumentation in a word or two. When Smith speaks of an "invisible hand" that brings private and social interest into harmony, he is not simply writing vividly; he is pinpointing an entire philosophy of economic life.

Smith is important not only because of his work, but because of the influence of that work on others. *The Wealth of Nations* became the rock on which a whole school of economists was founded. This school is usually called the Classical Economists, and it included, in the decades following Adam Smith, some of the most important writers in the history of the subject. There was Thomas Robert Malthus, the English parson whose ideas on population cast a pessimistic pall over nineteenth century thought and greatly influenced the evolutionist Charles Darwin. There was David Ricardo who published his *Principles of Political Economy and Taxation* in 1817 after a highly successful career in business. Ricardo was one of a small number of economists who really have done well on the stock market. His work in economic theory was rigorous and systematic. Although not well-known to the general public, he had an enormous impact on the development of technical economics. Even in the middle of the nineteenth century, Smith's influence was still strong, and John Stuart Mill, who once had Ricardo for a tutor, is often regarded as a Classical Economist. Mill, of course, was a many-sided genius whose works in philosophy and political science easily match his very substantial contributions to economics.

Smith's message, however, carried beyond his fellow economists, to the world at large. And this message was, in essence, that except for certain unavoidable responsibilities,[1] the State ought to stay fairly well out of the economic sphere. Laissez-faire was the motto: leave the economy alone; have the State keep a hands-off policy. Or in terms of our discussion in this chapter, let the society solve its economic problems largely through the functioning of a market economy.

Smith's general reasons for advancing this view are fairly clear. He combined a belief in the frugality and industry of private individuals with an insight into the ways in which competition among individuals could keep their actions in line with the interests of society. Smith said something like this: if you have everyone operating according to his own self-interest and if, at the same time, you have a great deal of competition among different individuals and businesses, then these private parties will be more or less forced to produce the goods that the consumers want and to make those goods available at reasonable prices.

Or we can state the same thing beginning at the other end: consumers have certain preferences with respect to, say, food and steel products. How are these preferences translated into economic reality in an economy in which everything is decentralized and works through the market? Smith's answer was that it will be in the self-interest of the producers to make the goods the consumers want (i.e., this will bring them greater profits); furthermore, the competition among these producers will be sufficient to keep profits moderate and to insure that no consumer is overcharged. He will have to pay only what, in Smith's phrase, "the good is worth."

The corollary was: if the private sector can handle things so well, then the State need not intervene except for rather special and limited functions.

The Demand Curve

Today we are aware of certain qualifications to the "classical" view of the world, but we can also state their own arguments more precisely than they could, because we have developed certain analytic tools that were not at their disposal. One of the most important of these tools is the *demand curve*. Together with the *supply curve*, which

---

[1] Smith acknowledged that the State had certain duties that would bring it actively into the economy: (1) national defense; (2) the administration of justice; and (3) the provision of certain socially necessary institutions—e.g., educational institutions—that private interests might neglect. Thus, neither he nor any of the Classical Economists advocated a truly *pure* market economy. The question was how much (or little) intervention was needed.

we shall take up momentarily, this tool will enable us to explain some of the essential features of a market economy.

A *demand curve* may be defined as follows:

A demand curve is a hypothetical construction that tells us how many units of a particular commodity consumers would be willing to buy over a period of time at all possible prices, assuming that the prices of other commodities and the money incomes of the consumers are unchanged.

The last phrase in this definition is of some importance. It is usually called a *ceteris paribus* or "all other things equal" phrase. It brings out the fact that we are isolating a particular part of economic life for close inspection and holding other areas in abeyance. This is clearly necessary here. How can we tell how many units of steak a consumer will buy at one dollar a pound if we do not know what his income is or what the price of lamb or chicken is? Hence the need to proceed in this one-step-at-a-time fashion.

In Table 2-1 we have set out the raw data for a demand curve for a commodity: apples. (We have chosen a food because ultimately we want to come back to the food–steel choice problem raised earlier in this chapter.) We have asked consumers to tell us how many dozens of apples they would be willing to buy in a given month at prices ranging from $1.00 to 1¢ per dozen. Notice that we must specify the period of time involved: presumably the number of apples purchased at a given price will be twelve times as much in a year as in a month, and so on.

TABLE
2 – 1

At price (per dozen apples)	Consumers wish to buy per month (thousand dozens)
$1.00	20
.90	90
.80	150
.70	212
.60	278
.50	340
.40	402
.30	465
.20	530
.10	590
.01	650

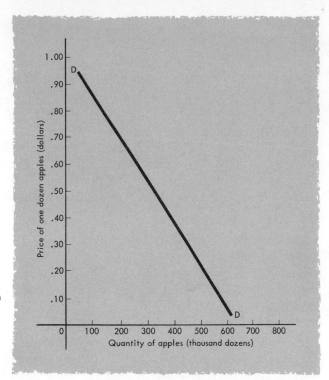

DD represents the consumer demand curve for apples. It is drawn on the assumption that money incomes of consumers are constant and that prices of other commodities (e.g., oranges) are constant.

FIG. 2-2

Figure 2-2 represents the material in Table 2-1 in a smooth curve. The procedure here is the same as in the case of our production-possibility curve of Chapter 1. The points from Table 2-1 are charted on graph paper and then joined together in a continuous line (as if, in fact, we actually had information on how many apples consumers would purchase at 31¢, 32¢, 33¢, etc., per dozen.) This curve is the consumer demand curve for apples.

Now you notice that the curve slopes downward from left to right. Why this particular shape? Actually, this is not too difficult to understand. At high prices for apples, the consumer will find that buying too many apples makes too big a dent in his budget; he will have to cut down his purchases. Furthermore, when apple prices are high, even the dedicated fruit lover will be tempted to substitute pears or peaches or oranges for apples. This, too, will mean fewer purchases. Thus, although we could imagine a few very curious exceptions if we wished to,[2] the customary shape of a consumer demand curve

[2] A famous (among economists) exception to the rule of a downward-sloping demand curve is the so-called "Giffen paradox," named after a nineteenth century British economist, Sir Robert Giffen. He noticed that when the price of potatoes goes up, very poor families may buy *more* potatoes. Why? Because the rise in the price of potatoes makes them poorer; and when they are poorer, they substitute potatoes for meat. This, however, is a very exceptional case and implies, among other things, that the commodity looms very large in the budgets of the consumers involved.

will be as we have drawn it: sloping downward toward the Southeast.

Before leaving the demand curve, the reader should test his understanding of the concept by asking himself what will happen to our demand curve if some of the "other things equal" items happen to change. Suppose all consumers have a 50 per cent rise in their money incomes? Suppose the price of bananas goes up? Suppose the price of oranges goes down? In each case, the answer is that the whole demand curve will *shift* its position. The reader should determine the direction of the shift and the reason why it shifts in each case.

The Supply Curve

The second tool we need for our analysis of the market economy is the *supply curve*.

This curve tells us not about the consumers of apples, but about the *producers* of apples. Instead of going around to consumers and asking, "How many apples would you buy this month at such-and-such a price?" we now ask producers, "How many apples would you produce and sell this month at such-and-such a price?"

We could, if we wished, draw up another table similar to Table 2-1, this time for producers rather than consumers. Since the principle is clear, however, we shall simply produce the results of our information survey in graphical form. The supply curve for apples, then, is given in Fig. 2-3. It shows us the quantities of apples that producers are willing to offer for sale at various prices over a given month.

Now in some respects the supply curve is a bit more complicated to grasp than the demand curve, or at least it seems so at first glance. Two problems arise: Under what assumptions can a determinate supply curve be drawn? What explains the upward (northeasterly) slope of the supply curve?

Assumptions
Behind the Supply Curve

One critical assumption is that apple producers take the prices of apples as given *by the market* and not as subject in any significant way to their personal control. They are price-takers, not price-setters. In technical economics terminology, they are *pure competitors*. We shall see in Chapter 5 that *pure competition* is by no means the only form of real-life market structure, and this is one of the reasons why

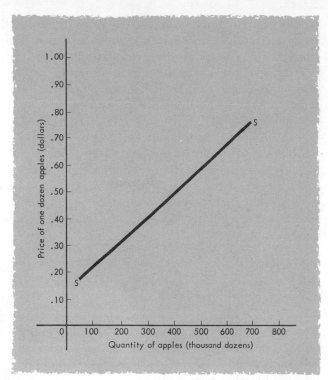

SS represents the producers' supply curve for apples. It tells us that producers are willing to supply more apples only if the price of apples goes up. A lower price, conversely, will lead to a smaller quantity supplied.

FIG. 2-3

our analysis of the market economy in the present chapter is necessarily only a beginning. For the moment, however, it is important only that we understand that such an assumption is, in fact, being made when we draw our supply curve. And this can be seen simply by reflecting a moment on the question we asked each apple producer: "How many apples would you offer for sale at such-and-such a price per dozen?" He is being asked to respond to a *given price*. If this were not the case, the only relevant question we could ask him would be: "What price do you plan to *set* for apples this month?" But that is not the question we asked. Our question—the question underlying the supply curve—does build in the assumption of price-taking or pure competition.

The curve is based on other assumptions as well, and we should not be surprised to find that each supply curve (like each demand curve) has its *ceteris paribus* clause attached. In the case of the supply curve, the meaning of this clause seems a bit more complicated, however, for it is so obviously affected by considerations of *time*. It was the late nineteenth century British economist Alfred Marshall who pointed out the great importance of the time period in speaking of producer behavior and the supply curve. In the very short run, when we allow virtually nothing to vary except the price of apples, the apple producer really has nothing to offer but his given stock of apples. The supply curve in this case might be practically nothing but a straight, vertical line—i.e., he would offer his given supply of apples at any price. In a somewhat longer run, he will have time to adjust production to different prices. When the price of apples goes up and stays up for a few months, he may hire more laborers to pick apples, to pack them, and to fill orders. In the still longer run, his adjustment may be more flexible yet. He may plant more trees, buy up more orchard land, acquire more farm machinery, and so on.

Thus, for any given supply curve, we must be careful to specify exactly what time period we are thinking of and, consequently, what factors we are holding constant and what factors we are allowing to change.

Shape of the Supply Curve

Considerations of the time period are also important with respect to our second problem—explaining the upward (northeasterly) slope of the supply curve—for the shape of the supply curve will also be affected by what factors are being held constant and what time period is envisaged.

Now the main *general* reason that the supply curve goes in this northeasterly direction is that costs tend to rise as the production of any particular commodity is increased. The argument is basically as follows:

1. The costs of producing more units of a product will generally increase as we expand the production of that particular product.
2. For a given price, producers will make most profits if they produce to the point where that price just covers the added cost of producing one more unit of the product.[3]

---

[3] Economists have a term to express the addition to total costs of producing one more unit of a given product: *marginal cost*. The statement above can therefore be rephrased as follows: Producers will maximize their profits if they produce up to the point where marginal cost equals price ($MC = P$). This will be true only under the assumption earlier made of pure competition. Under pure competition, then, the supply curve of a particular firm will, in fact, be a segment of its marginal cost curve. If a firm is producing at all (it always has the alternative of going out of business or temporarily halting production), then its supply curve and marginal cost curve in that range of production will be identical. In general, and especially in the short run, a firm's marginal cost curve (and hence supply curve) will be rising as production of the product increases.

3. Producers interested in maximizing their profits will therefore generally expand their production and sales when they are faced by a higher market price. This is the same thing as saying that the supply curve will be rising in a northeasterly direction away from the origin.

This is the *general* basis for the shape of the supply curve as we have drawn it. To be more specific, one would have to get more information about the time period involved, for the ways in which costs rise as production expands in the short run will be different from those in the long run. In the short run, the firm in question will not have time to adjust its productive apparatus fully to the increased level of production. It will be able to hire more laborers and buy more raw materials, but its fixed capital, its machines, its buildings, its land, etc., will not change. Therefore, it will be adding some new factors of production to a fixed stock of other factors of production, and the result generally will be increased costs or *diminishing returns.*[4]

By contrast, in the long run, all the fixed factors become variable. The firm can buy more land, build more plant, purchase more machinery. Furthermore, other firms, attracted by the prospect of high profits, will be able to enter the industry. It will still be the case that costs will generally rise as production of a particular commodity expands even in the long run;[5] however, the rise in costs will be less steep. Or to put it in other terms, the long-run supply curve for a firm and for an industry will generally rise less steeply than the short-run supply curve for such a firm or industry.

The "Law" of Supply and Demand

We have explained the general meaning and shape of both the demand and the supply curves. Now we are in a position to combine them. In Fig. 2-4, we have put the demand curve for apples and the

---

[4] We are dealing here with the famous "law of diminishing returns." We shall take up this law again (Chapter 14), but let us state it now: In the production of any commodity, as we add more units of one factor of production (say, labor) to a fixed quantity of other factors (land, machinery, etc.), the addition to total product with each subsequent unit of the variable factor will eventually begin to diminish.

[5] The ultimate reason that costs rise in the long run even when all factors of production are variable is that different commodities are produced by different kinds and combinations of the various factors of production. It was this reason, we recall, that explained the shape of our production-possibility curve in Chap. 1 (p. 13).

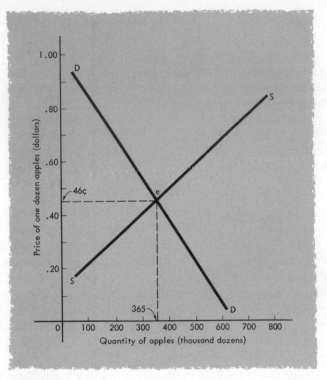

FIG. 2-4

Supply and demand are in equilibrium at point e, where the price of a dozen apples is 46¢ and the quantity bought and sold is 365 thousand dozens.

supply curve for apples in one diagram. With the aid of this diagram, we shall now be able to determine the equilibrium market price of apples and the quantity of apples that will be bought and sold. This determination of the price and quantity of a particular product is what the so-called law of supply and demand is all about.

Needless to say, it seems likely that the key point will be where the two curves intersect. And, indeed, it is at this point that the equilibrium price and quantity are determined. In our diagram, the market price will be 46¢ a dozen and the equilibrium quantity produced will be 365 thousand dozens.

The deeper question is: why is this intersection point significant? Why couldn't the price be somewhere else?

The answer to this, in essence, is that it is only at this particular price (46¢) that the quantity of apples consumers are demanding and the quantity of apples producers are willing to supply are exactly equal; i.e., supply = demand. At any other price, either the quantity supplied will be greater than the quantity demanded—in which case producers will be accumulating large quantities of unwanted and unsold apples —or the quantity demanded will be greater than the quantity supplied— in which case buyers will be clamoring for apples that producers simply do not have for sale. It is clear that neither of these alternatives could last long. If producers were accumulating unwanted apples, sooner or later they would decide to cut back on the production of apples. If, conversely, buyers kept asking for nonexistent apples, producers would sooner or later get the idea that it was time to raise prices and expand apple production.

It is only at this intersection point that these problems cannot arise. There is no accumulation of unsold apples; there are no queues of buyers trying to get apples that don't exist. We have then an equilibrium price—a price which will stay put unless some new fundamental change occurs—and this is the price at which supply and demand are equated.

Consumer Sovereignty
~a Simplified Example

Our analysis so far has shown how the price and quantity of a particular commodity are determined in a market economy, all other things equal. This is an important step in understanding how such a decentralized, private economy can function.

Now, however, let us use these tools to go a step further. We want to show how a market economy makes some of those fundamental economic choices which all societies must face. It will not be possible to do this rigorously in two or three pages, but we can illustrate the general process satisfactorily, and this is a matter of great importance to all students of economics.

One of those central choice problems, we recall, was whether to locate at point A (lots of steel; little food) or at point B (little steel; lots of food) on our production-possibility curve. Now in a market economy, as Adam Smith understood, the essence of the process is that producers will adjust their production of different commodities so that they are in accord with consumer desires. This is what is meant by the concept of *consumer sovereignty*. If the economy is at point A, and consumers prefer to be at B, the market will operate to shift production in the desired direction.

With our newly acquired supply and demand curves, we can give a bit more definition to this process. Let us imagine that we are dealing with two commodities. Apples will be our food commodity; our steel commodity will be, say, washing machines.

Now let us imagine that, for whatever reason, there is a shift in consumer desires from washing machines to apples. The example is a bit farfetched, but the principle is clear enough: consumer preferences have changed. How is this reflected through the market in changed production of these two commodities?

The general nature of the answer is given in our two diagrams, Fig. 2-5 (*a* and *b*). The increased demand for apples has resulted in an upward shift of the demand curve for apples. The decreased demand for washing machines has resulted in a downward shift in the demand curve for washing machines. The consequences of these shifts according to our diagrams are:

1. A greater production of apples at a higher price
2. A lesser production of washing machines at a lower price

Consumer preferences have shifted from washing machines to apples, and the result has been an increased production of apples and a decreased production of washing machines, and this without any planning or governmental intervention, but solely through the laws of supply and demand working in the marketplace.

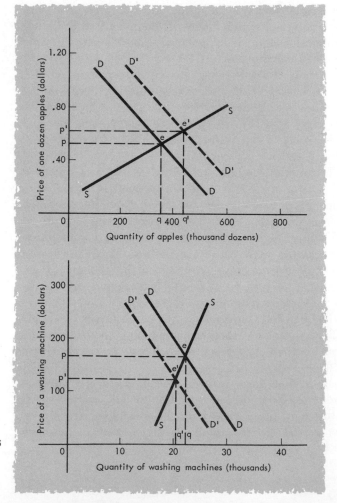

These diagrams represent a simplified example of how consumer sovereignty operating through the supply-and-demand mechanism can alter the composition of output in a market economy. In particular, a shift in demand from washing machines to apples has led to an increased production of apples and a decreased production of washing machines. This new equilibrium would correspond to a new point on the society's production-possibility curve.

FIG. 2-5

Now this example is simplified, and it should be taken as suggestive rather than definitive.[6] Actually, it wasn't until the late nineteenth century, 100 years after Adam Smith wrote, that economists began to pin down the full theoretical implications of a competitive market economy. Beginning around 1870, however, a number of important economists developed a very comprehensive view of such an economy. Alfred Marshall, whom we have already mentioned, was one of these. Another, less known to the general public but very highly regarded by professional economists, was a French–Swiss economist by the name of Léon Walras. Walras was one of the early breed of mathematical economists. He developed the kind of supply and demand analysis that we have been discussing in such an elaborate way that it could cover not only the supply and demand for products, like apples and washing machines, but also the supply and demand for the factors of production (land, labor, capital goods). What emerged in Walras' hands was a view of the interdependent structure of a market economy in a grand design known as *general equilibrium* analysis. And this whole structure—very theoretical, of course—could be expressed in mathematical terms as, indeed, an elaborate set of simultaneous equations.

The point of these remarks about *general equilibrium* analysis is to make us realize that to follow through any significant change in an economy—even a shift of tastes involving apples and washing machines—we ultimately have to inspect the whole system at once. Even though we cannot achieve this large objective here, our progress with the supply and demand apparatus has shown us the general nature of the process. We can see at least some of the links that join the consumer on the one hand with the productive apparatus of the society on the other. And in so doing we understand how the social miracle of the market economy is possible.

[6] In a more detailed treatment, we shall want to take into account some further consequences of a shift in consumer tastes. Such a shift would affect not only the quantities of different goods (apples and washing machines) produced, but also the methods of producing different goods and the distribution of income in the society. The reason is that when consumers shift their preferences, they are indirectly affecting the demand for the different productive agents (land, labor, and capital) that produced the different goods. In our example, we might imagine that apple production used a great deal of land (relative to labor), whereas washing machine production used a great deal of labor (relative to land). When consumers demand more apples and fewer washing machines, they are, in effect, creating an increased demand for land relative to labor. This will tend to raise the price of land relative to labor. And this, in turn, will affect (a) methods of production in the economy—businessmen will try to economize on the more expensive land by using labor whenever possible; (b) the distribution of income—landowners will receive increased income relative to laborers.

The Market
and the Public Interest

The market economy, then, is a possible system. Is it also, as Adam Smith was inclined to believe, the *best* possible system? It is with this second question that "economics" and the "public interest" come into critical confrontation.

The answer, as one might expect, is very complicated and subject to much disagreement among the experts. In a preliminary way, however, we can indicate at least two lines of argument that must affect all serious thinking about the subject.

The first line of argument really stems from the kind of analysis we have been presenting in this chapter. It emphasizes the essential viability of the market system. It says in effect: consider how beautifully the supply and demand apparatus works, how remarkable it is that, without governmental intervention or planning or forethought, all these thousands of individual decisions nevertheless do lead to such desirable social results. This is in the full tradition of classical economic thought.

A second line of argument leads in quite a different direction. It stresses that there are important areas of economic life where competition and markets do not produce the results we want. To take one simple example: the analysis in this chapter has not even touched on the problem of unemployment. Essentially, in our washing machines and apples example we were assuming a full-employment economy. But we do know that unemployment can exist. Will the market economy be able to solve that problem? The critics would tend to be pessimistic. In this area and, indeed, in many other areas, as will become clear in later chapters, they would point out significant divergences between private and social interest in a market economy.

History is partly on each side. The great industrial revolution of the late eighteenth and early nineteenth centuries was born at a time when the market system was triumphing over earlier forms of economic organization. On the other hand, it was true then and, as we have said, it is certainly true today, that a *pure* market economy was never a historical reality. In one way or another, citizens of this and every country in the world have asked that governments step in to change this or that aspect of the functionings of the price and market mechanism.

Thus, the crucial question, as far as the public interest is concerned, is not whether there should be *any* intervention—that question has really been settled by history—but what *degree* of intervention should be permitted. This question has been debated for over two centuries now. And as we shall see in the remaining pages of this book, the debate rages on with undiminished intensity to this very day.

Summary

A market economy is one in which the crucial economic decisions and choices are made in a decentralized fashion, by private individuals, operating through a price and market mechanism. In a *pure* form, such an economy does not exist in the modern world, but the study of its workings is fundamental to the understanding of modern economics.

The British Classical Economists of the late eighteenth and early nineteenth centuries, and especially Adam Smith, stressed the virtues of limiting government intervention in economic life so that private self-interest and competition could bring consumers the goods they wanted at reasonable prices. With modern analysis, we can give much sharper expression to Smith's views through the interaction of *supply* and *demand* curves.

A demand curve for a product shows the quantities of the product that consumers are willing to buy over a given period of time at different prices. A supply curve shows the amounts of the commodity that producers are willing to sell over a given period of time at different prices. Both curves are drawn under certain important *ceteris paribus* or "other things equal" assumptions. In the case of the supply curve, it is particularly important to notice the element of time, whether short-run or long-run, since, generally, costs will rise more steeply (and hence the supply curve will rise more steeply) in the short run than in the long run.

Equilibrium price and quantity are determined in a market economy where supply and demand curves intersect. This is the so-called law of supply and demand, a law valid only under the special conditions of pure competition.

Using supply and demand curves, we can illustrate in a general way how consumer preferences are carried through the price system to affect the kinds of goods produced in the economy. If consumers want more apples and fewer washing machines in a market economy, supply and demand will work to produce this general result.

To prove that the market economy is a "possible" economy is one thing; to prove that it is the "best possible" economy is another.

Economic analysis indicates points on both sides, as does historical experience. History does strongly suggest, however, that the issue is (and was) never one of a *pure* market economy, but rather one of what *degree* of government intervention should be allowed or encouraged.

Questions for Discussion

1 • Adam Smith was aware that certain businessmen, if given the opportunity, might overcharge consumers, but he felt that the forces of competition would ordinarily keep prices at a reasonable level. How might competition produce this result? Can you imagine circumstances in which the process would not work satisfactorily?

2 • The choice of methods of producing different commodities is not only a technological but also an economic question. Discuss.

3 • What does the phrase "other things equal" mean when applied to the ordinary consumer demand curve?

4 • Suppose that there is an invention that substantially lowers the costs of producing a certain commodity. What general effect would this invention have on the supply curve of that commodity? What would be the resulting effect on the equilibrium price and quantity produced of the commodity in question?

5 • Discuss the role of the time period of adjustment in analyzing producers' responses to changes in market prices. Might consumer responses to different prices (as shown by the demand curve) also be affected by the length of the time period under consideration?

6 • "When some people are very rich and others are very poor, the whole notion of 'consumer sovereignty' in a market economy is misleading and prejudicial." Discuss some of the issues raised by this statement.

Suggested Reading

DORFMAN, ROBERT, *Prices and Markets*. Englewood Cliffs, N.J.: Prentice-Hall, Inc., 1967, Chaps. 1-5.

HEILBRONER, ROBERT L., *The Worldly Philosophers*. New York: Simon and Schuster, 1953, Chap. 3.

LEFTWICH, RICHARD H., *The Price System and Resource Allocation*, 3rd ed. New York: Holt, Rinehart and Winston, Inc., 1966, Chaps. 1-9, 13.

MARSHALL, ALFRED, *Principles of Economics*, 8th ed. New York: The Macmillan Company, 1948, Book V.

SAMUELSON, PAUL A., JOHN R. COLEMAN, ROBERT L. BISHOP, and PHILLIP SAUNDERS, *Readings in Economics*, 4th ed. New York: McGraw-Hill, Inc., 1964, Chaps. 27-30.

SMITH, ADAM, *The Wealth of Nations*, Modern Library Ed. New York: Random House, Inc., 1937.

Economic planning, Marx, and the command economy

3

In the last chapter, we said that a *pure* market economy was something of an abstraction, not to be encountered in its pristine form in the real world. Much the same can be said of the kind of economic system we shall discuss in this chapter: the completely *planned economy* or the *command economy,* as it is sometimes called. Even in its closest approximation (the economy of the Soviet Union), important elements of a market system intrude—indeed with increasing frequency in recent years.

Nevertheless, as in the case of the market economy, the study of the pure form of planned economy is of great importance to the serious student of modern economics. For the mechanism of economic planning is in wide use in the present-day world. Elements of this mechanism appear in our own economy. In Western Europe, even in countries where the basic system is privately organized, planning is often an explicit part of public policy. Great Britain's Labor government has limited aspirations to "socialism"; France has developed an interesting mix of the public and private sectors through what she calls "indicative planning"; neutralist Yugoslavia has experimented with a system sometimes labeled "market socialism."

Furthermore, as everyone who follows the newspapers must be fully aware, there is a large fraction of the world's population who regard private enterprise and the market system with suspicion and, indeed, outright hostility. If we put together those uneasy (and perhaps incompatible) bedfellows, Russia and China, and add to them several Eastern European economies, we have a billion or more people who would like to reject the capitalistic system root and branch. Communism in all its varieties puts a considerable emphasis on governmental action, centralization of decision, high-level planning of fundamental economic choices. By referring to these systems as *command economies,* we emphasize the fact that the decision-making process generally goes not from individual consumers to individual producers but from central planning boards or commissions to enterprises that are either State-owned or highly regulated by the State. Consumer sovereignty largely gives way to the collective preferences of the central planners. It is this fundamentally different approach to economic problems that we shall consider in this chapter.

The Marxian Criticisms

In discussing the market economy, we went back to Adam Smith. In discussing the great planned economies of the modern world, we must go back to another early economist, the controversial Karl Marx (1818-1883). In all these countries, Marx is regarded as the true founder of scientific economic thought.

Actually, if we go to Marx in the hope of finding a detailed blueprint of how a planned economy should work, we shall be largely disappointed. Marx gave comparatively little attention to this important problem. What he did do was two rather different things. First, he provided a massive critique of the working of the capitalistic market economy. Second, he provided a revolutionary ideology that has proved very vigorous historically in leading to the overthrow of established economic systems and the installation of highly centralized economies.

Karl Marx, the man, was an activist and revolutionary. He took part in the Communist League of 1848 and summoned his followers to action with ringing phrases in his *Communist Manifesto*. But he was also a scholar—intense, very well-read, sometimes even pedantic. He was born in Germany, but he spent the latter part of his life in England working long hours each day in the British Museum in London. His major work, called *Capital*, is a vast document of literally thousands of pages of which he was able to complete only the first volume (1867) in his lifetime. The remaining volumes were published posthumously under the editorship of various of his followers, especially Friedrich Engels. Engels played a very important role in Marx's life, sustaining him spiritually and, at times, financially. The *Communist Manifesto* was actually a joint product of Marx and Engels, though Marx was the guiding light in the collaboration and clearly had the superior mind of the two.

Marx's first achievement was, as I have said, of a negative kind: to present a number of harsh criticisms of the capitalistic system. If he had perused the discussion of a market economy in our last chapter, he would have scoffed at its shortcomings as a description of historical reality. One objection he certainly would have made was that there was no reference at all to the different classes of society; in particular, that there was no reference to what Marx considered a fundamental feature of capitalism: the conflict between the capitalist class and the laboring class, between the owners of factories and machines and the dispossessed proletariat. For Marx, this *class conflict* was an absolutely central characteristic of capitalism and, indeed, he tended to view all past history as evidence of one kind of class conflict or another. To write about the beauties of supply and demand and how they reflected consumer preferences, but to ignore the struggle between the wealthy capitalists and the downtrodden laborers—this, in Marx's eyes, would be to shut out the fundamental facts of the real world.

Another objection he would have made was that we had failed to recognize the importance of *monopoly* elements in the price system. Our supply curve, we recall, was drawn on the assumption that producers were pure competitors or price-takers; i.e., each firm was too small to have any appreciable direct effect on the price of its product. As far as Marx was concerned, however, the result of free markets in the modern industrial and commercial world would almost certainly be that big, monopolizing firms would swallow up the small, individual producers. In his view, it was not the small firm but the giant industrial corporation that was characteristic of capitalism, particularly in its advanced stages. Indeed, he believed that these large firms would come to control not only the economies but to a great degree the gov-

ernments of capitalistic countries. In such a world, the notion of producers responding meekly to the will and wishes of consumers would
be a mockery.

Finally, he would have objected, as we ourselves recognized, that
our description of a market economy took no account of the *unemployment* problem. For Marx, this would have meant living in a fairy-tale
world. In his theoretical structure, unemployment was not an accidental
but an intrinsic feature of a capitalist economy. One reason for this was
quite simply that capitalists had to find some way to keep wages down.
The way they chose, according to Marx, was to introduce machinery in
place of labor whenever wages started to rise. This machinery displaced the laborers; consequently, there was serious general unemployment. If any laborer asked for a raise, his employer simply took him
to the factory window and showed him the line of workers who had no
jobs at all, a crude but effective method of settling wage disputes! In
terms of our production-possibility curve, Marx would have said that
a market economy characteristically operated at some point, *UE*, inside
the production frontier (see Fig. 1-5, p. 15). Indeed, Marx argued that
this problem would get worse and worse as time went on. Capitalism
would be subject to great crises and depressions. These crises would,
in fact, do much to make the Communist revolution inevitable.

History has shown that most of these criticisms of a capitalistic
market economy were seriously overstated. We would live in a fairy-
tale world far more fanciful than the one that Marx condemned if we
were to use Marxian analysis as a guide to what actually happens in
countries where, as in the United States, heavy reliance is placed on
the market mechanism. However, it would be just as misleading to
think that there is no truth whatever in the Marxian criticisms. There
clearly are numerous inequities in the distribution of wealth, income,
and power in a completely unregulated market economy. The large
industrial corporation with considerable influence over its markets is
a substantial feature of modern life. And as far as the displacement of
labor by machines is concerned, what workingman in an advanced industrial economy has not wondered at some time or other whether his
job may not give way to automation and the computer? The point is
that Marx did have a number of significant specific insights into the
workings of the capitalistic system. Where he went wrong was in missing the big picture of improvement and progress and evolutionary
change that such systems have proved capable of carrying forward, as
later chapters in this book will amply demonstrate.

The second major aspect of Marx's thought that concerns us is his
role as revolutionary. Marx was (and still is) the spiritual leader of

Communism, and his writings have served as inspiration for the revolutions that have created the major planned economies of the modern world.

Now in a sense, the most interesting and rather surprising point to be made in this connection is that the Marxist revolutions that have led to Communist governments have not been altogether in accord with Marx's own theory. Toward the end of his life, Marx once commented, "I am not a Marxist"; and, indeed, if he had seen some of the interpretations his doctrines have been subjected to since, he might have made the point even more emphatically. The problem is essentially this: Marx argued that the weaknesses in capitalism we have just been describing would cause the eventual collapse of the system after capitalistic evolution had run its full course. In theory, the revolution comes at, or toward, the end of the capitalist phase. In practice, the revolutions have not come in the advanced capitalistic countries but rather in poor, relatively backward countries which have scarcely had time to go through the capitalistic stage. Russia, in 1917, although she had made some economic progress by that time, was economically still far behind the advanced capitalistic countries of Western Europe and North America. The Chinese claim to be orthodox Marxists, yet they had their revolution in the 1940's before they could truly be said to have had any experience at all with modern industrial capitalism.

All this proves that Marx's theory was far from accurate in predicting when his own revolutions would occur. What happened, in effect, was that his doctrines were simply adjusted to the practical necessities of the situations at hand. In Russia, for example, there was Lenin, the great leader of the Revolution. Lenin had little time to worry about whether or not Russia was in the appropriate stage of development for the collapse of capitalism to occur. He was much more interested in the strategy of the Revolution itself. Or take Stalin. Stalin was fully aware that Russia in the 1920's was not an economically advanced country. On the contrary, he emphasized her need to catch up with the advanced countries and therefore proceeded to sacrifice everything to rapid industrialization. With him, communism became not the stage that follows modern development, but rather an ideology for promoting forced-draft industrialization and growth.

And the reinterpretation goes on today. The post-Stalin leadership in Russia seems to have a somewhat more flexible view of economic organization than did its predecessors. The Chinese, however, seem if anything more inflexible than Stalin himself; to them, of course, the new breed of Russian leaders are crass revisionists.

Indeed, the main common bond we can find in all these manifestations of Marxism is a built-in predilection for a much higher degree of centralization and economic planning than in the major economies of the Western world. And this takes us from the realm of ideology to the realm of economic organization and practice.

The Functioning
of u Command Economy

A centralized command economy must face the same fundamental economic problems as a decentralized market economy. Let us first say a few words about the general functioning of such an economy. And then let us make some specific comments about the actual experience of planning in the Soviet Union.

In the command economy, it is not the market but the central government or some branch of the central government that makes the basic decisions concerning the society's production targets, its allocation of resources, its distribution of income, and its desired rate of growth. In the pure command economy, the State would normally possess ownership of all the means of production and most of the property in the economy. It would determine the incomes of different kinds of labor and the salaries of production managers, doctors, artists, bureaucrats. It would determine the planned outputs of all the different productive enterprises in the economy and the allocation of resources to each. In terms of our earlier examples, it would set, and attempt to secure fulfillment of, targets for food production and steel production, for the output of apples and the output of washing machines.

Now such a task, if carried through into every single corner of a modern economy, would be hopelessly complex and really beyond the capabilities of any group of planners, however sophisticated. Consequently, in most real-life command economies, at least some of these decisions are decentralized either to lower levels of authority or, in some case, to what is a rough facsimile of a price-and-market mechanism. It is frequently the case that a command economy will direct its main planning energies to certain broad areas of the economy, or to certain particular targets that, for some reason, have special priority in the minds of the central planners.

Even when the task is limited in this fashion, it still involves a number of difficult and overlapping problems. These include problems of organization, coordination, efficiency, incentives, and basic goals.

1. *Organization.* The first and most obvious requirement of a command economy is a bureaucratic organization that makes it possible for

anything like effective planning to proceed. It is one thing to make decisions about what the pattern of economic activity in the society should be and another to see that these are carried out.

There must be, first, an organizational chain of command that makes it possible to transmit the decisions, targets, and directives of the central body *down* through the system to the level of the actual production units in the economy. There must be, also, an organizational structure that permits information and data from the production units to *rise up* through the system to furnish the ultimate decision-makers with the knowledge required for any kind of intelligent planning. It should be clear that many countries do not possess, or could build up only very slowly, the massive administrative mechanism necessary to carry out these vital functions. Even under the best of circumstances, there is a tremendous burden of bureaucracy to carry in the command economy, which is at least partially avoided in a more decentralized system.

2. *Coordination.* It is not enough that targets and directives be quickly communicated through the system; they must also be economically consistent. There is a serious problem of coordination in any command economy, arising from the interdependent nature of the modern industrial economy.

The problem may be put in terms of what economists refer to as *input-output analysis.*[1] The outputs of one industry in the economy can be thought of as inputs into some other industry in the economy. Machines are necessary to produce steel, but steel is necessary to produce machines. Actually, steel output will be used as inputs into literally hundreds of other industries in the economy: machines, tractors, automobiles, typewriters, building construction, and so on. And, indeed, a modern economy is an infinitely complex network of interdependence in which the production of one sector depends upon the inputs it can receive from a host of other sectors, while its own output will simultaneously be feeding back inputs into these and still other sectors. The point is that one cannot simply set a target for industry A and then, *independently*, set targets for industries B, C, and D. One must be sure that there is sufficient production of A, so that the input requirements of B, C, and D are met, and vice versa. With the large number of industries involved and their intricate interconnections, the coordination problem facing a command economy is necessarily extremely complex.

[1] For the standard reference on input-output analysis, see Wassily W. Leontief, *Structure of the American Economy, 1919-1939* (New York: Oxford University Press, 1951). Input-output analysis can be described as an attempt to apply "general equilibrium" theory (mentioned in the last chapter) to real-life economies under certain special assumptions. It has uses both in the West and in the more planned economies of the East.

3. *Efficiency.* Even consistency is not sufficient, however; for it is necessary or at least desirable that a command economy be *efficient*— that is, that it employ its scarce resources in such a way that it gets as much output as possible from them.

The subject of economic efficiency is a very large and difficult one.[2] Suffice it to say here that a market economy is provided with some rough guidelines for efficient use of its resources, since the prices of the factors of production— land, labor, capital goods—will reflect their relative scarcities; hence it will be profitable for firms to economize on the use of particularly scarce (therefore expensive) productive factors. In a command economy, difficulties may arise in this area, particularly if there is an aversion to using anything that may look like "capitalistic" market pricing. Historically, indeed, this has been a fairly serious problem for many actual command or near-command economies.

4. *Incentive.* In the command economy—as, indeed, in any economy—the workers, managers and executives, not the central planners, produce the goods. Hence, there must be sufficient *incentive* established, monetary or otherwise, to assure a vigorous labor force and intelligent managerial direction.

This problem is not necessarily as insurmountable as it may have seemed to some critics in the past. Many of these critics were doubtless going on the assumption that any form of socialism would characteristically involve a fairly equal distribution of income, and consequently a denial of special rewards to those producers in the society who contributed most to the social product. However, there is nothing intrinsic in the nature of a command economy that requires an equal distribution of income and, in fact, most command economies have set up fairly elaborate bonuses and other incentives to spur managers and workers to the fulfillment or, if possible, overfulfillment of their production targets.

5. *Basic Goals.* We have left to the last in this brief list what in some senses should have come first: the question of basic goals. If the central planners do not rely on the wishes and preferences of the consumers to set the basic economic targets for which they are aiming, what then do they rely on?

This is a complex question, for ultimately its answer depends on the particular political organization of the command economy and the psychology of its effective leaders. A rough generalization on the basis of historical experience

---

[2] For a discussion of the economist's use of the term *efficiency,* see Robert Dorfman, *The Price System* (Englewood Cliffs, N.J.: Prentice-Hall, Inc., 1964), Chap. 6.

would go something like this: In general, command economies, while not ignoring the preferences of consumers (including their preference for at least some choice in the goods they buy), have nevertheless usually set goals which were different from what might have been expected had the market mechanism had somewhat fuller play. In particular, and probably because most of these economies tended to be somewhat economically backward at the outset, there has been a heavy emphasis on achieving economic growth at as rapid a rate as possible. The objective of catching up with the West has been paramount. If this has required sacrificing present standards of living to the demands of the future, then the sacrifice has been made, sometimes with a vengeance.

In making this last generalization, however, we are speaking less of the intrinsic features of a command economy than of actual historical experience, especially that of the major exemplar of this general approach, the Soviet Union. Let us therefore now turn directly to the Soviet economy and make a few comments about its problems and accomplishments.

The Soviet Economy
~Successes and Failures

The Soviet economy, as we would expect, is not a pure command economy in every way. It is perhaps the closest approximation to such an economy that exists, however, and its durability (since the 1917 Revolution) gives us an important opportunity to inspect both the strengths and weaknesses of this form of economic organization.

All the problems that we have mentioned in the previous section have troubled the Soviet government at one time or another. In the very early days of the Communist regime, for example, organizational problems proved temporarily insurmountable. With the dislocation of the economy following World War I and the Revolution, stringent economic controls had to be abandoned in the early 1920's and a return to prices, markets, and capitalistic incentives had to be permitted in substantial areas of the economy. This was the period of the so-called New Economic Policy, a policy which, incidentally, was very successful in helping to restore the shattered Russian economy to its pre-World War I levels. Beginning in 1928, with the First Five-Year Plan, however, a near-command economy in most of the strategic sectors of the economy was established. Although this economy faced many difficulties, especially perhaps in the area of economic efficiency, and although, as we shall mention in a moment, modifications are now taking place, nevertheless the basic pattern of economic organization has remained fairly stable since 1928.

What conclusions, if any, can we draw from this experience? Has it been basically successful or unsuccessful? Economists will naturally differ on broad questions like this, but, in my own view, there are three important generalizations that can be derived from the Soviet record.

The *first* conclusion is that the command system of economic organization is, in fact, a workable system. In the past, many people had doubts about this. They felt that without the spur of markets, prices, and profits, without the advantages of the personal knowledge and involvement that decentralized decision-making can bring, the whole system might simply fall apart. And, indeed, given the complexities of planning under a command system which we have just outlined, that prediction would not seem completely unreasonable. But in fact, it hasn't worked out that way. Although there are definite flaws in the Soviet approach, her over-all economic record since the beginning of the First Five-Year Plan has been a very respectable one. The best Western estimates [3] are that Russian industrial output grew between 10 and 11 times from 1928 to 1961. This is a rate of growth of over 7 per cent per year for 33 years. Agriculture production grew less rapidly during this period, but it did show at least some increase and, consequently, the over-all growth rate of total national income was substantial.

This fact is proved when we compare the Soviet rate of growth with that of the United States during this same period. Figure 3-1 shows that the Soviet economy began at a level much lower than our own in 1928 but grew at a more rapid rate than ours from 1928 to 1960. Indeed, in the 1950's the Soviet growth rate was so much faster than ours that many people began to feel that Russia was, in fact, beginning to live up to her goal of overtaking this country. This view was overly pessimistic. In the 1960's, the relative rates of growth of the two countries became much more comparable. Furthermore, there is no doubt that a relatively less advanced country has certain advantages in the catching up phase (for example, she has the whole technological experience of the more advanced countries to lean on), and the Russian experience, when placed in the context of other semideveloped countries, does not seem quite so spectacular. [4]

[3] See Robert W. Campbell, *Soviet Economic Power,* 2nd ed. (Boston: Houghton Mifflin Company, 1966), pp. 124-25.

[4] Thus, for example, many countries in Western Europe—Germany, Italy, France —were growing at similarly rapid rates of growth in the 1950's. Indeed, if an economic growth prize had to be given at this time, it probably would have had to go to Japan, which sometimes showed yearly rates of growth in the neighborhood of 11 or 12 per cent. The meaning and measurement of such concepts as "industrial output" or "national income" are quite complicated (see Chapter 7).

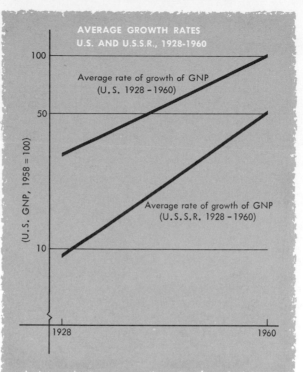

AVERAGE GROWTH RATES
U.S. AND U.S.S.R., 1928-1960

Average rate of growth of GNP
(U.S. 1928 – 1960)

Average rate of growth of GNP
(U.S.S.R. 1928 – 1960)

(U.S. GNP, 1958 = 100)

100

50

10

1928   1960

This diagram gives a very rough estimate of the relative growth trends of the U.S. and the U.S.S.R., 1928 to 1960. In the 1950's, some economists thought that these curves of growth were bound to meet in some future year. In the 1960's, however, more optimism developed toward the growth performance of the American economy.

FIG. 3-1

Still, the over-all conclusion does remain that a system relying heavily on the command mechanism has worked quite successfully over a fairly substantial period of time. And, indeed, this leads us to the next point.

The *second* main conclusion to be drawn from the Soviet experience is that there are *certain* aspects of economic life where the command economy may have advantages over its market counterpart. We have earlier said that most known command economies, and especially the Soviet Union, have placed enormous emphasis on achieving a high rate of growth. What the command mechanism has allowed them to do is to marshal a very high percentage of their national resources for this specific purpose.

This issue can be seen fairly clearly through the use of our production-possibility diagram. In Figure 3-2, we have drawn another such diagram, but this time we have placed "consumers' goods" on the *x*-axis and "capital goods" on the *y*-axis. One of the choices all societies face is how much of their output to devote to immediate consumption and how much to *invest* in machines, tools, equipment and plant—what we call *capital goods*—which will make possible a larger productive capacity in the future.

Now the Soviet leaders, with their urgency about raising the rate of growth, have, in fact, "commanded" that a very high proportion of their national income be devoted to such investment. Whereas in the

United States, say, something on the order of one-fifth of our total output might be devoted to investment purposes, in the Soviet economy, the figure would be closer to one-third. Considering that both economies also have heavy military and defense expenditures, this Soviet figure represents a very substantial direction of the economy toward

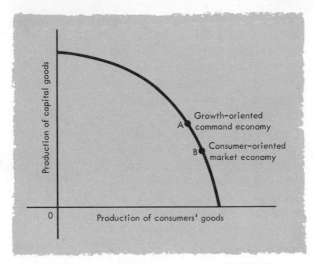

FIG. 3-2

In the determination of basic goals, most near-command economies in real life have put a heavy emphasis on investment and economic growth. They have moved in the direction of A (as opposed to B) on their production-possibility curve.

their desired targets. In Fig. 3-2, this is represented by the fact that the growth-oriented command economy may locate itself at point *A*, whereas the ordinary market economy, being more responsive to consumer preferences, may locate itself at point *B*.

But now we turn to the *third* main generalization, which is this: the Soviet experience also demonstrates clearly that the command economy has definite areas of weakness as compared to its more market-oriented counterpart. These weaknesses are of various kinds. Some observers, for example, may consider it a weakness that the Soviet leadership has been *able* to force a higher rate of growth than the consumers in the society would have freely chosen. The Soviet performance in the area of consumer good production has been much less satisfactory than her over-all growth rate would suggest, and her performance in agriculture, until fairly recently, was decidedly inadequate. The economic suffering that occurred, especially at the beginning of the Five-Year Plans, was acute and widespread, and it doubtless could have been alleviated had the growth "commands" been less insistent. Although it is not the economist's province to judge such matters, the political coercion that went with this attempt at forced industrialization must also be considered in human terms as deeply regrettable.

More generally, the weaknesses in the Soviet performance reflect precisely those problems of organization, coordination, incentives, and especially economic efficiency that we have mentioned earlier. The Soviet planners bought their high rate of growth in the early days not only at the expense of the consumer but at the expense of a more rational, careful, and efficient use of their scarce resources.

Indeed, the Russian leadership seems aware of this fact and aware, too, of the more threatening fact that the future growth of the economy may itself be jeopardized if more attention is not given to these neglected areas. It is highly instructive to note that this awareness has shown itself in a willingness to experiment—still cautiously and incompletely—with the introduction of what might heretofore have been considered capitalistic devices. A few years ago, several Soviet economists, especially E. G. Liberman, began to recommend the greater use of prices and markets in the Soviet system. Small-scale experiments were tried in 1964 and 1965, and it appears that some of these reforms will be extended throughout the entire industrial sector.

Although it is still too early to judge how far these measures will go, they are of great interest to all economists. They demonstrate the existence of definite flaws in the command approach to economic life. They suggest that, for all its defects, the market mechanism does have a surprising durability, a way of springing back into existence when one might least expect it. And finally, introduction of the new measures confirms the same general point that we made at the end of our last chapter: that neither a *completely* planned nor a *completely* market-organized economic system seems to be a viable way of arranging economic life. The real question in the modern world is how these elements are mixed together. The great debate is not about one pure form versus another but the much more complex (and interesting) question of the proper proportions of the mix.

Summary

In analyzing the heavily planned or command economy, we naturally go back to Karl Marx, who gave the ideological backdrop for most of these economies in the modern world. Marx did not, however, provide a blueprint for economic planning; rather, he provided a detailed critique of capitalism—because of its class antagonisms between capital and labor, its monopolistic elements, and its inherent tendencies to technological unemployment—and he developed an ideology which (when flexibly interpreted) could serve the purposes of communist revolutions.

In practice, the pure command economy must make difficult economic decisions which often require elaborate institutional arrangements in the modern industrial world. The areas in which problems are likely to occur are: (1) organization of an adequate planning bureaucracy; (2) coordination of economic targets in a consistent manner; (3) making production efficient in the economic sense; (4) securing proper incentives for workers and managers; and ultimately (5) setting proper goals for the economy when consumer sovereignty no longer provides the guidelines.

A near-approximation to the command economy has been the Soviet Union, whose economic experience over the past 50 years gives us our best case study of how the command mechanism works. Our suggested conclusions were that the Soviet record proved that a command economy could "work" and, indeed, that there were certain specific areas (for example, in marshalling productive resources for investment and economic growth) where it had advantages over its market counterpart. But we also noted the grave weaknesses that the effort at total planning involves; this helps explain why the Soviet Union in recent years has been turning more and more to experimentation with various market-type reforms. Although the future extent of these reforms is not known, those in operation give evidence of an increasingly mixed economy in the Soviet Union, which is what our Western experience would also lead us to expect.

Questions for Discussion

1 • Marx predicted an increasing class conflict between capitalists and the proletariat as the capitalistic system approached maturity. How well does this prediction stand up in the case of the United States, as judged by your general knowledge of American history? What economic factors may have moderated any tendency toward class conflict in this country?

2 • Marxian economics, in a technical sense, is based on what is sometimes called the *labor theory of value*. This theory states that the prices of different commodities are proportional to the quantities of labor involved in producing those commodities. This theory is generally believed to be inadequate because it neglects the fact that there are different *qualities* of labor and also the fact that there are *other* factors of production besides labor (e.g., land and capital goods). Remembering your general supply-and-demand analysis from Chapter 2, show how:

   a) a country with a shortage of cultivable land might generally expect higher food prices than a country where land was abundant;

   b) a sudden influx of highly skilled surgeons from abroad might lower the price of medical services.

3 • In a pure command economy, what takes the place of a market economy's "consumer sovereignty"?

4 • "The main problem with a command economy is that it has no way of providing incentives to its labor force and managers to work effectively and well." Discuss critically.

5 • It is said that the Soviet economy in the period from 1928 to World War II was often "inefficient" in its use of resources. Yet we know that the U.S.S.R. grew quite rapidly during this period. Is it possible to reconcile these points? How?

6 • The Russian Revolution is often attributed in part to the fact that the Russian economy was relatively "backward" in the early twentieth century. Communism also has an appeal for a number of economically "backward" countries today. What factors do you imagine may have created this appeal for such countries? List what you would consider to be possible advantages and disadvantages of a highly centralized economic system for an economically backward nation.

Suggested Reading

BERGSON, ABRAM, *The Economics of Soviet Planning*. New Haven: Yale University Press, 1964.

CAMPBELL, ROBERT W., *Soviet Economic Power*, 2nd ed. Cambridge: Houghton Mifflin, 1966.

GROSSMAN, GREGORY, *Economic Systems*. Englewood Cliffs, N.J.: Prentice-Hall, Inc., 1967.

MARX, KARL, *Capital*. Chicago: Charles Kerr & Co., 1906-1909, 3 vols.

SCHUMPETER, JOSEPH A., *Capitalism, Socialism and Democracy*, 3rd ed. New York: Harper & Row, 1950, Part I.

SWEEZY, PAUL M., *The Theory of Capitalist Development*. New York: Oxford University Press, 1942.

The mixed economy
–public sector

4

In the two preceding chapters, we have discussed forms of economic organization that lie at opposite ends of the politico-economic spectrum. At one extreme is the pure market economy in which all decisions are made in a highly decentralized fashion by private firms and individuals. At the other end is the command economy where the basic decisions are made by the central government and then passed on through directives setting various targets and objectives to the rest of the economy.

Now the striking fact, in both cases, is that the *pure* form, market or command, does not exist in actuality. Every market economy we know involves certain areas of government intervention and control. Every planned economy involves certain elements of prices, markets, and decentralized decision-making, as recent Soviet experience shows. In short, the characteristic modern form of economic organization is the mixed economy, an economy in which both public and private decision-making have a significant effect on the direction and well-being of the economy, where economic planning is often practiced by the large private as well as by the public enterprise, where, in general, the interaction among government, business, and labor is constant and complex.

Of course, the proportions of the mix may vary considerably, and this is a matter of importance. Still, the old-fashioned view that put market economies on one side and planned economies on the other and said, "Choose one or the other, not both!" is simply inaccurate. Most modern countries *have* chosen both—but in different degrees.

Since this is the case, we shall devote the next two chapters to a study of the mixed economy. In this chapter we shall concentrate on the governmental or public part of the mix; in the next, on the private sector. We shall use the United States' economy as our example throughout this discussion, both because we are familiar with it and because of its enormous importance in the world economy generally.

Growth of Government in the United States

Let us begin by getting a few facts under our belts. It is often said that governmental activity has been growing rapidly in this country in recent years. Has it? And if so, how rapidly, and in what ways?

One way of estimating the growth of the public sector in the American economy is to take all governmental expenditures—federal, state, and local—lump them together, and see how they have expanded over time. In Figure 4-1, the top line represents the sum of all governmental expenditures in the United States from 1929 to 1965. This chart is drawn on a semi-log scale, meaning that a straight line would represent a constant percentage increase. The strong upward drift of the curve makes it clear that the public sector has been expanding substantially in the United States—from about $10 billion total in 1929 to nearly $200 billion at the present time.

To understand the extent of this expansion, however, it is necessary to inspect these figures a bit more closely. The first thing to notice is that recent years have seen a particularly rapid expansion of state and local governmental expenditures. People often have a tendency to think of government intervention in the economy only as "big government"—the federal government. But after a period of relative stagnation from 1929 until the end of World War II, state and local expenditures have been expanding with great rapidity, well over threefold from 1950 to 1965. One of the reasons for this expansion is the large role state and local governments play in educational expenditures;

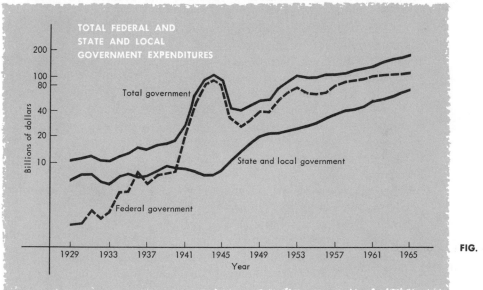

FIG. 4-1

Source: Economic Report of the President, 1966.

roughly a third of all state and local expenditures go into schools. With the "baby boom" of the early postwar period and the increased desire of American citizens to have more schooling for their young, the added burdens of educational financing have been unavoidable. An expansion of government of this sort is worth noticing, for it does not represent a new kind of government interference in the economy but simply an expansion of an area long considered properly within the public sector.

A second point to make about these figures is that they include at least two fundamentally different kinds of governmental expenditures. In addition to ordinary government expenditures on goods and services [1] they also include *transfer payments*. The difference is important.

---

[1] Sometimes called *exhaustive expenditures* by economists. It should be noted that these exhaustive expenditures include both direct governmental production— i.e., services of policemen and teachers—and also government purchases of goods— typewriters, buildings, etc. —from the private sector.

In the case of an ordinary government expenditure, the government pays a clerk for his services in the Defense Department or buys a truck or other commodity from a private firm. The payment is for a good delivered or a service rendered. A *transfer payment,* however, involves neither a good delivered nor a service rendered. In a typical form it simply represents a transfer of purchasing power from a taxpayer to the recipient of the transfer payment. Social security payments are transfer payments. So also are payments for unemployment compensation. So also are some of the payments made to farmers under our various agricultural programs. In each case, the key fact is that the government does not produce goods itself or direct private production into certain channels by its orders for goods. The elderly couples on social security do not have to provide any services to the government, and they are free to spend their money in such ways as they see fit.

In our present discussion, the relevance of this distinction derives from two considerations: (1) Although transfer payments necessarily involve a degree of government intervention in the economy, the degree is somewhat less than that of ordinary government expenditures, which represent a claim of the government on the nation's output of goods and services; (2) Transfer payments have grown very rapidly in recent decades, increasing as a percentage of total governmental expenditures. Actually, this growth of transfer payments, as we shall see in a moment, does represent some important new functions of government in the American economy. But it also means that our figures on the expansion of government in Fig. 4-1 may somewhat overstate the increasing impact of government on the economy during this period.

Finally, and perhaps most significantly, we should notice that while governmental activity has been growing over the past three or four decades, so also has the nation's economy as a whole. What we are interested in most directly is not governmental expenditures in isolation, but those expenditures in relation to the nation's total output of goods and services. Figure 4-2 represents the total of federal, state and local expenditures expressed as a percentage of the U.S. gross national product.[2] Now this diagram makes it clear that in this all-important *relative* sense, the growth of government in the American economy is somewhat less dramatic than one might have expected. Indeed, the striking thing about the curve is not so much the growth of government in recent years—the percentage has been relatively

[2] Gross national product is a common measure of a country's total output of goods and services. We shall discuss its precise definition in detail in Chap. 7, pp. 101-114.

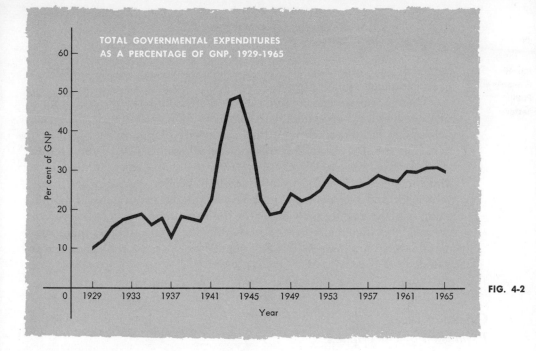

TOTAL GOVERNMENTAL EXPENDITURES
AS A PERCENTAGE OF GNP, 1929-1965

Per cent of GNP

Year

FIG. 4-2

stable in the last decade or so—but rather the extraordinary levels of expenditure reached during World War II. In 1943 and 1944, governmental expenditures were roughly *half* our total national output! There was a sharp cut-back immediately after the war, then a gradual upward drift that has continued since that time. Over-all, including transfer payments as well as ordinary expenditures, the general trend has definitely been upward—from 15 to 20 per cent of GNP in the 1930's to 30 per cent or so of GNP at the present time—but it is less drastic in this relative sense than the absolute figures had suggested; further, there is no evidence of any acceleration of the trend in recent years.

Of course, governmental expenditures are only *one* of a number of possible indicators of the role of the government in the economy as a whole. Actually, there are many functions of government that may affect the private sector very intimately and yet not show up in these particular numbers. For example: the Justice Department attempts to enforce various antitrust laws with respect to American business. In terms of national output percentages, the expenditure side of antitrust enforcement is trivial; but antitrust policy is a very important sphere in which the government is engaged in giving shape to the market economy. A similar situation exists with the many other regulatory functions of government, or with legislation such as the Wagner Act or the Taft-Hartley Act, affecting labor unions. Whether they are in the form of pure food and drug legislation or regulating airlines or requiring safety features on our automobiles, there are countless ex-

amples of government participation in the economy which do not show
up in our expenditure graphs.

There is no way to quantify these manifold activities, although a
rough generalization would be that they show very much the same
picture that has emerged from our expenditure diagrams; that is to say:
there has been a gradual expansion of these regulatory and other
activities from the 1930's to the 1960's. As with expenditures, these
other activities reached a great height in World War II when there
were price and rent controls, rationing of goods, and a general mobilization of the economy for war. After the war, there was a relaxation of
controls, and then, as with total governmental expenditures, there was
a gradual and undramatic, but still significant, increase from the prewar
period.

Causes of the
Expansion of Government

Some of the forces behind the expansion of the public sector have been
fairly clearly of an economic nature; others derive more from noneconomic considerations. An important example of a factor that seems
to stem largely from noneconomic causes is the great growth of defense expenditures in the American economy since the late 1930's. If
one adds together our direct defense expenditures, our international
programs, space research, and the interest payments and other costs
of past wars, one has about 60 per cent of all federal government expenditures in this country at the present time. Now it is probably true
that economic factors are reflected in these programs to some degree—
Marxists, of course, would claim that "imperialistic" wars stem largely
from economic causes!—and it is certainly true that these large defense
expenditures have a great economic *impact;* still, it seems fair to say
that the great pressures causing this part of federal expenditures to
grow so rapidly lie in the international political sphere. If the Cold
War in all its complicated ramifications were to end, this would certainly reduce many of the forces bolstering expansion in the federal
budget.

Thus, the biggest single item of government expense is largely
noneconomic in origin. Furthermore, it represents no new function of
government. This last, as we have already noted, can also be said about
most of our increasing expenditures on schools. A very great part of
the modern expansion of government in America, therefore, has either
resulted from noneconomic factors or has been in the traditional areas

of governmental responsibility, or both. (Adam Smith, we recall, charged the State with the responsibility for defense and with certain duties with respect to public education.)

However, there has also been an expansion of government activity into relatively new areas of our common life, and for what are largely economic reasons. These are of particular interest to the student of economics. Through an increase in the role of the public sector, these activities attempt to correct deficiencies (or, more accurately, what the majority of Americans regard as deficiencies) in the workings of a market economy.

A listing of these new programs would be very long. But certain general areas of concern stand out. One is the broad area of *income distribution.*

Private market forces operate efficiently with respect to many economic problems, but they often leave certain groups in the society without adequate protection. Elderly people, the disadvantaged, the uneducated, minority groups, the ill or the infirm—such individuals or groups will ordinarily receive a very small share of the nation's total output, and yet their economic needs may be as great as, or often greater than, their more fortunate neighbors. A great many of the government's welfare programs, ranging from the initial social security enactments of the 1930's to Medicare or the War on Poverty of the 1960's, have been designed to meet these needs. Not all transfer payments go from rich to poor, but many do, under these new welfare programs, and they consequently represent a redistribution of national income in favor of the needy.

Another broad area of concern is unemployment or, more generally still, the problem of *stabilizing the economy* in the aggregate and promoting its growth.

Ever since the 1930's, economists and, increasingly, public officials have recognized that an unregulated market mechanism does not ordinarily guarantee a full-employment economy. We shall be studying this problem in much more detail in Part II of this book, showing some of the underlying forces that bring about general unemployment or price inflation in a modern industrial economy. Suffice it to say here that many governmental actions in the past 30 years have been designed to cope with this problem. Part of the Social Security Act of 1937 set up a system of unemployment compensation. More recently, the government has been using its formidable fiscal and monetary policies to stabilize the economy in the aggregate. The tax cut of 1964 was aimed primarily at reducing unemployment and speeding up economic growth. The stringent "tight money" policy of the Federal Reserve Board in 1966 was designed to combat inflation. Even with active governmental intervention, these problems are not easy to handle, but it is now widely agreed that they do form an appropriate area for governmental concern and responsibility.

A third general field for government action has been in *providing certain goods or services that are valuable to society as a whole,* but are not likely to be produced by private market forces, or at least not in sufficient quantities.

Some goods are naturally *collective* as opposed to *private*, since it is difficult to withhold them from any citizen even if he doesn't pay for them (for example, defense, which shelters us all even if we do not pay a cent toward its cost).[3] But there are also many cases in which the marketplace will undervalue the actual social benefits to be derived from a particular act of production. A good example of this kind of problem is the construction of a dam. As a private party, I may build a dam on a river and find that a great many of the benefits of the dam go to other firms farther downstream. Now the dam may not be profitable for me to build, because although I must bear all the costs, I receive only *part* of the benefits. Yet if the government were to build the dam, the total benefits to society might be greater than the total costs. Whenever there is a divergence between the private and social benefits of an economic undertaking, there is a prima-facie case for governmental intervention.

We could list a number of other items that have influenced the expansion of the role of the American government in recent decades. Rather than going on, however, let us take one particular example of government intervention and show more specifically its various causes and effects. In this way, we shall get a better sense of the complexity of the interaction between the public and private sectors in our mixed economy.

An Example of Government Intervention ~ U.S. Agriculture

American agriculture is a particularly good example of some of the paradoxes of a mixed economy. In some respects, the agricultural sector affords the closest approximation to a purely competitive market economy we have in this country. There are several million farm families, the average size of farming units is quite small, and, in general,

[3] For a fuller discussion of the distinction between *collective* and *private* goods, and also of the general issues treated in this paragraph, see Otto Eckstein, *Public Finance,* 2nd ed. (Englewood Cliffs: Prentice-Hall, Inc., 1967), pp. 8-14.

the conditions for "responding" to the impersonal market seem to be met. Furthermore, we often think of the American farmer as particularly individualistic and independent and determined to shape his own fate.

Yet for many years the United States government has been extremely active in this area of our economy. Governmentally subsidized agricultural research has been a major factor in the modern technological revolution in farm production. Furthermore, the government has been involved in a whole series of programs affecting the level of production, the accumulation of surpluses, the international disposal, and the setting of prices of farm products of various kinds. We cannot go into all these different programs here, but let us take an example—governmental price supports—and suggest why they have come into being and what are some of their effects.

The problem that has led to government action to support certain farm prices is roughly this: there has been a tendency for the supply of American farm products to outrun the demand for them, despite a considerable movement of the farm population out of agriculture. In an unregulated market economy, this would have the effect of bringing a fall in farm prices and, in ordinary circumstances, a fall in farm incomes relative to the incomes of the rest of the society.

The effect of these tendencies can be illustrated by shifts in the demand and supply curves for a hypothetical farm product. In Fig. 4-3, the solid curves show us the initial supply and demand conditions for our farm product; the dotted curves show the positions of the curves

If the supply curve,
over time, shifts out
more rapidly than the
demand curve, the result
will be a fall in
the price of the product.

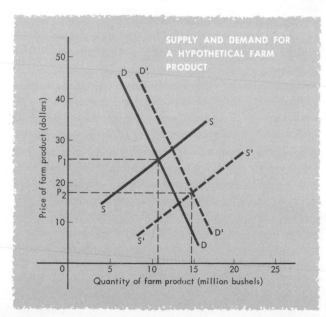

SUPPLY AND DEMAND FOR A HYPOTHETICAL FARM PRODUCT

FIG. 4-3

after a period of time—say five years later. Supply has outrun demand in the sense that the supply curve has shifted outward much farther than has the demand curve. The consequence has been a substantial fall in the price of the farm product from P_1 to P_2.

Why this tendency for the curves to shift out in this particular way? Actually, there are many factors involved. As far as the supply curve is concerned, the most important factor has been the technological revolution in farm production, which we have already mentioned. Because of new techniques of production, farmers have been able to supply substantially increased quantities of their product even while there has been a dramatic shrinkage in farm employment (e.g., over-all farm employment fell by nearly one-third in the 11 years between 1953 and 1964). On the demand side, an important factor has been what the economist calls the low *income-elasticity* of demand for farm products. There has been *some* outward shift in the domestic demand for farm products because our population and incomes have been rising rapidly in recent years, but this shift has been relatively moderate because, as we get richer, we tend to spend a relatively smaller part of our income on food and other agricultural products. This is what is meant by a low *income-elasticity* of demand: for a given percentage increase in our incomes, the percentage increase in our demand for the particular product is small.[4] As a consequence of these and other factors, we have

---

[4] Technically, *income-elasticity* is defined as the percentage change in the quantity of a good demanded at a given price divided by the percentage change in our incomes. Suppose my income goes up by 10 per cent and my purchases of corn at 10¢ an ear go up by 2 per cent: the *income-elasticity* of my demand for corn would be .2 or one-fifth. There is another even more common use of the *elasticity* concept in connection with demand curves. This is the concept of *price-elasticity* of demand: the percentage change in the quantity of a commodity demanded over the percentage change in its price. It is also believed that many farm products have a low price-elasticity or are in relatively *inelastic demand*. In the figure, I have drawn three demand curves: the center one has a price-elasticity of 1; the steeper one is less price-elastic (more inelastic); the flatter one is more elastic. The reader should determine why this is so, given our definition of price-elasticity of demand.

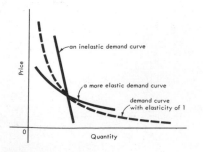

faced a tendency toward substantial decreases in farm prices and incomes, a tendency which would have been very strong indeed had not there been some form of government intervention.

Should the government have intervened? There are arguments on both sides. Some economists have pointed to the inefficiencies of many government farm programs and have argued that the changing levels of prices and incomes are simply the mechanisms by which the market allocates scarce resources into their best possible uses. Other economists have claimed that the arguments for a free market in agriculture are simplistic; they have urged attention to important social facts: the low level of farm incomes (average personal per capita farm income in 1964 was about $1500, compared to $2600 in the cities); the high incidence of poverty on the farms (43 per cent of farm families as opposed to 17 per cent of nonfarm families); the inadequacy of health, educational, and housing facilities in many poor rural areas; and so on.

Whatever the merits of these conflicting arguments, the fact is that the government, working through our normal political processes, has indeed intervened in a number of ways. We can illustrate the workings of one of these general methods—price supports—through our supply and demand analysis. The basic mechanism of a price support program is shown in Fig. 4-4. We suppose that the government proposes to keep farm prices at some particular level, say, our original price, P_1. Now when the supply and demand curves shift, the quantity supplied at this price will far exceed the quantity demanded. The government then will

The government supports the price at p_1. When supply and demand curves shift, the government will have to purchase AB million bushels of the farm product, the excess of supply above demand at the publicly supported price.

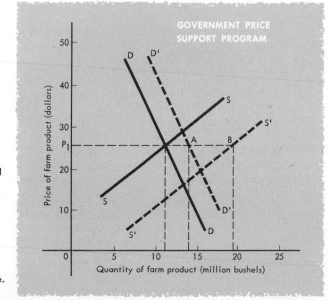

FIG. 4-4

buy up the difference and add the surplus to its stock of the farm product in storage. Does this involve a violation of the law of supply and demand? Yes, of course it does. We have already seen that supply and demand would give a different price and a different quantity produced (Fig. 4-3). The violation of the law can occur because the government is willing to buy up surpluses and keep them in storage. Of course this is not because it wants the surpluses, but because it wants to keep up farm prices and incomes.

Now there are many other ways in which the government could achieve this same objective of raising farm incomes. (The reader should use our diagram to show, for example, how a production limitation program—only so much of the crop can be produced—could also keep farm prices up.) [5] Instead of going into these, however, let us make two important general points about this area of government intervention in the American economy.

The first point is that the future shape of the farm "problem" in the United States may be somewhat different from what it has been in the past, depending very much on what happens in other countries of the world. Ultimately, with huge and growing populations, the underdeveloped countries of Asia will need far more food than they are at present capable of producing. Already, many of our surplus stocks of farm commodities have been substantially reduced through our programs of food aid (under Public Law 480) to the underdeveloped world. The final impact of this factor is impossible to predict, but it seems at least possible that, in two or three decades, the problem of "excess" supply in American agriculture may be of historical interest only.

The second point is more immediately relevant to our discussion in this chapter: it is simply to reiterate the complexity of the public-private relationship in the mixed economy. In a certain sense, as we have said, there is nothing more ruggedly independent and individualistic than the American farmer. In another sense, however, as we have just seen, it is clear that for many years now the government has been an effective partner to most farmers in their economic operations. And

[5] The reader will find it fairly easy to show that a production limitation program will keep prices up; but will it keep farm *incomes* up? After all, even though the program means a higher price, it also means a lower quantity sold. Actually, the answer largely depends on the price-elasticity of the demand curve for the farm product. If the reader will look back to the figure in the previous footnote, he will find that the total revenue (price X quantity) for the farm product will be higher with a higher price and smaller quantity as long as we are dealing with a low-elasticity (inelastic) demand curve. The opposite will be true with a high-elasticity demand curve. Since most farm products are judged to have inelastic demands, production limitation programs will generally result in higher farm incomes. (Also, the critics would say, in fewer goods and higher prices to the consumer.)

this is a good note on which to end this chapter, for it brings home clearly how intricate the relationships between the public and private sectors are in real life, how far removed they are from the simple stereotypes we sometimes imagine them to be.

Summary

The characteristic form of the modern economy is the *mixed economy* in which both government and the marketplace have important roles, though in different degrees in different countries.

In the United States, the public sector has grown substantially in the past three or four decades, though not so dramatically as is sometimes imagined. Total expenditures of governments at all levels have grown from about 20 per cent of GNP in the 1930's to about 30 per cent or less in the late 1960's. The growth in recent years has been particularly rapid in state and local expenditures, in governmental transfer payments, and in the very large federal expenditures in defense and defense-related areas.

Much of this expansion is due to noneconomic forces, and it represents no particularly new areas of government responsibility (e.g., defense, schools, etc.), but there has doubtless also been a growth of the role of government in the economy for economic reasons as well. These reasons involve concern for (1) welfare of the needy and income redistribution; (2) stabilization and growth of the economy in the aggregate; and (3) provision of collective goods and other goods where private and social benefits diverge.

Among the many specific programs of the government is its agricultural policy. Farm price supports do violate the law of supply and demand in agriculture, and some critics would say that they disrupt the efficient allocation of resources possible under a market system. But they also raise farm incomes, and many observers argue that low average farm incomes and the high incidence of poverty in farming justify intervention. In any case, the government has intervened, thus providing an example of the complex interrelationships between public and private sectors in the mixed economy.

Questions for Discussion

1 • Although government expenditure figures give an important indication of the degree of government intervention in the economy, they are not the

only measure of government activity. What are some other forms that public intervention may take? Give some specific examples from the experience of the United States or of other modern mixed economies.

2 • What are transfer payments? Why have governmental transfer payments been growing rapidly in recent years?

3 • Show how in the case of industrial air and water pollution there may be a significant divergence between private interest and the social welfare. Does this have any relation to arguments for or against public intervention in these areas?

4 • Suppose that we have a farm product with a relatively inelastic demand curve and a perfectly inelastic supply curve as follows:

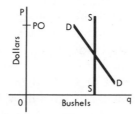

The government has two (politically feasible) alternatives:

a) support the price at Po by buying up all the product that consumers will not buy at that price;

b) guarantee the farmers the same total revenue as under the price support program, but do this by direct subsidy after the farmers have sold their entire crop to the public at the supply-and-demand determined price.

Which program will cost the government more money?

Can you see any possible advantages to the more expensive program?

5 • Considering the major economic problems facing the United States in the 1960's, do you consider it likely that there will be a) further growth in federal government expenditures, b) further growth in state and local expenditures, or c) resurgence of private initiatives? Try to think of at least one example that might lead to expansion in each of these spheres.

Suggested Reading

ECKSTEIN, OTTO, *Public Finance*, 2nd ed. Englewood Cliffs, N.J.: Prentice-Hall, Inc., 1967, Chaps. 1-3.

HATHAWAY, DALE E., *Government and Agriculture*. New York: Macmillan, 1963.

HARLAN, H. C., ed. *Readings in Economics and Politics*. New York: Oxford University Press, 1961, pp. 7-69.

PHELPS, EDMUND S., *Private Wants and Public Needs*. New York: W. W. Norton & Company, Inc., 1964.

SHONFIELD, ANDREW, *Modern Capitalism*. New York: Oxford University Press, 1965, Chaps. V-X, XIII-XIV.

The mixed economy
—private sector

5

Despite the growth of government in the
American economy, described in the last chapter, our mixed economy remains heavily oriented to the private side. If government
expenditures amount to something near 30
per cent of our gross national product, private
expenditures amount to over 70 per cent.
Furthermore, many government expenditures
are for the products of private industry, so
that although government orders may determine the direction of certain areas of production, the organization of that production remains overwhelmingly in private hands. In
this chapter, we shall look at some of the
characteristic institutions of the private sector,
attempting also to show some of the ways in
which this and the public sector interact.

The Market Economy Re-examined

It is tempting (and it would be very convenient) to describe the private sector of the American economy in terms of what we have earlier called a *pure market economy*. Unfortunately, this is not really possible, and for reasons that go deeper than the important fact that public and private sectors in our economy are mixed together. There is also the fundamental fact that the organization of business and labor in our economy is not as simple as our supply-and-demand markets might have indicated.

To bring out the critical assumptions more clearly, let us very briefly re-examine our picture of the pure market economy and indicate the foundations it presupposes.

The main features of the market economy are that economic decisions are made individually and are brought to bear on the economy as a whole through a price system operating in terms of a supply-and-demand mechanism. In this economy, we thought of every individual commodity—apples or washing machines—as having a demand curve drawn on the basis of consumer preferences and also a supply curve derived from producers' responses to various possible market prices. The equilibrium price and quantity for each commodity were then determined where supply and demand curves intersected.

We also suggested that this same kind of mechanism could be applied to the factors of production, as had been shown by the great general equilibrium theorists of the late nineteenth century.[1] Thus, let us suppose that we are dealing not with a commodity—washing machines—but with a kind of labor—electricians. In Fig. 5-1, we have drawn supply and demand curves for electricians. In the pure market economy, the price of electricians—which we would normally call their wage—and the number of electrician-hours employed would be determined by the intersection of these two curves.

Of course, we should not imagine that these supply and demand curves for the services of a factor of production are the same curves that we would draw for a commodity. When we were talking about washing machines, the demanders were the consumers who wanted to buy washing machines for their homes. When we are talking about electricians—or about welders or truck drivers or machine tools or blast furnaces—the demanders are typically not consumers but business firms that will produce the products that we shall ultimately buy. The business firm, in other words, is characteristically a *supplier* of products

[1] See Chap. 2, p. 33.

to the consumer but a *demander* of the services of the factors of production.[2]

We are not interested here in going further into the details of this process, but rather in asking about the assumptions on which it is based. And all these assumptions can be summed up in what we earlier

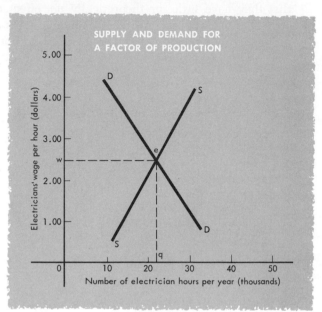

In a market economy, we determine the price of the services of electricians (or welders or machinery) by supply and demand curves analogous to those determining prices of commodities. In the factor supply and demand curves, however, the business firms are the main demanders, and the suppliers are the owners of the factors of production (in the case of labor, the workingmen of the economy).

FIG. 5-1

called the concept of pure competition. Our pure market economy functions in the way we have described only if it is a purely competitive economy; unfortunately, the private sector of the American economy does not in general fulfill the conditions of this kind of economy.

I say "unfortunately" here not as a value-judgment (though a small number of economists would argue that the purer competition

[2] Although we cannot derive these factor supply and demand curves here, a few hints as to their derivation should help make their meaning clear. The *demand curve* for electricians will ultimately reflect how profitable it is for firms to hire electricians. This, in turn, will be influenced by the consumer demand for electrical products and by the productivity of the electricians hired. The *supply curve* for electricians in a pure market economy will reflect, in the short run, the attractiveness of this kind of work compared with other employment opportunities or leisure for those who possess the necessary skills as electricians. In the longer run, if the wages of electricians remain very high, then more young men will seek to acquire the special skills required. If electricians' wages happen to be very low, then in the long run fewer people will head into this line of work. All this, of course, assumes that a pure market economy is functioning up and down the line.

is the better), but quite simply because it is much easier to *analyze* pure competition than the other, more realistic market structures. In economics, as in all social sciences, the closer one gets to reality, the more difficult things tend to become for the pure theorist.

Now the special feature of a purely competitive economy is that the various economic units in the society are assumed to be so small that they have little, or theoretically *no,* effect on the prices that are set in the marketplace. All these economic units simply *respond* to impersonally determined market prices; they do not *set* prices themselves. Thus, when a consumer goes to the store to buy a product, he is assumed to take the store price of a product as given and independent of any of his actions. And the same is also assumed to be true of the businessman and the laborer in their markets. The laborer does not set his own wage under pure competition; he simply decides whether or not to work at the going market-determined wage. Similarly, the businessman does not set a price for his product; this is done by the market. What the businessman does is to decide how much he is willing to produce and sell at that market price. As we have already noticed (Chapter 2), this assumption is built into our ordinary supply curve which tells us how producers will respond to various hypothetical prices.

Now pure competition works—or, at least, is a reasonable approximation to the facts—as long as the economic units in the society are quite small. If individual consumers do not league together, if laborers approach their employers as individual workmen without collective action, if the typical business firm is small in relation to the over-all market—if all these assumptions are fulfilled, then pure competition will serve as a fairly good description of reality. But, as we have said, these conditions are not typically fulfilled in the modern American economy. To show this, let us say a few words about the actual structure of American business and labor organization.

The Modern Corporation

Perhaps the most striking feature of industrial organization in the United States is its enormous variety. There are something like 5 million business units in this country today, some of them infinitesimally small. Even if we look at the specific business form known as the *corporation,*[3]

---

[3] The *corporation* is the main form of business organization in the United States, accounting for about two-thirds of our privately produced income. It differs from a single proprietorship or a partnership in that the stockholders who own the corporation are *not* liable for the debts of the corporation beyond their original

we find that over half of them have assets of less than $100,000. At the
other extreme, however, is the great modern corporation with assets
and annual sales running into the billions of dollars. In 1960, for example, there were 14 American firms that had assets of over $2 billion
each; more than a hundred American corporations have assets of over
$1 billion. Table 5–1 lists 10 of these large giants ranked according to the
assets of each. A similar picture would emerge if we considered annual
sales. In 1960, for example, General Motors had sales of $11.2 billion,
or over $60 per man, woman, and child in the country (more than the
total per capita incomes of some modern underdeveloped countries!).
Altogether, the 250 largest nonfinancial corporations in the United
States control nearly half of all our nonfinancial corporate assets.

TABLE / ASSETS OF SOME LEADING
5 – 1 / AMERICAN CORPORATIONS (1960)

Corporation	Assets (in billions)	Corporation	Assets (in billions)
American Telephone & Telegraph Company	$20.8	Gulf Oil Co.	$3.6
Standard Oil of N.J.	9.9	Socony-Mobil Oil	3.3
General Motors	7.9	Texaco	3.3
U.S. Steel	4.7	Pennsylvania Railroad	2.9
Ford Motor Co.	3.9	General Electric	2.6

To look at the extremes of very small and very large firms is one
way of showing the variety of modern American industry. Another way
that economists find helpful is to look at something they call *concentration ratios*. These concentration ratios show how much of the sales
of a particular industry are accounted for by the larger firms in the
industry. Thus we might ask: what percentage of the sales of an industry are accounted for by the four largest firms, what percentage by
the eight largest, and so on? Figure 5-2 presents a selection of indus-

---

investment (this is "limited" as opposed to "unlimited liability"). Although the
stockholders own the corporation, much of the control rests with management, leading to what is often called the "divorce of ownership and control." A famous early
study of the modern corporation and its economic significance is A. A. Berle and
Gardiner C. Means, *The Modern Corporation and Private Property* (New York: The
Macmillan Company, 1934). For recent provocative views on the modern corporation, see John Kenneth Galbraith, *The New Industrial State* (Boston: Houghton
Mifflin Company, 1967).

tries with different concentration ratios. Variety is again apparent. In the electric light bulb industry, the top 4 firms accounted for 93 per cent of total shipments. In the fur goods industry, the top 4 firms accounted for only 4 per cent of total shipments; indeed, the top 20 firms accounted for only 11 per cent of the shipments in fur goods.

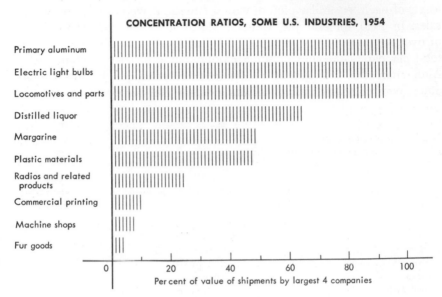

CONCENTRATION RATIOS, SOME U.S. INDUSTRIES, 1954

FIG. 5-2

Per cent of value of shipments by largest 4 companies

This chart shows the great variety of ratios in American industries in 1954. Many of our characteristic modern industries, however, have very high concentration ratios. (Source: *Concentration in American Industry*, Report of the Subcommittee on Antitrust and Monopoly, U.S. Senate Judiciary Committee, 85th Congress, 1st Session, Washington, 1957.)

This variety, in itself, should make it clear that any simple set of assumptions, such as pure competition involves, would be inadequate to the rich reality of American industry. But the problem is even more complicated. For one thing, even the relatively small firms in American industry are often found to have at least *some* control over the prices of the commodities they sell. We know from our own direct experience that even that smallest of all units, the corner grocery store, often charges prices that are different from those of not only the supermarket but other corner grocery stores. Most firms, however small, have a tiny "monopoly" on something, whether it be the way they package goods, special brand names, trade-marks, even something as elusive as good will. The term *monopolistic competition* has sometimes been used to describe these cases in which "monopolistic" and "competitive" elements combine even where there are large numbers of quite small firms.[4]

But the greatest problem comes from the giant modern corporations we have been describing. Some of the highly concentrated industries are among the largest and most characteristic industries of the modern American economy. The top 4 firms control over half the shipments in industries such as primary aluminum, breakfast cereals, cigarettes, motor vehicles, steel, electrical appliances, and so on. The list goes on and, in total, represents a sizeable fraction of all industrial production in the United States.

The significance of these facts is great:

1. In a negative sense, the existence of giant corporations and heavily concentrated industries clearly means that the assumptions of pure competition do not hold for much of American industry. These large firms do not simply respond to the prices set by an impersonal market. They clearly have at least some discretion in the prices they charge consumers. General Motors does not have total freedom in the price it sets for, say, Chevrolets, but it would be quite false to say that it had no freedom at all. Ford, Chrysler, and other automobile manufacturers are in similar positions.

Now the fact that these firms have at least some control over their markets means that they can try to affect these markets by a whole variety of means that would not be characteristic of purely competitive firms.

These large firms can introduce special features, gadgets, designs, improvements in comforts, appearance, or safety, or other changes in the quality of their products, to try to separate their particular product from that of their rivals in the eyes of the consumer. This is what economists call *product differentiation*. The large modern industrial firm may often choose to compete through such changes in its product rather than by lowering its price and outcompeting its rivals in that way.

Another common form of competition between large firms is through *adver-*

---

[4] Since "monopoly" and "competition" are opposites, the very phrase "monopolistic competition" may seem a contradiction in terms. The meaning becomes clear, however, if we imagine an example of brand-name competition. Take laundry soaps and detergents as an example. There is clearly a competition involved among Tide, Rinso, Lux, and other such products. Yet the producer of each of these products has a complete monopoly on the sale of each. No one but the producers of Tide can sell Tide, and so on. The reader should think of other areas of competition he knows—cigarettes, automobiles, etc.—and determine whether there is not both a "monopoly" and a "competitive" element in each case.

The classic reference in this area of monopolistic competition is Edward H. Chamberlain, *Monopolistic Competition* (Cambridge, Mass.: Harvard University Press, 1933).

tising. The expenditure on advertising in some American industries is very large. In 1962, for example, over $12 billion was spent on advertising by American industry. Advertising is a kind of competition that one would not find in our *pure* market economy, because it involves at least some ability to influence the market for one's product. Though, of course, it is a *form* of competition.

The first point, then, is that the ways in which firms compete with each other when there are small numbers of large firms is, in general, quite different from those we would expect in our simple supply-and-demand model.

2. Our second point is that the *analysis* of these different forms of competition is really very complex when there are highly concentrated industries. Economists speak of what they call the *oligopoly problem.* The word *oligopoly* comes from the Greek and means "few sellers." It is from the same root as *monopoly* which means "a single seller." Actually, pure monopoly, as a form of market structure is not so difficult to analyze, but pure monopoly is rare. But oligopoly, as we have seen, is not rare, and it involves considerable difficulty for the economic analyst. One of the main reasons for this is the fact that these large firms cannot help being aware that each one's actions are likely to affect, and produce a reaction from, its rivals. Here are firm A, firm B, and firm C. A knows that when he does something it may produce a reaction from B and C. B and C, in turn, know that what each of them does will produce a reaction from the other two. But what reaction? If, as firm A, I know that firms B and C will definitely react in such-and-such a fashion, I may know exactly what to do. But suppose they react in some other fashion. May I not find myself losing out altogether?

Suppose I believe that the other two firms will go along with a price rise if I make one on my product. If I believe this, I may decide that we shall all make more profits if I raise my price. But then suppose I am wrong and that one of the other firms decides that it will not go along, that it will keep its price just below mine, cutting me out, taking over my customers, increasing its share of the market. In this case, I would find that I had made not a good move but exactly the wrong move.

In short, the pattern of action and reaction that can take place when there are a few large sellers is enormously complex. Instead of relying on the grand generalizations of supply-and-demand theory, economists have to content themselves with very careful studies of particular industries, trying to judge from their past behavior how these firms are likely to behave in the future.

3. A third and final point about this problem of highly con-

centrated industries is that they raise a number of difficult questions for public policy and action. Now it must not be assumed automatically that because these firms do have and exercise market power that they are therefore running against the public interest. In some industries it is the very small firm that is inefficient and wasteful and the large firm that produces the cheaper and better quality product. Furthermore, some economists would argue that the large firm with its capability for research and development may contribute greatly to the growth of the economy as a whole. Nevertheless, there is one respect in which this departure from pure competition removes an important public safeguard. In the world of Adam Smith, the consumer was protected ultimately not by the government but by the competition of hundreds of rival firms that would rush into any market if the producers there were overcharging the consumer and making exorbitant profits. When this kind of competition is absent, we are forced to ask what safeguards *does* the consumer have, or must the government intervene to protect his interest?

Before going into the public policy issue, however, let us first take a brief glance at the other major aspect of the private sector: American labor organization.

Unions and Modern American Labor

Just as the existence of the large modern corporation means a deviation from supply-and-demand in the "product market" so does the existence of organized labor mean a deviation from supply-and-demand in the "factor market." Again, this is not necessarily undesirable, but it does mean that a more complicated analysis is required.

Actually, even if there were no labor unions, the American labor market would hardly work in the smooth fashion that a pure market economy requires. There are all sorts of possible imperfection: laborers may not generally know about jobs in other localities or occupations; there may be discrimination against minority groups; there may be general unemployment in the economy as a whole; the individual laborer faced with the necessity of having some sort of job may be at the mercy of a locally *monopsonistic* [5] employer; and so on.

---

[5] As *monopoly* means a single seller, *monopsony* means a single buyer. In a given locality where there may be only one large industrial firm, the employer of labor in that area may effectively have some monopsonistic control over the labor market.

Labor unions, however, do represent a particular and especially important form of labor organization in the American economy, and we should say a word about their economic significance.

Figure 5-3 shows the growth of labor union membership in the United States in the course of the twentieth century. The trend has

FIG. 5-3

clearly been upward during this period although there have been notable ups and downs, and, in recent years, union membership has been relatively stagnant. With the increase in the number of white-collar, as opposed to blue-collar, workers in the American economy, labor unions actually face some difficult organizational problems in the years ahead.

Difficult problems, however, are nothing new to the American labor movement. In one sense, as the diagram shows, their progress has been fairly continuous. In 1886, the American Federation of Labor (AFL) was founded under the leadership of Samuel Gompers. In 1935, the Congress of Industrial Organizations (CIO) joined the fray under the leadership of the controversial John L. Lewis. In 1955, under George Meany, the two large organizations joined together into the massive present-day AFL-CIO. Organized labor now accounts for about 30 per cent of the nonagricultural labor force in the United States. In *another* sense, however, this progress has been pock-marked by problems and crises. This was especially true in the early days when American industry can hardly be said to have welcomed the new unions with open arms. Moreover, the attitude of the government was by no means friendly. The courts interpreted the Sherman Act of 1890 to restrict unions that were organizing in "restraint of trade"; and in the Danbury Hatter's case of 1908, the union was made to pay extensively for damages caused by a strike. It was not until 1914 that the Clayton Act stated explicitly that unions were not to be considered in "restraint of trade," and it was really not until the Wagner Act and other favorable legislation of the 1930's that the labor movement came strongly into its own.

Unions have an impact on many different aspects of the labor market. They have what we may think of as a primary objective—to raise wages for their members—but they bargain collectively about many more issues than this: seniority systems, hours and conditions of work, methods of production, job tenure, and so on. They are complicated institutions with their own meetings, elections, organizational structures, and often their own political views.

Let us examine one aspect of the economic impact of unions—raising wages—and show, first, how it can cause a departure from the market-determined wage and second, why we must use caution in interpreting this piece of analysis.

Figure 5-4 shows the effect of a wage increase for electricians above the supply-and-demand determined price. W_1 is the wage that would obtain if there were no external intervention in the market. The union's objective is to raise the wage to W_2. If it succeeds—

If one union in the economy succeeds in raising its wage (W_2) above the supply-and-demand determined wage (W_1), the consequences for those workers will be less employment but higher wages for those employed. One must not generalize this effect to the action of unions in the economy as a whole, however, since these curves are drawn on ceteris paribus assumptions that do not hold when all unions are acting together.

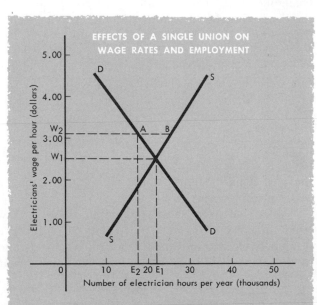

EFFECTS OF A SINGLE UNION ON WAGE RATES AND EMPLOYMENT

FIG. 5-4

and if everything else remains unchanged (our familiar *ceteris paribus* clause)—then, when the wage rate is raised to W_2, business firms will cut their employment from E_1 to E_2. Actually, the measure of unemployment among electricians would be greater than the difference between those formerly employed and those now employed. The reason is that at the new and higher wage rate, more electricians' services would be offered than before. (This is what the supply curve tells us.) Consequently, the amount of unemployment is measured by the horizontal distance between the demand and supply curves at the new wage (W_2), or the distance AB.

Now it would seem from this analysis that the main impact of unions in this area of bargaining would be to raise the wage rates of their members and to curtail the employment of their members. And, indeed, the objective of securing a wage that is high relative to other income-receivers in the economy is an important one for most unions.

We must not conclude that this effort will be successful *in the aggregate,* however. And this is where we must exercise some caution in interpreting our results. For we cannot say that when one union does something alone, the same results will be achieved for that union as when *all unions together* attempt a similar thing. The relevance of the *ceteris paribus* phrase is particularly important here. When *all* unions are attempting to achieve wage increases, then this clause is no longer appropriate for any one labor market—other things *are* changing. In particular, if all wages go up, this will have an effect on the demand for most products in the economy; and when the demand for products goes up, this, in turn, will have an effect on the demand for labor. We could, in fact, imagine a case where everything more or less canceled out: there were higher wages in general, higher prices in general (so that the higher wages would purchase the same number of goods in the economy as before), and no change in the employment of workers throughout the economy.

This might seem like an argument against unions, since it would mean that they hadn't achieved much for all their pains. On the other hand, it can also be used to combat an argument frequently used in the past against labor unions: namely, that they are responsible for mass unemployment in the economy.

What we have actually done in these last two paragraphs has been to move on from a particular part of the economy (washing machines, electricians, and so on) to a consideration of the economy in the aggregate. Thus, we are foreshadowing matters that we shall be taking up in some detail in Part II of this book, beginning with the next chapter.

Government, Business, Labor, and the Public Interest

What should be our attitude toward "big business" and "big labor" and, for that matter, to "big government" in the modern mixed economy? As we might expect, the industrial countries of the West have taken many different attitudes toward these modern institutions. In the United States, the characteristic preference has been to view the growth of government with some concern and to rely on private enterprise when possible. However, there are many economists who argue that this preference is inadequate for the needs of our present-day society.[6] And, in fact, even in the United States, there are literally thousands of pieces of legislation that in one way or another prescribe or circumscribe the behavior of business and labor organizations.

Perhaps the most well-known form of governmental intervention in the sphere of American business is that of what are loosely called the antitrust laws. We have already mentioned the two most important of these laws, the Sherman Act of 1890 and the Clayton Act of 1914.

The Sherman Act prohibits "every contract, combination in the form of trust or otherwise, or conspiracy, in restraint of trade or commerce" and prescribes punishments for "every person who shall monopolize, or attempt to monopolize, or combine or conspire with any other person or persons, to monopolize any part of the trade or commerce" in the United States or with foreign countries. The Clayton Act contains a proviso outlawing business policies that might "substantially lessen competition or tend to create a monopoly."

Now these laws have been subject to many different interpretations in the courts, and, indeed, the standards by which offensive conduct is to be judged are extremely difficult to formulate in an economically satisfactory way. Nevertheless, it is fairly clear that the basic intent of these laws is to try to protect society from the worst abuses of monopoly power and to move the economy *in the general direction* of a somewhat more competitive, slightly less impure market economy than might exist if private forces were allowed completely free rein. In some ways, these laws are very much in the spirit of Adam Smith; for although they do involve governmental intervention in the economy, they are designed to promote what he would have considered the beneficent forces of competition.

[6] We shall consider some of these views later on when we discuss the problems of the affluent society in Chapter 16.

The antitrust laws are by no means the only way in which the American government intervenes in the business sector. Nor, for that matter, can it be said that this intervention reflects any consistent over-all pattern. In the last chapter, for example, we showed an instance—agricultural policy—where the government was attempting to *interfere* with the normal workings of competitive markets. Other examples could be cited in which the government has attempted to correct a deficiency in a particular market by making it not more but *less* competitive.[7]

Some of these interventions—as is unavoidable in a political democracy—represent simply the play of special interests to which the majority has acquiesced. In a deeper sense, however, it is not surprising that our laws should display a complex character in this area, because the area is itself complex. There are economic advantages to competition, but there also are economic advantages to larger-scale production. In attempting to protect the consumer, while still recognizing the realities of modern industrial organization, even the wisest and most public-spirited government must walk a finely strung tightrope.

Governmental policy towards "big labor" has also displayed a number of ambiguities. Furthermore, as we have seen, it has swung back and forth over the years:

In the early days, the policy tended to be restrictive of union activities. In the 1930's, the tide turned. The Wagner Act of 1935 set up the National Labor Relations Board to protect unions against "unfair labor practices," and it unequivocally supported the workers' right to "bargain collectively through representatives of their own choosing." During World War II, strikes were at a minimum; but then immediately after the war, in 1946 and especially in 1947, strikes reached an all-time high in terms of the percentage of man-hours lost in American industry. Congress responded with the Taft-Hartley Act in 1947, which defined unfair *union* practices, set an 80-day cooling-off period for some types of strikes, and restricted certain other union activities. The other major piece of labor legislation since World War II was the Landrum-Griffin Act of 1959 designed to combat corruption in unions. Both these measures, especially the Taft-Hartley Act, were strongly opposed by organized labor at the time they were passed. Thus it can be said that, in contrast to the permissive attitude of the 1930's, governmental policy in the past two decades has been slightly more restrictive. The pendulum has swung back, though only part of the way.

[7] For example, the Robinson-Patman Act of 1936, which was designed to protect the small retail store against the competition of the chain stores. For a good discussion of government policies towards business in the United States, see Richard Caves, *American Industry: Structure, Conduct, Performance*, 2nd ed. (Englewood Cliffs, N.J.: Prentice-Hall, Inc., 1967), especially chaps. 4-6.

As in the case of the business sector, we should not be surprised that labor legislation in this country is complex. For again, the problem is complex. Labor unions in one form or another are clearly here to stay. It would be inconceivable—particularly in an economy that has giant corporations like General Motors, Standard Oil, General Electric, and others—to ask that the individual laborer, by himself, meet and bargain with his "employer." The inequality of the two parties to the bargain is self-evident. Labor will, and should, organize collectively, if only to bring a rough parity of bargaining power to the conference table.

But what of the "public interest"? One of the grave dangers of our economy, as we shall see in Part II, is that industry and labor are so constituted that it is very difficult to get full employment in the economy without wage–price inflation. No one wants unemployment, but no one wants inflation either. Furthermore, most people do not want the government stepping in to check on either business or labor at every turning of the way.

These problems are not hopeless, but they are difficult. For the central fact is that when economic institutions, whether labor unions or business corporations, become big, then (unlike the tiny firm of pure competition) their actions are drenched with the public interest. And when the public interest is involved, sooner or later people will ask that some branch of the government make sure that their interests are not being abused. Thus, to the other reasons we mentioned in the previous chapter, we can add this further explanation of why the modern industrial society is characteristically of the mixed form.

Summary

Despite the growth of government in the American economy in recent decades, our economy remains heavily oriented toward the private sector. This private sector cannot, however, be characterized in the simple supply-and-demand terms of a pure market economy. Supply-and-demand analysis typically assumes the existence of small business and labor units, none large enough to affect the prices at which goods are bought and sold.

This is patently untrue in the case of large areas of American business. The industrial sector of our economy displays an enormous variety, from the tiny firm to the giant modern corporation with its billions of dollars of assets. Even quite small firms usually show at least some ability to influence their local markets in a form of *mo-*

nopolistic competition. More significant perhaps is the *oligopoly problem:* the case of industries where a few large firms substantially dominate the markets involved. When this happens, competition seldom takes a supply-and-demand form but involves many other elements such as changing the quality of the product or advertising. The analysis of oligopoly is particularly complex because it is difficult to know how firms will react when they recognize their mutual interdependence.

Nor does American labor fit the purely competitive model. There are imperfections in this market quite apart from formal labor organizations, but unions are clearly an important economic institution in this country. They currently account for 30 per cent of our nonagricultural labor force. They have many different objectives, though raising the wages of their members is an especially important one. In analyzing a particular union's attempt to raise wages, we found that the union might be able to raise the wage, but at the expense of higher unemployment for that type of worker. This conclusion is not, however, generalizable to all unions acting together or at the same time, for this would violate the *ceteris paribus* clause on which the labor supply and demand curves are drawn. The analysis of this kind of *aggregative* problem belongs in Part II.

The growth of big business and big labor in this country poses interesting problems in protecting the public interest. In the business sector, much legislation, notably our antitrust laws, has been designed to prevent the worst abuses of monopoly power and to stimulate competition where possible. Our policies in this area, however, have by no means been consistent, which also can be said for our policies toward labor, fluctuating as they have from repression of unions in the early days to strong encouragement in the 1930's to moderate regulation in the post-World War II period. These ambiguities of policy are not simply accidental; they reflect genuine difficulty in coping with the problem of "bigness" in the industrial and labor spheres, for when economic units are large, private actions almost always have significant public consequences.

Questions for Discussion

1 • Business firms under pure competition are said to take the price of their product as determined by the impersonal market. Show that this statement is equivalent to saying that the firm in pure competition faces a horizontal (perfectly elastic) demand curve for its product:

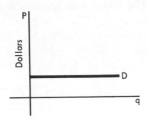

Why is such a demand curve unlikely unless the firm is very small in relation to the industry as a whole?

2 • Demand curves for factors of production are often called "derived demand curves" since they depend on consumer demand for the products that the factors produce. Describe the general process whereby an increase in consumer demand for diamonds might increase the demand for, and consequently the wage of, diamond-cutters.

3 • Show how the oligopoly problem is made difficult to analyze by virtue of the fact that the firms recognize their mutual dependence on each other's actions. Can you think of any reason why it would be difficult to draw a demand curve for the products of a single oligopolist?

4 • "The existence of large, even giant, corporations means that American business does not respond to the dictates of the market, but rather manages the market for its own purposes. For this very reason 'consumer sovereignty' is largely a myth in the modern industrial world." Discuss.

5 • Write an essay giving the pros and cons of advertising expenditures in the American economy.

6 • The distinguished American economist Thorstein Veblen (1857-1929) once called the struggle between business and labor a mere game "played between two contending interests for private gain." How might the leader of a modern labor union respond to such a criticism?

7 • Why is it impossible to generalize from the effects of one union, acting alone, to the effects of all unions, acting simultaneously, on real wages and employment in the national economy?

8 • Enumerate some of the ways in which the U.S. government attempts to protect the public interest in the face of the growth of big business and big labor. What do you consider to be the major difficulties in defining an effective policy in this area?

Suggested Reading

ADAMS, WALTER, ed., *The Structure of American Industry*, 3rd ed. New York: The Macmillan Company, 1961.

CAVES, RICHARD, *American Industry: Structure, Conduct, Performance*, 2nd ed. Englewood Cliffs, N.J.: Prentice-Hall, Inc., 1967.

GALBRAITH, JOHN K., *American Capitalism, the Concept of Countervailing Power*. Boston: Houghton Mifflin Co., 1952.

Mixed
Economy—
Private
Sector

MASON, EDWARD S., *The Corporation in Modern Society*. Cambridge: Harvard University Press, 1956.

PHELPS, EDMUND S., ed., *Problems of the Modern Economy*. New York: W. W. Norton & Company, Inc., 1966, pp. 7-106.

TAFT, PHILIP, *Organized Labor in American History*. New York: Harper & Row, 1964.

WEISS, LEONARD W., *Case Studies in American Industry*. New York: John Wiley & Sons, Inc., 1967.

WILCOX, CLAIR, *Public Policies Toward Business*, rev. ed. Homewood, Ill.: Richard D. Irwin, Inc., 1960.

II

THE ECONOMY IN THE AGGREGATE
National Income, Employment,
Inflation, Money, Trade

Keynes and
the New Economics

6

In Chapter 5, when discussing American labor, we ran into a difficulty. We found that even if we analyzed one union's actions in a particular market, our analysis would not allow us to draw general conclusions about the effect of unions on the economy as a whole. This is not a special difficulty; it is a general one. It is a very big step, surrounded by pitfalls, to move from the particular union, firm, or industry to the economy in the aggregate. Analyzing the economy in the aggregate indeed requires a rather new and different point of view.

Economists have recognized this problem by dividing their subject into two related but nevertheless distinguishable areas: (1) *microeconomics*, the study of the particular units (consumers, individual business firms, laborers, etc.) that make up the economy, and of how they are inter-related; and (2) *macroeconomics,* the study of the economy as a whole. In the second area, the consumption, production, and employment of individual consumers, businesses, and laborers are "aggregated" to form grand totals for the nation at large.

Most of our analysis in Part I was of the *micro*economic variety. "Other things equal," a phrase that occurred frequently in our discussion of supply-and-demand analysis, was indeed a way of isolating a particular part of the economy from the rest of its surrounding environment.

In Part II, we shall be concerned with *macro*economics. The following chapters form a roughly logical progression as we move from a consideration of problems and concepts to an analysis of the workings of the economy as a whole, and then, finally, to the public issues involved in applying governmental monetary and fiscal policies to areas such as unemployment, inflation, and international trade.

Problems of the
Economy in the Aggregate

Another, more controversial name for certain aspects of modern macroeconomic analysis is the "new economics." To the public at large, this term has gained wide currency in the 1960's as a description of various policies of the federal government in the monetary and fiscal fields. For economists, the phrase has an older lineage. In 1947, Seymour Harris of Harvard edited a book called the *New Economics.* This book, in turn, was dedicated to an analysis and evaluation of an economist whose main work had been done a decade earlier. The "new economics" stems ultimately from *The General Theory of Employment, Interest and Money* (1936) written by perhaps the most famous economist of the twentieth century, the late John Maynard Keynes.

Like Adam Smith and Karl Marx, Keynes was one of a half-dozen economists whose work profoundly influenced large numbers of other economists and, indeed, the actions of statesmen and nations. Before studying his contribution, however, let us be clearer in our own minds about what kind of problems macroeconomics involves.

The first step is to alter somewhat the point of view that we gain almost automatically from our daily participation in economic matters: a view of particular jobs, particular firms, particular industries. We know that it is sometimes hard to find a job, or that some particular business firm may be having troubles; but now we ask: Might the nation sometimes face conditions when businesses *in general* were failing, when people *in general* could not locate work? Actually, the question need not be put pessimistically. We could also ask: Are there times when everyone has work, when labor is in great demand, when prices, profits, and wages are all high? The point, of course, is that these questions are about the performance of the economy as a whole.

Now if we look at the past in our own country or in other industrial countries, we can find many instances to prove that national economies do, indeed, suffer ups and downs in their general economic well-being. All of us know from our reading of American history of the great number of "panics" that have seized our country at one point or another. There were panics in the United States in 1819, 1837, 1857, 1893, 1907, 1914, 1920-1921, and, of course, the "great crash" in 1929. Various statistical measures of these ups and downs are also common. In Figs. 6-1 and 6-2, we present some diagrams of unemployment in the United States and the United Kingdom at various times in the past. These diagrams measure unemployment as a percentage of the labor force, and they indicate how variable this factor has been

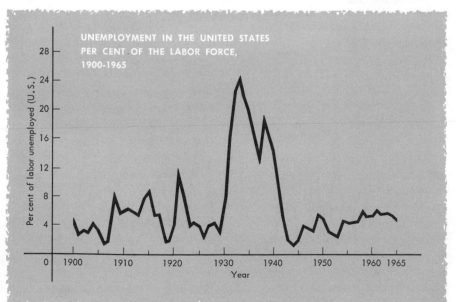

UNEMPLOYMENT IN THE UNITED STATES
PER CENT OF THE LABOR FORCE,
1900-1965

Per cent of labor unemployed (U.S.)

FIG. 6-1

historically. The great leap in the unemployment percentage in the United States in the 1930's is a less picturesque but still telling way of describing the Great Depression, which we mentioned in our very first chapter.

But economies can get out of gear in other ways besides unemployment. In the first chapter we also talked of the German hyperinflation of the 1920's, when the price level soared to the trillions.[1] This was truly an exceptional incident, but no more exceptional than completely stable prices would be. Almost all industrial countries have had some experience with inflation in the twentieth century and, in many underdeveloped countries, rapid inflation is a week-to-week phenomenon. Figure 6-3 shows the general course of consumer prices in the United States from World War I to the present.

We must remember that when we talk about the price *level*, we are talking about something slightly different from the price of apples or the price of washing machines. When the price of apples alone goes up, our demand curve tells us that we will buy fewer apples because, among other reasons, it will be cheaper for us to satisfy our desire for fruit with peaches and pears. When we talk about the price *level* rising, however, we are referring to a rise not only in apple prices but in the prices of peaches and pears and washing machines as well.

Similarly, in the case of unemployment: if the wage of electricians

[1] See the chart of the German inflation, Fig. 1-1.

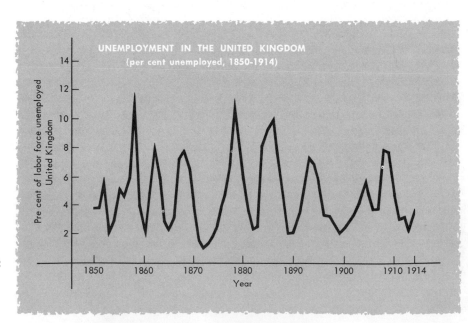

FIG. 6-2

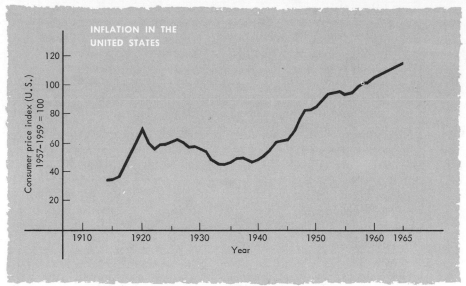

INFLATION IN THE UNITED STATES

The United States has experienced nothing like the
German hyperinflation in the 1920's; nevertheless, like most countries,
we have had a general rise in prices during the twentieth century.

FIG. 6-3

goes down, people will turn toward other occupations, and fewer will
offer their services as electricians. But suppose there is unemployment
in all industries at once? What happens to the wage then? Where do
people turn?

These are the heartland questions of macroeconomics. What
determines the general level of employment? What determines the
short-run level of national income? [2] What determines the over-all level
of prices? These are the problems of the economy in the aggregate.

Early Views

Our diagram of unemployment in the United Kingdom (Fig. 6-2)
indicates that aggregative problems were around long before the

---

[2] The adjective *short-run* has been inserted here purposefully. The analysis of
national income (or total production) that we shall consider in Part II is largely
concerned with the utilization of a *given* labor force and productive capacity. In
the short run (one or two years), this is a permissible assumption. In the long run,
the labor force, the productive capacity, and the economy in general *grow,* and
the problem changes. This problem of long-run economic growth will be our prin-
cipal focus in Part III.

1930's. What then did earlier economists have to say about them? What kind of analysis did they offer?

Now the truth is that until fairly modern times the economics profession did not do very well in this particular department, especially when it came to the problem of unemployment. There are some exceptions, but, for the most part, prevailing economic theory in the nineteenth century tended either to ignore the problem—i.e., to proceed on the *assumption* of a full employment economy and then to go on to analyze other problems—or to argue that theoretically there could not be a general unemployment problem except in a temporary or "frictional" sense.

This argument was not simply a personal whim on the part of these early economists; rather, they had certain systematic reasons for believing that an unfettered market economy would automatically solve any short-run aggregative problems. Hence they could direct their attention to other areas, either to microeconomics or, in the case of the early Classical Economists, to population growth and other long-run factors.

These systematic reasons are sometimes summarized in what is called Say's law, after a French economist, Jean Baptiste Say (1767-1832). Say's writings were well-known to the eminent British economists of the period such as David Ricardo and Thomas Robert Malthus, whom we have mentioned earlier. Ricardo fully subscribed to Say's law, though Malthus, as we shall see, had serious reservations about it.

Say's law states that, in the economy as a whole, supply creates its own demand. When we produce goods, according to this law, we create a demand for other goods; consequently, there can be no over-production of goods in general. Since there can be no overproduction of goods in general, there can be no unemployment problem in general. To put it in different words: since there is always a market for the goods we produce, there is no over-all limit on the number of jobs the society can sustain. If people are unemployed, then it can be only because they make unreasonable wage demands or prefer leisure or are simply in transit between one job and another.

This is simply a statement of the law, not a defense. But Say and Ricardo, and in fact most nineteenth century economists, also felt that they had a good defense for the law. The defense really had two parts.

The first part consisted in relegating "money" to a minor role in the economy.

They said in effect: "Money is just a veil that covers the realities of economic life. Money is simply a medium of exchange. In order to understand what really goes on, let us look at potatoes, steel, wheat, shoes, and so on. Then we will not be deceived by mere monetary changes and we will reach the fundamental phenomena involved."

If the first step was to underplay the role of money, the second step was more positive.

They argued: "Now look at this real, non-money economy. In this economy, when I put a laborer to work producing, say, more potatoes, I am increasing the supply of potatoes, but I am *also* increasing the demand for other goods. What will I use the potatoes for? Either I will consume them myself (my demand is increased), or I will offer them in exchange for some other commodity, say, clothing, and this will mean that the demand for clothing has increased. Either way, the added supply has created an added demand; thus, in general, supply creates its own demand. Hence, there can be no such thing as *general* overproduction or *general* unemployment. Q.E.D."

These arguments are not nonsense. In fact, they are rather persuasive and, for most of a century, they did persuade most economists that aggregative economic problems could be set to one side.

Not all economists, however. Malthus worried about the problem and remained unconvinced. He saw the possibility that there might be a "universal glut" of commodities in the economy as a whole and that this might lead to widespread unemployment. He tried to argue the point with his friend, Ricardo; but Malthus's own arguments were far from airtight, and Ricardo won out on debating points, fairly easily. Marx was another economist who remained unconvinced. As we have already seen, Marx made increasing unemployment an intrinsic part of his analysis of capitalism. This unemployment arose from the technological displacement of labor by machines, but Marx also spoke generally about an over-all inadequacy of markets. The capitalistic system, he thought, might produce more goods than it was constituted to absorb. This could also contribute to crises and depressions.

Neither Malthus nor Marx, however, made much of a dent on this part of the main body of economic analysis, and it wasn't until the very end of the nineteenth century that really serious thought began to be given to these problems. Here special credit should be given to the Swedish economist Knut Wicksell (1851-1926), who anticipated many of the elements in the "revolution" in economic analysis that was soon to take place. The economists of Sweden were, indeed, generally in the vanguard of this particular development, although the great breakthrough must be attributed to the man we shall turn to now. It was his theory that really did the trick.

That man was John Maynard Keynes.

Keynesian Analysis

Keynes (1883-1946), the man, was a most remarkable and versatile figure. He was at one time or another a businessman, teacher, college administrator, high government official, patron of the arts, and, of course, the foremost economist of his age. His wife was Lydia Lopokova, a prima ballerina, and she and Keynes were members of the famous Bloomsbury group that included famous artists such as E. M. Forster and Virginia Woolf. Even in his academic work he was versatile. His first book was on the theory of probability. His economic writings included controversial comment on current issues—like his *Economic Consequences of the Peace,* which made such a stir after World War I—and also highly abstract theoretical works that are quite incomprehensible to the general public. His *General Theory of Employment, Interest and Money* is in the latter group. It has to be studied hard, and a background in technical economics is required if the reader is to make much headway with it.

Actually, during the next few chapters, we shall be developing much of the essence of the analysis from this book, and also bringing in some modern modifications of that analysis. In the remainder of this chapter, we shall simply suggest a few of the central features of Keynesian thought, and comment about some of the controversy surrounding his work.[3]

What, then, in essence, was it that Keynes tried to do that sets his work off from that of most preceding economic theorists? Let us mention five characteristics of his work and make a brief comment on each:

1. Keynes put his emphasis very clearly on the kind of problems we have just been discussing, problems dealing with the *economy as a whole.* His work was fundamentally macroeconomic in approach, meaning that his key variables were total national output, the general level of employment, the price level, and the like. Insofar as most preceding economic theory had had a strong weighting towards micro-analysis, this represented something of a break with the past.

2. Keynes emphasized the key role of *aggregate demand* in determining the level of national income and employment in the economy as a whole. In Part I, we spoke of supply and demand in particular industries. Keynes spoke of supply and demand in the aggregate. He felt that aggregate demand in a given economy might be high or low in relation to aggregate supply. In other words, he rejected the

[3] For a somewhat more extensive discussion of Keynesian theory along the lines suggested here, see my *Evolution of Modern Economics* (Englewood Cliffs, N.J.: Prentice-Hall, Inc., 1967), Chap. 6.

theory behind Say's law that suggested that supply invariably created its own demand in the economy as a whole.

3. He believed that the economy might come to rest at a position of *unemployment equilibrium;* that is, a position where there would be no natural forces operating to restore full employment to the economy. Suppose, he said, that aggregate demand falls short of aggregate supply at the full employment level. What will happen? According to Keynes, the shortage of demand would mean that businessmen in general would cut back on production and jobs. He believed this cutting back process would go on until an equilibrium of supply and demand had been achieved. But this equilibrium might involve a great deal of unemployment in the economy as a whole. Indeed, Keynes felt that this analysis helped explain why such a phenomenon as the Great Depression, in full sway while he was writing, could occur in a modern industrial economy.

These last two points indicate that Keynes rejected not only the conclusions of Say's law but, necessarily, the argument that lay behind it. One of these arguments, as we know, was that it was permissible to relegate "money" to a minor role in workings of an economy. And this brings us to a fourth characteristic of Keynesian analysis.

4. Keynes tried to bring "money" back into economic analysis in a rather pivotal role. He attempted to perform a *synthesis of real and monetary analysis.*[4] More particularly, he argued that "money" was not simply a convenient medium of exchange. He called particular attention to a characteristic of money named *liquidity.* By *liquidity,* he meant "command over goods in general." If I have money, I can exchange it for goods or services or bonds or securities in any direction I choose. It is a perfectly generalized way of holding purchasing power. Now all commodities have some elements of liquidity. When I own a house, I can exchange it for some other goods if I so desire; however, I can never be quite sure what the house will sell for. Similarly, with securities (stocks and bonds): I can quickly turn them into money with which to buy other goods and services; still, it is never quite certain at what price I shall be able to sell them. They are nearly perfectly liquid, but not quite. In short, Keynes said that "money" had certain special properties that gave it an important role in the functioning of the economy. By recognizing this role, he argued, one could explain the possibility of a discrepancy between aggregate

---

[4] We use the term *real* here, as is customary in economics, to refer to the goods and services (potatoes, automobiles, etc.) which underlie their customary representation in money terms. The role of money, or *monetary* phenomena, is a complex one both in measuring and in analyzing this "real" goods-and-services world, as we shall see in succeeding chapters.

demand and aggregate supply in the economy, and hence the possibility of general unemployment.

5. Finally, Keynes argued that since a market economy could not guarantee full employment by its own devices, it might be necessary to have a somewhat greater degree of *government intervention* than had been thought desirable in the past. The government could remedy the problem directly, in the Keynesian view, by affecting aggregate demand by its own purchases of goods and services. On the other hand, it could also influence aggregate demand indirectly by lowering taxes (or raising them if the problem was too much demand) and thus stimulating private consumer and business demand. Still more indirectly, the government could affect the level of aggregate demand by altering the supply of money available to the economy. In general, however, the point was that since the market alone could not be counted on to do the job, the government might have to take a more active participating role.

And this leads us directly to the controversial aspect of Keynesian writing and of the "new economics" generally. For, even today, more than three decades after the *General Theory* was published, these matters are still very much under public debate.

Controversies
Surrounding Keynesian Theory

There are really two quite different kinds of controversy that surround the work of John Maynard Keynes. The first is based on a failure to read or at least to understand what Keynes actually wrote and said. The second is based on differing judgments about the actual and important limitations of the Keynesian theory.

The most extreme form of the first type of criticism (fortunately heard less frequently these days) is the charge that Keynes was attacking the capitalistic system in more or less the same manner as Karl Marx had attacked it 75 years earlier. Actually, it is closer to the truth to say that Keynes provided the main alternative *to* Marxism. For the fact is that the approaches of these two economists to the capitalistic system were radically different. Marx argued that the diseases of capitalism were intrinsic, inevitable, and fatal; they could be removed only by the overthrow of the entire system. By contrast, Keynes argued that the basic features of the capitalistic system could be preserved and its problems eliminated by modifications of that system. The mixed economy—which we actually have in the United

States and Western Europe—is the natural heir to Keynesian analysis; but it is anathema to the good Marxist. For if, through modification of the system, one can forestall serious problems from arising and can make the economy "work," then one has completely undercut the ground from the Marxist who believes that things *must* get worse and that "revolution" is the *only* cure.

No one would argue that the *General Theory* is a "conservative" book in the usual sense of the term; but it is not a "radical" book—certainly not in the Marxist sense—and, indeed, it does hope to "conserve" certain features of a private enterprise system. Keynes deeply prized individual liberty and also the economic efficiency of the market economy; he hoped that when one had solved the problem of depressions, these virtues might be preserved.

If this first line of criticism is of little interest to the serious student, the second line of criticism is quite a different matter. For the fact is that there *are* important limitations on the Keynesian analysis (it could hardly be otherwise, given the vast amount of economic research done in the past 30-odd years) and, consequently, there are good grounds for debating both his arguments and his conclusions. A listing of these limitations would be very long, but even a short list would include obviously important matters:

Keynesian theory is basically static; it is very much concerned with short-run problems, and it leaves to one side the whole matter of growth and changes in fundamental conditions.

Keynesian theory dwells in a purely competitive world where the real-life market structures of the modern corporation or labor union hardly figure at all.

Keynesian theory is based on rough "psychological" generalizations which are inadequate for the complexities of economic behavior revealed by subsequent research.

Keynesian theory does not recognize some of the complications and difficulties of applying governmental expenditure, tax, and monetary policies to the solution of unemployment, inflation, and other problems of the modern economy in the aggregate.

It is apparent, even from this short list, that there is much ground for disagreement and debate even among serious students of Keynesian analysis.

Having said this, however, we should add there are also some matters that really are not subject to much question among economists. For one thing, there is no doubt that Keynesian theory has had an enormous impact on the development of the subject of economics in the past 30 years. Even his harshest critics have been stimulated enormously by the challenge to new research which his work provided. For another thing, it is clear that a majority of economists (including those aware of the limitations of this theory) accept his general contention that there are serious problems in keeping an economy at or near the full employment level and that there are times when only government intervention (of one sort or another) will have sufficient impact to turn the trick.

Finally, there is the important fact that most governments in the Western world now tend to accept: (a) the fact that governmental actions do have a substantial effect on the health of the economy as a whole, and (b) a governmental responsibility for maintaining at least a reasonably close approximation to a full employment economy.

Thus, despite its critics, the "new economics" is very much in business in the modern mixed economy. And it is essentially because of the "new economics" that one can predict with a high degree of certainty that such a thing as the Great Depression of the 1930's could not happen again in the United States or in Western Europe. Considering the hardship and despair that that Depression caused, this is no small tribute to the accomplishments of the late Lord Keynes.

Summary

We shall be concerned in Part II with the economy in the aggregate. Our interest now shifts from the area of individual consumers, firms, and industries to broad questions concerning the level of national income, the general level of employment and unemployment, and the over-all level of prices.

The history of modern industrial economies makes it quite clear that there have been fluctuations in the levels of employment and prices in various countries over the past century or two. Early economists (with some exceptions such as Malthus and Marx) tended on the whole to set aggregative problems, and especially the unemployment problem, to one side. They were confident that they could rely on Say's law to guarantee no major problems. Say's law depicted a "money-less" economy in which supply always created its own demand, thus preventing any problems of general overproduction or general unemployment.

In the twentieth century, many economists began to criticize this point of view, and the great theoretical breakthrough was made by John Maynard Keynes. Keynesian theory departed from its predecessors by (1) its heavy emphasis on macroeconomics, (2) its stress on the role of aggregate demand, (3) its acknowledgment of the possibility of underemployment equilibrium, (4) its synthesis of real and monetary analysis; and (5) its recognition of the important role of government in curing unemployment and other aggregative problems.

Keynesian theory has been subject to many valid criticisms and also to some not so valid (e.g., the false identification of Keynes and Marx). Despite the critics, however, there is general agreement about his impact on the development of economics as a field and about the influence his work has had on the actual policies of governments in the Western mixed economies. The "new economics," in one form or another, is widely accepted and utilized by modern nations to avoid such harrowing disasters as the Great Depression of the 1930's.

Questions for Discussion

1 • "The Great Depression of the 1930's made forever obsolete the view that an unregulated market economy could guarantee, save for a few minor frictions, full employment of the nation's labor force." Discuss.
2 • What are the assumptions behind Say's law? Show how, given these assumptions, an economy would be able to find markets for an expansion of its total output caused, say, by a sudden immigration of labor from abroad.
3 • What is meant by macroeconomics? Microeconomics?
4 • John Maynard Keynes said of his *General Theory of Employment, Interest, and Money* that the critics would fluctuate "between a belief that I am quite wrong and a belief that I am saying nothing new. It is for others to determine if either of these or the third alternative is right." What grounds might be offered today to support the third alternative?
5 • Compare the views of John Maynard Keynes and Karl Marx on the problems facing capitalism and their prospective cures.
6 • What evidence do you find today of the influence of the "new economics" on actual governmental policies in the United States and in other modern industrial economies? Give as many specific examples as you can.

Suggested Reading

HANSEN, ALVIN, A Guide to Keynes. New York: McGraw-Hill, Inc., 1953.

HARRIS, SEYMOUR, ed., The New Economics. New York: Alfred A. Knopf, Inc., 1947.

HARROD, R. F., The Life of John Maynard Keynes. New York: Harcourt, Brace, and World, Inc., 1951.

KEYNES, JOHN MAYNARD, The General Theory of Employment, Interest and Money. New York: Harcourt, Brace, and World, Inc., 1936.

LEKACHMAN, ROBERT, The Age of Keynes. New York: Random House, Inc., 1966.

RICARDO, DAVID, Notes on Malthus's Principles of Political Economy, ed. P. Sraffa. Cambridge: Cambridge University Press, 1951, pp. 301-452.

The concept of GNP

7

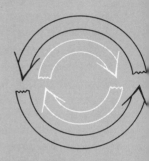

Having outlined the general area of macro-economics, we shall now turn to a concept that is central to this field: the concept of *gross national product,* or GNP. The term GNP is widely used in our daily press, but the concept is somewhat complicated, and it is worth spending some time with it.

Total Output
and Its Fluctuations

The basic idea behind the gross national product is simple enough. This is one of the important measures economists use when they try to estimate the total output of goods and services produced in the nation over a given period, say a year.

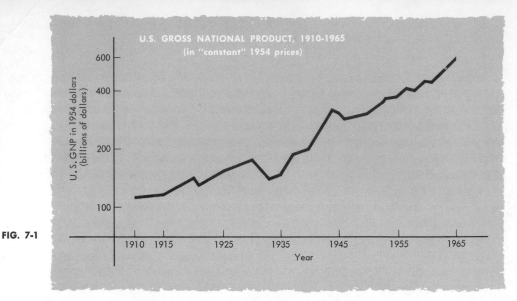

FIG. 7-1

Growth and fluctuation of total output in the United States
are brought out sharply in this diagram of 55 years.

Furthermore, it is apparent that some such concept of total output is indispensable to the field of macroeconomics. For example, we have talked about the Great Depression of the 1930's, but wholly in terms of unemployment. We could just as readily have spoken about a fall in the nation's total output, its GNP, during that period. Indeed, we should generally expect that when there is heavy unemployment in an economy, its total output of goods and services would fall, or at least would not rise as rapidly as might otherwise be the case.

In Fig. 7-1, we have charted the changes in the United States' GNP since 1910. Two things about this diagram should strike us immediately. The first is the pronounced upward trend in our GNP over this period of time: our annual total output of goods and services has risen some five times in little over a half-century. The second striking feature is the irregularity of the upward movement. The curve does not move upward continuously, but with spurts and pauses, with occasional downward movements followed by rapid accelerations, and so on.

Now the first feature of this diagram, the long-run growth of our total output, will be of primary interest to us in Part III, where we will take up various factors, such as population growth, capital accumulation, and technological change, that bring about long-run gains in a country's productive capacity. The second feature, however, is of central interest to us now. It tells us that there has been, in addition to long-run growth, a considerable *short-run fluctuation* in the level of GNP in our country. Another way to put this is to say that there has been a changing gap between the total output our nation was actually producing in any given year and what it had the capacity for producing.

In Fig. 7-2, we show the gap between actual and potential gross national product in the United States for the decade, 1955-1965, as estimated by the President's Council of Economic Advisers. This gap reflects underutilization of our productive capacity, and, as the bottom half of the figure shows, the size of the gap in percentage terms and unemployment of labor in percentage terms are very highly correlated.

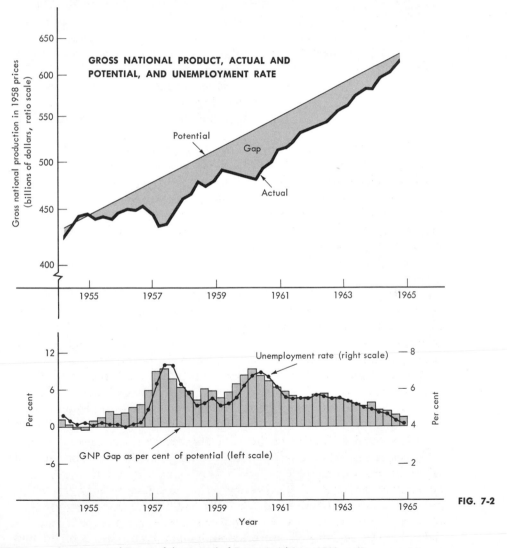

FIG. 7-2

Source: Annual Report of the Council of Economic Advisers, 1966, p. 41.

Similarly, two questions are very closely related: What determines our level of GNP in the short run? What determines our level of employment in the short run?

Measuring Total Output

Having observed that GNP is an important concept, we now have to ask the more difficult question: Is it a meaningful concept? What is this thing, "total output," and how would we go about measuring it?

The difficulty is an obvious one; in fact, it takes us back to elementary school days. We were told then that we cannot add oranges and apples and pears. But the total output of our economy includes oranges, apples, and pears, *plus* lathes, tractors, toy balloons, soft drinks, and several thousand other commodities. How can these different commodities be added together to form a single numerical total?

What is needed is a common denominator, and the common denominator in our particular economy is dollars. Oranges have a price; apples and pears have prices; so do tractors, lathes, and toy balloons. What we do is to give a money valuation to the production of each particular commodity, then add up the total of these money values, and this will give us a number in dollars for our total output during the given year.

Say that 600 million oranges are produced in the country in a certain year and that the price of oranges is 5¢ each. Then the value of orange output will be determined:

$$5¢ \times 600 \text{ million} = \$30 \text{ million}$$

We can then do the same thing for apples, pears, and lathes, and come up with money figures for each. We would then add these money figures together to form an estimate of aggregate output. To be specific: Suppose there is, in addition to oranges, only one other commodity in our economy: toy balloons. Toy balloon production is 50 million units a year at a price of 10¢ apiece.

Total output in this fictitious economy might then be defined as equal to

$$P_o \times Q_o + P_b \times Q_b,$$

where P_o, Q_o and P_b, Q_b are price and quantity produced of oranges and balloons, respectively. In numerical terms, we should have:

$$\text{Total output} = 5\cancel{c} \times 600 \text{ million} + 10\cancel{c} \times 50 \text{ million}$$
$$= \$30 \text{ million} + \$5 \text{ million}$$
$$= \$35 \text{ million}$$

It is fairly obvious that what we have done for these two commodities, we could do for the remainder of the commodities in a real-life economy: shirts, missiles, secretarial services. They all have prices and can all be added together in this fashion.

Components of Total Output

Now there are some serious problems in the kind of measurements we have just performed, and we must attend to these in a moment. First, however, let us mention in passing the basic component parts into which the total output of the economy can be divided. The most common breakdown, and one we shall be referring to often in the future, is in terms of three main categories of goods and services:

1. *Consumption.* There are first of all the goods bought by ordinary consumers like ourselves: clothing, food, automobiles, tennis racquets. These include consumer expenditures on services as well as commodities, and on durable as well as nondurable consumers' goods. The category of durable consumers' goods has grown very rapidly in recent decades as we have expanded our purchases of automobiles, television sets, washing machines, and the like. In total, consumption expenditures in the United States currently average between 60 to 65 per cent of our GNP.

2. *Investment.* Part of the goods produced in the economy each year are funneled back into the productive process either to replace worn-out buildings, machines, and so on, or to add to our general stock of capital goods. Gross investment in our economy includes these replacement items and the net additions to our capital stock.[1] Investment expenditures in the United States may run in the neighborhood of 15 or 16 per cent of GNP, though this percentage is subject to a fairly high degree of variability. The term *investment* in the sense we are now using it is, of course, different from the kind of investing we do when we buy a stock or a bond. It is better to regard the latter as *financial investment,* and to think of *investment* (unmodified) as indicating those goods devoted to building up the real productive capacity of the economy. The main categories of investment ex-

---

[1] We shall come to the distinction between "gross investment" and "net investment" in a moment (pp. 109-10).

penditure are fixed business investment (machinery, factories, etc.), residential construction (apartments and also private homes), and additions to inventories (stocks of products kept on hand to meet orders from other producers or consumers).

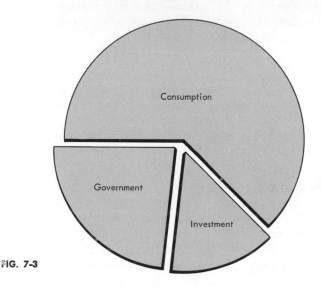

MAJOR COMPONENTS OF UNITED STATES' GNP

These are average proportions of GNP. Remember that they change from year to year, investment being a particularly variable item.

FIG. 7-3

3. *Government.* The third main category is governmental expenditures. If we exclude transfer payments—which, as we recall, do not represent governmental purchases of goods and services—then government expenditures currently run at something above 20 per cent of GNP. We have already indicated (Chapter 4) that a great part of these government expenditures at the federal level are related in one way or another to defense. Educational expenditures are the most important single category at the state and local level. For our present purposes, the important point to note is that when the government buys goods and services, the destination it provides for the total output is exactly analogous to that provided by private investment or consumption purchases.

These then are the three main categories by which the total output of the society can be classified: consumption, private investment, and government expenditures.[2] We shall be mentioning each of these categories often in the pages that follow.

[2] A further category would be *net* exports of American goods abroad. We will mention this category again later; it is a very small category, however, perhaps 1 per cent or so of GNP. See Chap. 14.

But now it is time to return once again to the basic concept of total output. We said that our procedure of simply adding together the dollar values of different outputs involved a number of problems. Let me now mention two specific and major problems. The first is that of *constant prices;* the second is the problem of *double-counting.*

The first problem, the problem of what is happening to the price level in our economy as we try to measure total output, is a complicated one. The difficulty arises when we try to compare total output or GNP in two different years. To return to our simplified world of oranges and toy balloons:

In our earlier example (p. 105), we determined that the total output of oranges and toy balloons in our economy was worth $35 million. Let us suppose this was for the year 1950. Suppose someone now comes along and tells us that the combined money-value of orange and toy balloon production in 1960 had risen to $70 million. The question is: what can we conclude from this fact? Can we conclude that both orange production and toy balloon production had doubled from 1950 to 1960? Or that if one product less than doubled in quantity, the other more than doubled? Or does the given information actually enable us to conclude nothing at all about the production of oranges and toy balloons in this period?

The correct answer, unfortunately, is the last. We can conclude nothing whatever about orange and toy balloon production in 1960 as compared to 1950 unless, and until, we know what has happened to the prices of these goods during that period. To take an obvious case: suppose the prices of both goods had *quadrupled* in this ten-year period. A rise in total output from $35 million to $70 million would, in this case, represent not an increase in real GNP, but a *halving* of GNP from 1950 to 1960. If, on the other hand, prices had remained absolutely constant, then it would be clear that real GNP was expanding; indeed, if prices are constant, then the changes in the money value of GNP would reflect changes in the real output value of GNP.

The problem thus becomes one of finding some rough equivalent to constant prices when prices are, in fact, changing all the time. The way economists do this is by taking prices for some given year and using these prices throughout the series of measurements of GNP in different years. Thus, you will notice that in the charts of United States' GNP (Figs. 7-1 and 7-2), prices in Fig. 7-1 are "1954 prices," and in Fig. 7-2, "1958 prices." More generally, we should have to amend our formula for calculating total output to indicate a specific date for the prices involved. Using 1950 prices throughout, our comparison of the total output of oranges and toy balloons in 1950 and 1960 would look as follows:

1) Total Output $(GNP)_{(1950)} = P_{o(1950)} \times Q_{o(1950)} + P_{b(1950)} \times Q_{b(1950)}$
2) Total Output $(GNP)_{(1960)} = P_{o(1950)} \times Q_{o(1960)} + P_{b(1950)} \times Q_{b(1960)}$

In this way, by using 1950 prices throughout, the problem of fictitious changes in total output due to mere changes in the price level is removed, and the focus is put on changes in the actual outputs of the goods involved.

The reader should notice that the prices and quantities in equation 2 are differently dated; from what we have said, he should be able to explain this fact fully.[3]

Problem of Double-counting

A second major problem arises in measuring GNP because many of the goods we produce in a given year are actually already included in the value of other goods being produced.

Suppose we are using all the oranges to produce frozen orange juice. Then we have:

Stage 1	Value of oranges produced (as sold by the grower)	$30 million
Stage 2	Value of canned orange juice (as sold by the canner)	$40 million
Stage 3	Value of canned orange juice (as bought by the consumer from the retailer)	$48 million

The double-counting problem arises here because the $48 million of final output produced includes the value of the oranges and canned orange juice at the earlier stages of production. If we were to add them all together, we would get a fictitiously large total because of "double-counting."

How does one avoid this problem, given the great number of different industries and different uses for their products in an economy

[3] Before leaving the "constant prices" problem, it should at least be noted that when we are making comparisons of GNP over long periods of time, it is by no means easy to handle this problem. Prices are changing not only absolutely, but *relatively* (i.e., the price of oranges relative to the price of toy balloons), and when this happens, changes in "total output" do not have an unambiguous meaning.

Problem of Double-Counting

like ours? One way (and the simplest conceptually) is to be careful to avoid all kinds of "intermediate" products when adding up GNP, and to concentrate wholly on "final" products in the various lines of production (i.e., to count only Stage 3 orange juice at $48 million and to exclude Stage 1 and Stage 2 orange products).

An equivalent, though more roundabout, way of achieving the same result is through what is known as the *value added* method of calculating GNP. A firm's or an industry's *value added* to total output is the value of its sales minus its purchases of products from other firms or industries. If we assume for simplicity that the orange growers in our example purchased no inputs from other firms, then we could represent *value added* at each stage of orange production as follows:

Stage	*Value of sales*	minus	*Purchases from other Firms*	equals	*Value added*
1	$30 million		$ 0		+ $30 million
2	$40 million		$30 million		+ $10 million
3	$48 million		$40 million		+ $ 8 million
			Sum of *Values added*	=	$48 million

The reader should notice that the sum of the values added equals the value of the final products ($48 million). He should prove to himself that this is not an accident but will necessarily be the case. The ultimate reason, of course, is that in both methods we have scrupulously avoided counting intermediate products.

Before we leave the double-counting problem, however, we should remark on one aspect of measuring GNP where double-counting is in fact countenanced. The reader by now must have wondered why the *G* (gross) is always prefixed to this measure of national production. The answer has to do with the way we evaluate the *investment* category mentioned earlier.

It should be clear that the proper way to evaluate the total output of machines, say, in a given year, would be to take the number of machines produced in that year and to subtract from it the number of machines that have become worn out, obsolete, and have been discarded during the year. Put it this way. We have been using machines throughout the year; when we produce a quantity of new machines, at least some of those machines are necessary to replace those that have become worn out through use; they do not all constitute a net *addition* to our stock of machines.

This is a problem that all businessmen are familiar with: the problem of depreciation and replacement. The difficulty, however, is that really accurate and meaningful depreciation figures are hard to come by, and even hard to define. Hence, economists and government statisticians often include *all* the machines produced in a given year without making the depreciation adjustment. This figure is called *gross invest-ment*. When *gross investment* is added to consumption and govern-ment expenditures, we call the total *gross* national product. If the depreciation of the country's capital stock is estimated and deducted, we would get *net* investment and, correspondingly, *net* national product (NNP).

Product, Income, and the "Circular Flow"

In a sense, everything we have done so far in this chapter has been a matter of defining terms. Definitions are important in any subject; but now let us try to use our new definitions to gain some important insights into macroeconomic problems. Indeed, with the tools now at our disposal we can move fairly quickly into the heart of a significant area of modern analysis.

Much of this modern analysis proceeds from the recognition of a fact that we should be able to understand easily now, though it might have been obscure before. This fact is that there is a *basic equivalence between the national product or output of a society and the real national income of that society.* "Annual total output" is really another name for "annual total income." The latter, in turn, is the sum of all incomes earned in the production of this "total output": i.e., wages, profits, interest, and rents. These are basically two dif-ferent ways of looking at the same thing.

The simplest way to convince ourselves on this point is to recall our *value added* method of measuring GNP. At each stage of produc-tion, we subtracted from the value of the products a firm sells, the value that it has paid out to other firms for their products. Now the sum of these *values added* is our total "product," but it is also clearly our total "income." For to what uses are these *values added* put? Since, by definition, they do not represent sales to other firms, they must represent either payments to the factors of production—wages to labor, rent on property, interest on borrowed funds—or profits to the firm. Indeed, profits can be thought of as being precisely the surplus of value added after payments are made to other factors of produc-tion. If we subtract all other incomes from our national product, we get profits as the residual, and profits, of course, are income. Hence the point is established: national product and national income are essentially equivalent concepts.

In present-day practice in the United States, we actually have a great number of related but still distinct "product" and "income" concepts for use in different connections. If we start with GNP and work downward, we get the following definitions:

Gross national product − Depreciation = Net national product
Net national product − Indirect business taxes = National income

$$\text{National income} - \left\{ \begin{array}{l} \text{Retained profits} \\ \text{Corporate profit taxes} \\ \text{Contribution for social} \\ \quad \text{insurance} \end{array} \right\} + \begin{array}{l} \text{Transfer payments} = \\ \text{Personal income} \end{array}$$

Personal income − Personal taxes = Disposable personal income

Incidentally, it is only when we come to this last category (Disposable personal income) that most consumers actually begin to see the income they have produced.

In the pages to come, we shall use the term *national income* in a less technical sense than in the above definition, as a symbol of the whole family of *total output* concept. Where a more specific definition is called for, we shall note it explicitly in the course of the analysis.

As we think about it, the basic equivalence of income and output in the aggregate is not too difficult to understand. For what determines how much income you and I and our neighbors will have to share amongst ourselves? Ultimately, it has to be what all of us together have produced. Barring special cases where there is aid from abroad, there is simply no other source from which our incomes in the aggregate can emanate.

Now with this fact clearly in mind, we can illustrate the general workings of a modern economy in a fairly dramatic, pictorial way. Figure 7-4 presents what is sometimes called a *circular flow* diagram. What this diagram does is to picture the macroeconomic process as consisting of two opposite flows: (1) a money-income-and-spending flow; and (2) a national-product-and-factor-services flow.

The money-income-and-spending flow is in the outer circle. It shows business firms paying dollars to households for the use of their labor, their land, their machinery. This is the flow of wages, rents, interest, and other incomes. As we follow this flow around the circle, we see that the households pay this money back to the businesses in return for the products they buy from these businesses—oranges and toy balloons, if you will. So the money income flow circulates around as incomes to the public in general, who then spend this income buying the goods that businesses have produced.

The national-product-and-factor-services flow goes in the opposite direction (it is made to go clockwise in Fig. 7-4 which, of course, is perfectly arbitrary; it is not arbitrary, however, that it goes in the opposite direction from the money-income-and-spending flow). In

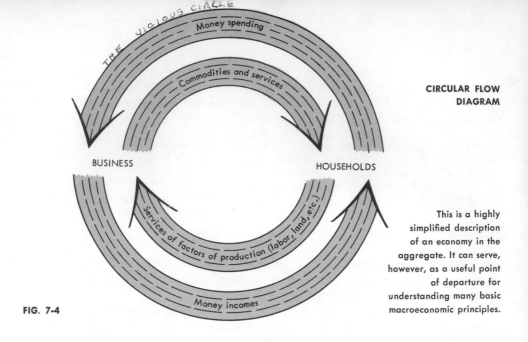

CIRCULAR FLOW
DIAGRAM

BUSINESS   **HOUSEHOLDS**

This is a highly
simplified description
of an economy in the
aggregate. It can serve,
however, as a useful point
of departure for
understanding many basic
macroeconomic principles.

FIG. 7-4

this circle, we show business firms taking the services of the factors of production—land, labor, and capital—and transforming these into commercially saleable goods which they then sell to the general public.

This diagram, of course, is a very simplified way of looking at a complex modern economy; and if we were to make any pretense at accuracy, we should quickly have to draw numerous little subcircles and interlocking canals and what-have-you. Even from this primitive picture, however, we can see intuitively how macroeconomic problems arise.

Let us try to imagine a case in which these nice smooth flows may not be so smooth after all. For example, let us suppose that consumers in general decide that they wish to *save* (i.e., not spend on consumption) a healthy percentage of their money incomes. Businesses, let us say, have paid out $100 million in incomes to the households. But the households now decide that they want to spend only $75 million for the goods and services offered by the business firms. They want to lay aside $25 million for a rainy day.

The first question that occurs to us is: Is this really possible? Can we have $100 million going out in the income loop of the flow and only $75 million coming back in the spending loop? The answer, essentially, is no, because incomes are created by customers spending on the products of businesses. What might happen in this case is that businessmen might find that they themselves were spending the missing $25 million. They would do this by not selling $25 million worth of the goods they had produced and thus automatically accumulating $25 million of added inventories.

This accumulation of added inventories would make the flows come out all right arithmetically, but it would hardly make sense *economically*. These added inventories are unwanted and unsought. What they tell the businessman is that he has produced more of his products than the market will bear. His natural reaction: to cut back output and employment until he finds himself producing just the amounts that his customers want.

The reader should recognize that what we have just done has been to describe what is nothing more nor less than a deficiency in aggregate demand. We recall from the last chapter that Lord Keynes attributed the major causes of depressions to precisely such deficiencies. What we have shown is that one reason why aggregate demand may be too low is that consumer spending may be too low (or, equivalently, consumer saving may be too high).

Still in this preliminary way, we might ask: Can we also describe a situation where aggregate demand is too high? The answer is yes. Let us suppose this time that consumers want to spend all of their incomes on consumption goods (i.e., to save nothing). Let us suppose that at the same time businessmen, realizing that markets are good, want to divert part of the national product to investment, either in buildings and machinery or in added inventories. The consumers, then, want to spend the whole $100 million on consumption goods. But businessmen want to spend some sum—say $20 million—on investment.

Again, we ask: Is this possible, and if it is possible in some mechanical way, is it economically possible? That is, what will the economic repercussions be?

The answer is that consumer and business behavior in this instance will create a situation in which "something has to give," and that the economic consequences of this behavior would normally be an *expansion* of national output and employment. Essentially, we have $120 million of spending coming around and trying to buy $100 million worth of goods. If we assume that prices are constant (actually, they would probably rise), the only way businessmen could meet the demand would be by selling off some of their inventories of goods in stock. Now this is a good thing from the point of view of the businessman—he has all these customers clamoring for his goods—but it is not something he will simply sit back and watch without doing anything. In particular, he will try to increase his employment and output to the point where he can not only meet consumer demands but also maintain (or add to) his stock of inventories. An excess of aggregate demand, then, will generally lead to a business expansion.

We have moved now from definitions into the very core of the modern theory of national income determination. We have seen that consumer decisions on consumption and saving may be crucial; we have also just seen how business investment decisions can influence the macroeconomic outcome. In short, we are now in a position to move ahead in a systematic way into this very important area of modern economics, and this will be our central task in the next chapter.

Summary

In studying the modern economy in the aggregate and its short-run fluctuations, we need some measure of annual total output. *Gross national product* (GNP) is such a measure. Its major components are (1) consumption, (2) gross investment, and (3) government expenditures on goods and services.

The common denominator used to make possible the adding together of the various outputs in the economy is the price of each of these goods expressed in money terms. In performing this aggregation of outputs, however, two significant problems arise. The first is the problem of constant prices, or ruling out changes in GNP which derive simply from inflationary (or deflationary) changes in the price level and do not reflect changes in the real output value of GNP. To accomplish this end, prices in some one base year are used; e.g., "constant 1954 prices." The second problem is that of avoiding double-counting in adding up the outputs of different industries in the economy. This may be done by rigorously excluding intermediate products and concentrating on final goods and services only. Or, equivalently, it may be done by the *value added* method of calculating national income.

The value added approach has the virtue of bringing out quite clearly the fundamental equivalence of national product and national income. In our society, our real income in the aggregate (wages, salaries, rents, etc.) is nothing but our total production in the aggregate.

This equivalence of product and income leads, in turn, to a circular flow representation of a modern economy. A money-income-and-spending flow, representing households as they sell their services (labor, land, etc.) to business firms and then buy the products of the business firms with their incomes, is matched by an opposite national-product-and-factor-services flow, showing the business getting the services of the factors of production and transforming these into useful commodities. With the circular flow diagram in mind, we can begin to understand more vividly how deficiencies or excesses of aggregate demand may make their presence felt in the modern economy.

Questions for Discussion

1 • Show the equivalence of the final-product and the value-added methods of measuring GNP.

2 • An increase in real GNP can be defined unambiguously only when the prices of all goods or the quantities of all goods change in the same proportions. If relative prices change and the relative quantities of goods produced change, then the change in GNP will be different depending upon what set of prices is used to make the measurement. This is known as the *index number problem.*

In the following example, determine the percentage change in GNP from 1950 to 1960 as measured (1) in 1950 prices and (2) in 1960 prices:

	1950		1960	
	Oranges	Toy balloons	Oranges	Toy balloons
Price	$.10	$.05	$.15	$.10
Quantity	1,000	2,000	3,000	2,500

Which measure—in 1950 prices or 1960 prices—gives the larger percentage change in total output? Can you see why this problem might pose some difficulties for measuring changes in GNP over long periods of time?

3 • Distinguish *financial investment* from *investment* as a component of GNP. What is the difference between *gross investment* and *net investment?*

4 • In a private economy, total output consists of consumption and investment while total real income consists of consumption and saving. Since total output and total income are equivalent, saving and investment must always be equal. However, *decisions* to invest and *decisions* to save are not the same. Is there any inconsistency in saying that saving must always equal investment but that decisions about saving and decisions about investment are often made by different people for different reasons? (Hint: Remember the supply and demand diagrams of Chapter 2. The quantity of a good bought and the quantity of a good sold must always be equal. However, the decisions of buyers, reflected in the demand curve, are quite different from the decisions of sellers, reflected in the supply curve.)

5 • Using the circular flow diagram as a guide, show how a decision of consumers to save more than businessmen want to invest can lead to a deficiency of aggregate demand. Show, conversely, how a decision of businessmen to invest more than consumers wish to save can lead to an excess of aggregate demand.

Suggested Reading

Economic Report of the President (Washington: U.S. Government Printing Office, 1967), Appendix B. ("Statistical Tables Relating to Income, Employment, and Production").

HANSEN, ALVIN, *Business Cycles and National Income.* New York: W. W. Norton & Company, Inc., 1951, Chaps. 1-2.

RUGGLES, RICHARD and NANCY RUGGLES, *National Income Accounts and Income Analysis.* New York: McGraw-Hill, Inc., 1956.

SCHULTZE, CHARLES L., *National Income Analysis,* 2nd ed. Englewood Cliffs, Prentice-Hall, Inc., 1967, Chaps. 1-2.

The theory of
national income
determination

8

We have been setting the stage for the analysis we shall undertake now. It has to do with what economists usually call "the theory of national income determination," but a somewhat more vivid description might be: an analysis of the root causes of depressions or inflations in the modern industrial economy.

The Problem and Some Clues

What we have done so far has been to state the problem and to provide a few clues to its solution.

The problem, briefly, is this: Given the basic productive capacity of the nation, how can we determine where the actual level of

GNP will be? We know historically that there have been gaps between actual and potential GNP in our own and in other industrial economies. What determines the size of these gaps?

To assist in the approach to this problem, we have developed a number of important clues to the nature of the solution.

We noticed that John Maynard Keynes, in his theorizing about these matters, placed great stress on the role of *aggregate demand*. If aggregate demand fell short, Keynes argued, actual GNP would be below potential GNP and there would be substantial unemployment in the economy.

We showed that national income and national product are basically two different views of the same object. This led us to the *circular flow* approach to economic life. Businesses pay incomes to the owners of labor, land, etc., who then use these incomes to buy the goods and services that businesses have produced.

We observed that the three main categories of GNP are: (1) *consumption* expenditures, (2) *investment* expenditures, and (3) *government* expenditures.

We showed how a deficiency in one of the spending categories (say, consumer spending) might lead through the circular flow to business troubles and thus to a contraction of output and employment. Such a deficiency in the spending flow, we said, was really what Keynes meant when he talked about inadequate aggregate demand. We also suggested how aggregate demand might be "too high," as it would be when businessmen want to invest more than consumers wish to save.

These clues give us the basic structure for analyzing the problem of national income determination. We must first determine the factors that influence the three main categories of spending: consumer spending, private business investment, and government expenditure. Then we must "add up" these expenditure items and see whether they will provide us with sufficient aggregate demand to sustain GNP at its full employment potential level. If they will not sustain full employment GNP, then we must ask: What *is* the level of national income that can be sustained? When we have answered these questions, our theory of national income determination will be basically complete.

We shall follow this suggested structure except for one point. In this chapter, we shall consider the theory of national income determination in a purely private economy—i.e., we shall assume that there are no government expenditures or taxes and that our only sources of aggregate demand are consumer spending and business investment spending. Having presented the theory in this simplified case, we shall introduce government once again in the following chapter. This procedure, besides being easier to follow, also has the advantage that it enables us to show very clearly and explicitly what the impact of various government policies on the economy will be.

Consumption Demand

The level of national income that can be sustained in a private economy will be determined by the strength of (1) consumer demand for the various categories of consumption goods the nation can produce, and (2) business demand for goods to invest, i.e., to add to the stock of machines, buildings, inventories, and other capital goods in the economy. We shall consider these two components of aggregate demand in order.

What are the factors that influence consumption demand in a modern industrial economy? Can we generalize about them in any way?

Of course, the truth of the matter is that there are countless elements that may influence our demand for consumer goods to at least some degree. An advertising campaign may affect our buying habits and preferences. So may a medical report on the virtues or harmfulness of certain products. There may be consumer fads that sweep the nation, changes in ladies' fashions, new sports that interest either spectators or participants. In some societies, there may develop a general philosophy of "Eat, drink, and be merry"—spend as much of your income on consumption today as possible! In other societies, there may be a puritanical and thrifty code: "A penny saved is a penny earned."

It is worth mentioning the great variety of factors influencing consumer demand because this makes it clear that if we single out any one factor as all-important, we are doing a certain injustice to the facts. Any generalization we get will be only in the nature of an approximation.

Still, even rough generalizations can be important—indeed, we seldom do much better than that in the social sciences—and many economists feel that such is the case in the area of consumer demand. The basic generalization, in this instance, states that consumer spending can be usefully related to consumer income. If you wish to know how much a family will spend on consumption, find out what their family income is. If you want to know how much the nation will spend on consumption in general, find out what the national income is. It is this *income-consumption* relationship that has played a pivotal role in the modern theory of national income determination.

The roots of this, as we would expect, were in Keynes' *General Theory*. In this book Keynes expressed his belief in a "psychological law" that as an individual's (or society's) income rises, that individual (or society) will spend part, but not the whole, of the increase in income on added consumption. Another way of putting this is to say that individuals or society will divide any increase in income into (a) added consumption and (b) added saving. (Since saving is defined as that part of income that is not consumed, $a + b$ will necessarily equal the given increase in income.)

Today we can go somewhat further than this and suggest that, in the short run, saving will tend to increase as a percentage of national income as national income increases. A typical shape for the curve relating consumption to national income is shown in Fig. 8-1. In this diagram, you will notice that we have drawn a 45° line from the origin. On this 45° line, vertical and horizontal distances from the axes are equal, meaning that the vertical distance is equal to national income. Since, in our simplified economy, consumption plus saving equals national income, we can calculate saving by measuring the distance between the consumption function and the 45° line.

What does the shape of this so-called *consumption function* mean? And on what kind of empirical evidence is it based?

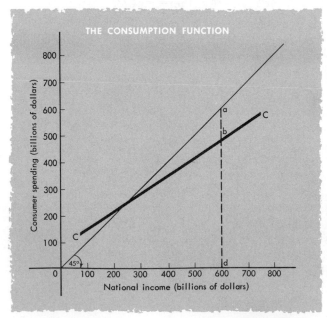

FIG. 8-1

This diagram shows a fairly typical consumption function. The line CC shows how much consumers will want to spend on goods and services at various levels of national income. The reader should understand that any line (e.g., *ad*) drawn from the 45° line to the horizontal axis will be equal to national income as measured at its point of intersection with the horizontal axis (in this case $600 billion). He should also understand that the distance *ab* will represent anticipated consumer saving.

The shape, as we have said, indicates a rising percentage of income devoted to saving and a declining percentage devoted to consumption as income increases. At a rather low level of national income ($250 billion), consumption expenditures equal the whole of national income. At still lower levels—and here we must imagine the nation in a condition of general poverty—people would, in the aggregate, spend more than their entire incomes on consumption. In the economist's phraseology, at very low levels of income, people will *dissave*. They will go to their past savings; they will live on their capital assets, their homes and personal property, without replacing them; they will be consuming on the average more than they have actually produced that year. This is a pathological case (though not an unknown case since there *was* net dissaving in the depths of the Great Depression in 1932 and 1933), and hence the more interesting part of the curve lies to the right of $250 billion. In this range, we can see that consumption is continually rising with income but that saving is increasing as a percentage of income.

The evidence for this general shape of the consumption function is both macro- and microeconomic in nature. In Fig. 8-2, we have plotted out personal consumption expenditures in relationship to disposable personal income in the United States for each year from 1929 to 1965. The shape of the line we have fitted to this data is roughly what we should expect, although there are years that obviously need special explanation—for example, the years during World War II when voluntary saving was quite high even after large income taxes.

Another quite different kind of information is provided by microeconomic studies of family spending at different income levels. Thus, we should expect that families with higher incomes will generally save more than families with lower incomes, not only absolutely, but also in percentage terms, and various studies have confirmed this general tendency. Thus, in 1950, a family with a disposable income of $4,000 a year probably saved little if anything on the average, while a family with $10,000 a year might save close to 20 per cent of their larger income. In 1960, as everyone's incomes had risen, the percentages changed—at $4,000 a year, families were *dis*saving on the average; at $10,000, they were saving not 20 per cent but closer to 10 per cent— but the general relationship of higher percentage savings with higher levels of family income still remained valid.

It must be stressed that none of this evidence is absolutely conclusive. One problem that makes this whole area so difficult is that of distinguishing between long-run and short-run effects and causes. We do know that in the long run, a consumption function such as we have drawn in Fig. 8-1 will shift upward. At a given level of income, as we have shown, families spent more in 1960 than in 1950, and they will presumably spend still more at that same level of income in 1970. Why? Because there were many new products in 1960 that hardly existed in 1950, and we can expect still more product changes in the 1970's. Even more significant, perhaps, is the fact that we are in a society in which

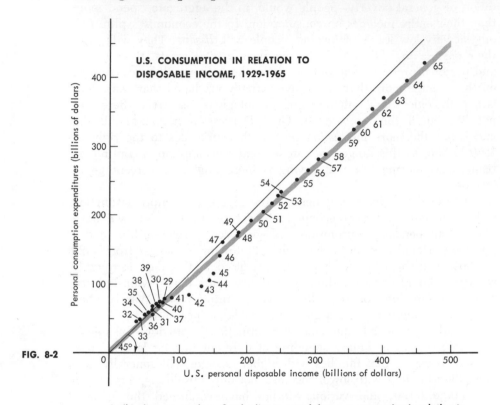

FIG. 8-2

In this diagram, we have fitted a line to actual data on consumption in relation to income in the U.S. for each year, 1929 to 1965. In general, the data show the same pattern exemplified in our hypothetical consumption function, Fig. 8-1.

everyone's family income (on the average) is rising. Insofar as our consumption expenditures reflect our relative position in the income distribution, then, if we stay at the same absolute level while other families around us are improving their positions, we may feel relatively poorer, and this may lower our willingness to cut consumption and save for the future.[1] To complicate matters still more, some economists, like

[1] The dependence of our consumption habits on our relations to other consumers was stressed forcefully by Thorstein Veblen nearly 70 years ago. In his

Milton Friedman of the University of Chicago, have argued that our income is really of two sorts: "permanent income" and "transitory (or windfall gain or loss) income." Saving and consumption patterns will generally be different depending on which sort of income we are talking about.

There are, in short, many complications in this area, and no one should take any statements about the income–consumption relationship as though they were established beyond possibility of doubt. Still, the view that makes consumption demand depend substantially on the level of national income has proved quite a durable one.

Our first question, then, is answered as follows: Consumer spending in a private economy will be largely determined by the level of national income in the general manner described by the consumption function of Fig. 8-1.[2]

Investment Demand

We now turn to our second question: What factors will determine the level of investment spending in our hypothetical economy?

Now the determinants of investment demand are, if anything, even more complicated than those which influence consumer demand. Indeed, while economists often stress the relative dependability of consumer spending at a given level of national income, they usually point out the great variability of business investment spending. For this reason, changes in investment spending are often seen to be pivotal in causing upswings or downswings in a modern economy.

To appreciate the problem, put yourself in the place of a business-

---

Theory of the Leisure Class (1899), Veblen emphasized the concept of "conspicuous consumption"—i.e., consumption to prove our superior status to our neighbors. More recently, another American economist, James S. Duesenberry added the notion that our consumption may be a function not of our absolute level of income but of our relative position in the income distribution of the society.

[2] This discussion of consumption and saving has been limited to household consumption and saving out of personal disposable income. In a fuller discussion, we should have to take into account the fact that business corporations also save and that their savings form an important source for business investment in the modern American economy. These corporate savings arise when businesses pay out less in dividends than their after-tax profits. These retained profits are part of national income but do not go to the consumers as personal income. The reader who wishes to follow through in this matter should consult the excellent treatment of the subject in Charles L. Schultze, National Income Analysis, 2nd ed. (Englewood Cliffs, N.J.: Prentice-Hall, Inc., 1967), especially Chap. 3.

man and ask what are the factors that are likely to influence you in a decision to expand the size of your factory, to add new machines, equipment, and so on. There are a host of obvious factors that you would have to take into account at the outset. Basically, you would be trying to judge the future profitability of the investment. This would involve an assessment of your present position. Are sales good? Is demand for your product high? Is the extra machinery needed to produce more output? But it also requires an assessment of the future: Are sales likely to expand or contract over the life of the new machinery? Demand may be buoyant today, but does the future look bright or gloomy? In other words, the first thing one would have to do would be to formulate some general opinion about the future market for one's particular product. *Business expectations* are a crucial factor influencing investment spending.

But it is not just the state of the market that one has to estimate. As a businessman, you would also have to investigate whether there are new productive methods and processes available to you that will make the investment profitable in terms of reducing costs of production or producing an improved product. The kinds of plant, tools, and machinery we have in the economy today are vastly different from what they were fifty years ago, and this is a consequence of the fact that businessmen invest not only in more of the "old" machines, but also in replacing "old" machines with "new" machines. Here we enter the whole area of *technological progress*. If there is an important new invention, for example, this may create a wide range of opportunities for profitable business investment. The great Austrian–American economist, Joseph A. Schumpeter (1883-1950) emphasized the pivotal role of new products and new productive methods as stimuli to business investment. He considered the introduction and absorption of innovational advances to be the mainspring of the major fluctuations of a modern economy. The judgment on whether investments in a new line of business or new productive process will work is not a mechanical one; it involves considerable uncertainty and, indeed, Schumpeter felt that those who took the lead in innovations had to have certain special qualities of character and leadership ability.[3]

Even if you were aware of the future state of demand and also the full range of technological possibilities open to you, however, you still would not have solved the problem of whether or not to invest in a particular factory or piece of machinery. For you would now come up against the problem of financing the new investment. Does your firm have a great sum in the form of retained profits that can be used to

[3] For Schumpeter's theory, see his *Theory of Economic Development* (Cambridge, Mass.: Harvard University Press, 1949).

purchase the added capital equipment? Or will you have to go to the money markets to raise funds from the outside? In either case, the cost of borrowing money—the *interest rate*—will have to be a factor in your decision.[4] If interest rates are high, this will mean that you will have to pay more to borrow money and, consequently, that you will be more reluctant to undertake any vast expansion schemes. High interest rates are often associated with "tight money." It is difficult to get loans from the bank, and when one does get a loan, the interest charge is very stiff. In such circumstances, business investment is likely to be considerably curtailed.

In short, we have a whole series of factors that are likely to lead to more or less investment spending in the economy. Current demand for our product, pressure on our plant capacity, future expectations, technological progress, our profit position, the rate of interest—all these are factors which may significantly affect this second great component of aggregate demand, business investment expenditure.

We shall return to some of these factors later, especially when we come to our discussion of the economic effects of changes in the rate of interest (Chapter 11). For the moment, however, so that we can get on with our argument, let us simply assume that business investment spending has been determined. Let us suppose that all these various factors have done their work and that the net result has been to give us a level of investment of, say, $100 billion. This is a short cut, but it will help us get the over-all picture in the clearest possible terms.

Very well then. We have (1) a consumption-function (Fig. 8-1) relating consumer spending to national income, and (2) a given $100 billion of investment demand. How then is the level of national income determined?

Determination of the
Level of National Income

The determination of the equilibrium level of national income takes place basically in the following way:

We add up the sum of consumer spending and business investment spending at each level of national income and determine whether this sum exceeds the

---

[4] It might seem that the interest rate would affect our decision only if we had to borrow money from outside, say, take a bank loan, and not if we already had the funds ourselves. However, this is not so. If the machine promises us a return of 4 per cent a year, and we can get 5 per cent in a savings account, are we likely to purchase the machine? What will we do with our money?

level of national income or falls short of it. If there is an excess, it will mean that aggregate demand exceeds aggregate supply. In this case, forces will be set in motion to produce an expansion of national income. If, however, there is a deficiency, this will mean that aggregate demand is less than aggregate supply and this will bring about a fall in national income and, with it, of course, a fall in employment.

In short, the root cause of depressions, at least as far as our simplified economy is concerned, is a sum of consumption and investment spending that falls short of national income at the full employment level.[5]

It is one thing to state the conclusion, another thing to demonstrate it in a convincing way. Actually, there are several approaches, all of which we have already suggested in our various clues along the way. One approach, for example, would be to return to our *circular flow* diagram of the last chapter and to show that consumers and businessmen will be content with what they are doing only when the sum of anticipated consumer spending and planned business investment in the spending flow is equal to the national product flow. We shall leave this approach to be worked out by the reader with two additional hints. (1) It is important to remember the words *anticipated* and *planned* in the previous sentence. The sum of *actual* consumption and investment expenditures in our private economy *must* equal the national product, since there is no other place for output to go. (2) The reader may wish to introduce another loop in the diagram showing part of the output of the economy going directly back to business in the form of business investment. He should then show that there will be over-all equilibrium only when an amount equal to this planned investment is drained off from the household spending flow in the form of saving.

An equivalent, and somewhat clearer, approach is to build on the basis of the consumption function diagram (Fig. 8-1). In Fig. 8-3, we have taken this earlier diagram and made two additions to it. The first addition is the vertical line *FE* drawn at the level of national income of $760 billion. This line tells us what national income (or product) would be if all the factors of production in the economy were fully employed. Actually, full employment national income is not quite so definite a concept as this single line would suggest. The size of the labor force seeking jobs in the labor market is itself a function of economic conditions to some degree. Hence, we could, if we wished, think of *FE* not as a line but as a band of a certain width suggesting the range of possible full employment outputs.

[5] In the remainder of this chapter, we shall speak only of the depression or unemployment problem. The opposite problem, inflation, will be taken up in a separate chapter (Chap. 12).

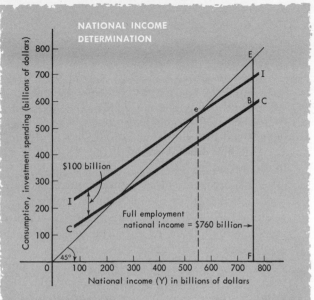

Consumption, investment spending (billions of dollars)

National income (Y) in billions of dollars

$100 billion

Full employment
national income = $760 billion→

45°

FIG. 8-3

Equilibrium national income will be determined in this private economy at point e, where the CC+II curves intersect the 45° line. The equilibrium level of national income in this example will be $550 billion.

The second addition is the line *II*, which has been drawn above our *CC* curve. The vertical distance between these two lines is $100 billion. This represents the amount of planned business investment which we are taking as determined by the host of factors influencing such investment. The vertical distance from the *x*-axis to the *II* line at each level of national income represents the sum of investment and consumption demand at that level of national income.

How then will the equilibrium level of national income be determined? To see the process involved, let us start out at the full employment level, or at the national income of $760 billion. We now ask: What is the level of aggregate demand when the economy is fully employed? The answer can be read off from the diagram. Consumption demand is equal to the distance, *FB*, or $590 billion. Investment demand, of course, is $100 billion. The sum of the two therefore is $690 billion. This is $70 billion less than the value of full employment national income.

Now it does not take any very sophisticated analysis to show that this is an untenable situation. Businessmen are paying out into the income stream far more than consumers (through their consumption expenditures) and businessmen (through their own investment expenditures) are willing to pay back to them. The effects of this will be direct and compelling. If we assume that prices remain unchanged (they might actually start to fall somewhat under these circumstances), businessmen in general will find that they are accumulating unwanted inventories of goods in stock. This is investment, but it is unplanned and unwanted investment. Furthermore it is a kind of investment that the businessman knows how to respond to directly: he will start cutting production and employment. This will be true of businessmen throughout the economy. There will be general cutbacks in national output and employment. Full employment national income, in short, has proved unsustainable; employment and income will have to fall.

But how far? Where will the equilibrium level of national income in our economy be?

The answer is that equilibrium national income will be at the level determined by the intersection of the $C + I$ lines with the 45° line (point e). At this level of national income, aggregate demand will equal aggregate supply. Since the distance between the CC curve and the 45° line equals the amount of their incomes consumers wish to save, this equilibrium level of national income is also one at which planned business investment and anticipated consumer savings are equal. In this instance, the amount businessmen want to invest and the amount consumers want to save are both equal to $100 billion.[6]

To prove that the point e has significance, we must show that levels of national income either higher or lower will not work. We must also show that higher levels will set in motion forces bringing national income *down*, whereas lower levels will set in motion forces bringing national income *up*.

Actually, we have already done half of this by showing the unsustainability of full employment income and the way in which businessmen would react to unwanted inventories of their goods in stock. This logic can be applied to all points to the right of e in our diagram. In each case, there will be some accumulation of unwanted inventories and consequently a further reduction of production and employment.

[6] Another graphical way of showing equilibrium national income is precisely by showing the intersection of the planned savings and investment schedules. This method is given in the following figure. The reader should test his understanding of this subject matter by (1) showing for himself exactly how the figure is derived from Fig. 8-3; and (2) analyzing the process of national income (Y) determination (which we have done largely in terms of $C + I = Y$) in terms of savings and investment decisions (or $I = S$).

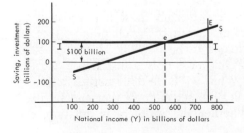

DETERMINATION OF EQUILIBRIUM NATIONAL INCOME BY SAVING AND INVESTMENT SCHEDULES

Similarly, we can show that points to the left of e will not work either, though for an opposite reason. Here the sum of $C + I$ *exceeds* the level of national income (Y). This fact would manifest itself to producers in the form of clamoring buyers who would be trying to purchase more of the firm's product than had been produced in the given period. If, again, we assume that prices remain unchanged (in this case they would have a tendency to rise), the consequence would be depleted inventories, empty store shelves, unfulfilled orders, and the like. The effect of this, in turn, would be to suggest to businessmen that they ought to expand production and employment. In short, at all levels of national income lower than e, we would have forces working for an expansion of national income.

Thus, at lower levels, national income will expand; at higher levels, national income will contract; at point e, aggregate demand will be just sufficient to match the output the economy is producing and thus there will be no forces effecting any change in the level of national income. Q.E.D.

At point e, do we have an equilibrium level of national income? Yes. No consumer, businessman or laborer can improve his situation by an indicated change in his pattern of actions. Do we have general contentment in the economy? Definitely no! Our equilibrium level of national income is short of full employment income by \$210 billion. Translated into employment figures, this amount means that our economy is suffering from massive unemployment. We are, indeed, precisely at the kind of "underemployment equilibrium" we mentioned in our discussion of Keynes. There are people who want work, but there are no jobs. There is, to use a phrase current in the 1930's, "poverty in the midst of plenty."

This, then, is the basic theory of national income determination in a purely private economy. Before one could apply such a theory to a real-life economy, he would have to develop it in a number of ways. First, one must bring in government expenditures and taxes; second, one must show the relationship of "money" and governmental monetary policy to this analysis, while also developing further the theory of investment demand; third, one must extend the analysis to cover closely related topics such as inflation and the macroeconomics of international trade. These topics are precisely those that we shall be taking up in a roughly logical order in the remaining chapters of Part II.

The enumeration of what remains to be done is in itself a clear indication that the analysis of this chapter is only a first step along the way. It is, however, a major step. What we have done here is to equip ourselves with an important and flexible set of tools that can be used in many different connections. Whether the problem is inflation, the balance of payments, unemployment, or what have you, modern macro-economic analysis essentially begins with the instruments we have provided in this chapter. Thus if careful attention is necessary here, that attention will have its reward in the numerous applications of the analysis we shall be able to make in the chapters ahead.

Summary

In this chapter, we have presented the essentials of the theory of national income determination in a simplified private economy.

In such a private economy, the main components of aggregate demand will be consumer spending and business investment spending. Consumer spending is related to national income through the *consumption function*. This function tells us that consumers will consume more as their income increases, but that they will also save more. The evidence is that, in the short run, saving increases as a percentage of income as income rises.

Investment spending is a function of many different factors including such important elements as business expectations, technological progress, the amount of profits available for investment purposes, and the cost of borrowing funds, or the rate of interest. Investment spending is, on the whole, a more variable and unpredictable factor than consumer spending. In our simplified analysis, we take a certain amount of planned investment as already determined by the workings of these various factors.

The equilibrium level of national income is determined at the level where aggregate supply equals aggregate demand or, equivalently, where the sum of consumption and investment spending equals national income (or output) or, equivalently still, where savings and investment decisions are equated. At levels of national income higher than this equilibrium level, forces will be set in motion to bring about a contraction in output and employment. At levels of national income below the equilibrium level, forces will be set in motion to bring about an expansion in output and employment. This equilibrium level is not necessarily a "full employment" level and, indeed, is compatible with major mass unemployment in the economy.

Although simplified at this stage, the present analysis is fundamental to modern thinking about macroeconomic problems and has a wide range of reference to everything from the monetary and fiscal policies of the government to the problems of inflation, employment, and trade.

Questions for Discussion

1 • State in your own words the basic theory of national income determination as you have understood it from this chapter.

2 • Define the *consumption function*. What cautions should be kept in mind in employing this important tool?

3 • In our analysis in this chapter, we have assumed that all saving is done by households and that all investing is done by businesses. In reality, however, households also invest (e.g., building homes) and businesses save (corporate saving now provides a substantial percentage of the funds for business investment in the United States). How might these facts modify the general analysis of national income determination as we have presented it?

4 • In the pre-Keynesian era, it was sometimes argued that the main reason for unemployment in the economy was that labor was making unreasonable wage demands. If wages were lower, it was argued, employers would find that they could afford to hire more workers and the unemployment problem would be solved. Do you find this argument satisfactory? If not, why not? (Hint: Think back to the supply-and-demand curve for electricians of Chapter 5. If electricians and all other workers accepted lower wages, would this be likely to affect the demand curves for electricians and for other workers? In what direction?)

5 • If you were going to use the analysis of this chapter to help gain an understanding of the Depression of the 1930's, what are some of the facts that you would look for in your research?

Suggested Reading

DUESENBERRY, JAMES S., *Income, Saving, and the Theory of Consumer Behavior*. Cambridge: Harvard University Press, 1949.

MUELLER, M. G., *Readings in Macroeconomics*. New York: Holt, Rinehart and Winston, Inc., 1966, pp. 3-133.

SCHULTZE, CHARLES L., *National Income Analysis*, 2nd ed. Englewood Cliffs: Prentice-Hall, Inc., 1967, Chaps. 3-4.

SLESINGER, REUBEN E., MARK PERLMAN, and ASHER ISAACS, eds. *Contemporary Economics*. Boston: Allyn and Bacon, Inc., 1967, pp. 155-246.

Fiscal policy
and the multiplier

9

In Chapter 8 we presented the basic tools of the modern theory of national income determination. In this chapter and the next, we shall sharpen those tools and also apply them to an analysis of governmental expenditure and tax policies. Collectively, these policies are usually referred to as a nation's *fiscal policy*.

With the study of fiscal policy, we approach the heart of one of those areas of economics in which the public interest is very much at stake, and also in which controversy is rife. For the past three decades, a great debate has raged in this country about the effective use of fiscal policy. What we might call the classical view has been that the government ought simply to keep its own house in order and allow the rest of the economy to manage its affairs privately. In contrast, the "new economics" has argued that government policy in a modern mixed economy should be guided at least in part by the objective of maintaining the over-all health of the economy with respect to full employment, the price level, and economic growth.

The historian will record that the "new economics," if it has not won an outright victory, has certainly made much headway during these decades. Economists still differ on the precise measures the government ought to use in implementing its goals, and there are still a very few economists who adhere to something close to the classical position, but the great majority of economists accept the fact that the market itself does not guarantee the fulfillment of important macroeconomic objectives and, consequently, that the government must shoulder a share of the responsibility. More significantly, political leaders, both here and abroad, have generally come to the same over-all conclusion.

All this does not mean that everyone must immediately become an enthusiastic partisan of the "new economics"; it does mean, however, that everyone should keep an open mind in studying these matters, particularly when the analysis seems to conflict with the traditional, common-sense view.

Introducing
Governmental Expenditures: G

In our discussion of a purely private economy in the last chapter, we dealt with only two components of aggregate demand: consumption, C, and investment, I. Now we shall introduce a third major element: government, G. To make the analysis as straightforward as possible, we shall deal separately with government expenditures and government taxation, and then combine them. In the course of this discussion, we shall introduce an important *general* tool of macroeconomic analysis: *the multiplier.*

We begin then with government expenditures. In a mixed economy, the government, along with households and private business investors, is purchasing goods and services. What will the effect of this government demand be?

The fundamental answer is that this demand will have precisely the same effect as any other demand. To the business firm producing, say, automobiles and trucks, it makes no essential difference whether the buyers are consumers, other business firms, or the United States government. In each case, the added demand means added sales and added profits.

Since this government demand is to be treated in the same general way as any other demand, we can represent it in our diagram by simply adding it on to our $C + I$ curve, just as, earlier, we added investment spending to our consumption function. Again, let us pull a number out of the hat. Suppose that in our hypothetical economy, government expenditures for goods and services are running at $50 billion a year. Neglecting the tax side, what will happen?

The answer is given in Fig. 9-1, where $50 billion of G has been added vertically to the $C + I$ curves. The consequence is that the equilibrium level of national income has been changed. Before, the equilibrium was at $550 billion; now it is where the $C + I + G$ curve intersects the 45° line, or at $700 billion. As a result of governmental expenditures, this particular economy is much closer to full employment national income than before.

In its most primitive and fundamental form, this is the justification for those who argue that the government ought to act to bring the economy as near as possible to the full employment level.

But this is still a bit too primitive. We have not touched on taxation yet. Also, we have not explained exactly why the government expenditures have just this much impact and no less or no more. This second question, indeed, brings out a rather interesting feature of this whole analysis. One might have expected that a $50 billion addition of government expenditures would increase national income by the same amount, $50 billion. But, in fact, as our diagram shows, the equilibrium level of national income has gone up by a multiple of G—in our particular case by $150 billion.

In this diagram, we add government expenditures of $50 billion and get an expansion of national income from $550 billion (without G) to $700 billion (with G). We have not, however, taken taxes into account at this point in the argument.

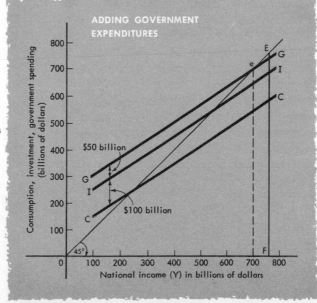

FIG. 9-1

Why this magnified effect? How can we determine whether an extra dollar of government expenditure will increase equilibrium national income by $1, $2, $5?

We reach here one of the most basic tools of modern analysis: *the multiplier.* Let us analyze this important concept.

An Important General Tool
~ the Multiplier

The *multiplier* tells us by how much an increase in spending will raise the equilibrium level of national income. If a $1 increase in spending leads to a $5 increase in equilibrium national income, the multiplier = 5; if the increase is $2, the multiplier = 2.

It is important to stress at the outset that the multiplier is a *general* tool applying to all categories of spending: consumption, investment, or government. So that there will be no mistake about this matter, let us first discuss the multiplier with respect to a change in investment demand, and then return to our example of government expenditures.

In Fig. 9-2, we have gone back to a private economy again with the purpose this time of showing the effects of a change in investment demand on equilibrium national income. Investment demand was originally $100 billion. But now we imagine that some change has taken place (perhaps there has been an improvement in business confidence, owing to some international development, or perhaps there has been a

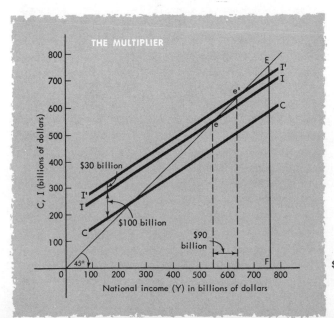

FIG. 9-2

The principle of the multiplier is here illustrated in increased investment spending. A $30 billion increase in *I* leads to a $90 billion increase in Y.

new technological breakthrough, or perhaps the Federal Reserve System has lowered the interest rate), and planned investment spending has risen to $130 billion. The increase in investment is $30 billion, measured by the vertical distance between II and $I'I'$. The effect of this change has been to raise equilibrium national income from $550 billion to $640 billion or $90 billion. A $30 billion increase in investment spending has brought about a $90 billion increase in national income. The *multiplier*, then, is 3.

Why 3? The geometrically-minded reader will see that the size of this number depends very much on how steep the consumption function (*CC* curve) is. Indeed, everyone can see this in a general way. Imagine that the *CC* curve in our diagram were perfectly horizontal, i.e., running parallel to the x-axis. In this case, a rise in investment of $30 billion would raise the intersection with the 45° line by $30 billion only and, consequently, would raise the national income level by only $30 billion. Here the multiplier $= 1$. If we imagined the *CC* curve as very steep, however, we would get the opposite effect. Suppose the curve ran almost parallel to the 45° line; then one can see that even slight changes in investment spending would raise national income by great multiples.

Thus, we can see that the size of the multiplier in general depends on the steepness of the *CC* curve. But we can be more precise than this. Let us first state our conclusion and then offer two different demonstrations of its validity.

The conclusion is that the multiplier (m) will in ordinary circumstances obey the following rule:

$$m = \frac{1}{1 - \text{MPC}}$$

where MPC refers to the "marginal propensity to consume" or, geometrically, the *slope* of the consumption function.

The meaning of this conclusion can be elaborated with reference to Fig. 9-3 where we have blown up a small fragment of the *CC* curve. The *marginal propensity to consume* is defined as that part of an extra dollar of income that consumers will wish to spend on consumption. In Fig. 9-3, we give an example in which a $1 increase in income increases consumption demand by 67¢, roughly ⅔. The same result would be obtained if the numbers were not written in, but we simply measured distance BC and divided it by distance AC. This term BC/AC is the *slope* of the *CC* line, meaning that the *marginal propensity to consume* is the slope of consumption function. The multiplier in this example can be worked out as follows:

$$m = \frac{1}{1 - \text{MPC}} = \frac{1}{1 - \dfrac{BC}{AC}} = \frac{1}{1 - \dfrac{2}{3}} = 3$$

Another way of stating the same conclusion would be in terms of the *marginal propensity to save* (MPS). The MPS is defined as the part of an extra dollar of income that consumers wish to save. Since the extra dollar of income will be either saved or spent on consumption,

$$MPS = 1 - MPC \text{ (by definition)}$$

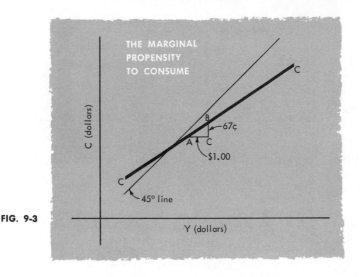

FIG. 9-3

The marginal propensity to consume (MPC) is equal to the slope of the consumption function or BC/AC. In this case,
$$MPC = \frac{67}{100} \text{ or } \frac{2}{3}$$

This means that we could, if we wished, rewrite the multiplier very simply as:

$$m = \frac{1}{MPS}$$

What we have stated here (but have yet not proved) is that the multiplier in our simplified private economy will be equal to the reciprocal of the marginal propensity to save, or, equivalently,

$$\frac{1}{1 - MPC}$$

When we ask *why* this is so, we come to the matter of proof. Let us show in two different ways why the multiplier will follow this rule.

The first is a geometrical demonstration:

Figure 9-4 is simply Fig. 9-2 with some additional notation. Say that we have an increase in investment of the amount *b*. The diagram tells us that this leads

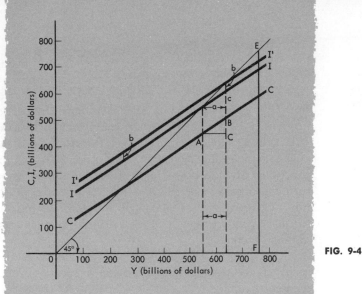

FIG. 9-4

to an increase in national income of the amount a. By definition, then, the multiplier is:

$$(1) \qquad\qquad m = \frac{a}{b}$$

Our 45° line tells us that $a = b + c$; hence equation 1 can be rewritten:

$$(2) \qquad\qquad m = \frac{a}{a-c} = \frac{1}{1-\dfrac{c}{a}}$$

The *marginal propensity to consume* (MPC), we know, is measured by the slope of the CC curve, or, MPC = BC/AC. Since the investment curves are drawn parallel to the CC curve, we can also say that MPC = c/a. Substituting for c/a in equation 2, we get:

$$(3) \qquad\qquad m = \frac{1}{1-\text{MPC}}$$

And this was what we set out to show.

This geometrical demonstration is useful enough, but it gives us little insight into the economic logic of what is going on. The second demonstration, which we shall take up now, will make this clearer. For it is based on observing what happens at each stage of the game as the increase in investment or other expenditure makes its way through the economy. The *economics* of what happens is essentially this: When businessmen decide to invest in a new factory, they buy products (iron, steel, machinery, etc.) from other people, thus creating *income* for these people. This is in the first stage. But now these people have more income than before, and *they* will want to spend more on consumption. So in the second stage, consumption spending increases. *But not by the whole amount of the increase in income.* That is to say, they will spend part, but also save part. In particular, the marginal propensity to consume tells us what fraction of this extra income they will want to spend. But then we go on to a third stage. The additional consumer spending (on food, shoes, etc.) creates more income for the producers of food, shoes, and other consumers' goods. This income, in turn, will also be spent in part (determined by the MPC) on consumption. The process repeats itself indefinitely and, at each new stage, further income (though in increasingly smaller amounts) is added to national income.

Our second demonstration of the theory of the multiplier simply involves adding together all these successive rounds of additionally created income:

Let us suppose that there is a $100 increase in investment spending, and that the MPC = ⅔. The amount of income created at each stage will be as follows (to the nearest dollar):

Stage 1: $100 (the original added investment)
Stage 2: ⅔ ($100) = $67   (MPC × $100)
Stage 3: ⅔ ($67) = $44   [(MPC)^2 × $100]
Stage 4: ⅔ ($44) = $30   [(MPC)^3 × $100]
Stage 5: ⅔ ($30) = $20   [(MPC)^4 × $100]
* * * * * * * * * * *
Stage $n + 1$: (⅔)^n ($100)   [(MPC)^n × $100]

The total of all these stages of added income will be the increase in the equilibrium level of national income. If we use the term ΔY to signify the total increase in national income, then:

(1)$\qquad \Delta Y = \$100 + \$67 + \$44 + \$30 + \$20 + \ldots \ldots$

or

(2)$\qquad \Delta Y = \$100 \ (1 + \frac{2}{3} + (\frac{2}{3})^2 + (\frac{2}{3})^3 + \ldots + (\frac{2}{3})^n + \ldots)$

or, most generally, where ΔI is the added investment,

(3)$\qquad \Delta Y = \Delta I \ (1 + MPC + MPC^2 + MPC^3 + \ldots + MPC^n + \ldots)$

Since the multiplier is equal to $\Delta Y / \Delta I$, we get:

(4)$\qquad m = (1 + MPC + MPC^2 + MPC^3 + \ldots + MPC^n + \ldots)$

Knowing that MPC is less than 1, we can conclude from algebra that [1]

---

[1] The general formula, where $|a| < 1$, is:

$$1 + a + a^2 + a^3 + \ldots + a^n + \ldots = \frac{1}{1 - a}$$

(5)
$$m = \frac{1}{1 - \text{MPC}}$$

Which again is what we set out to prove.[2]

Both these demonstrations prove the same point about the multiplier, but the second is perhaps more vivid in bringing out the economic aspect of what is going on. We must always imagine the successive rounds of expenditures and incomes created by any new act of spending. A businessman invests in an additional typewriter. This creates income for the seller of typewriters, who spends part of his increased income in buying a pair of shoes. This creates income for the producer of shoes, who now buys himself an umbrella. And on and on and on, the amounts getting smaller and smaller each time, as part of the added income leaks into added savings. Indeed, it will be precisely when savings in total have increased by the same amount as business investment that the process finally ends. This the reader can verify by looking at Fig. 9-2 again. Notice that, at the new equilibrium level of national income, saving, like investment, has increased by $30 billion.

The Multiplier Effects of Increasing G

With the multiplier concept in hand, we can now return to the mainstream of our argument which was concerned with the effect of government expenditures on national income. Our original question was: why is it that the introduction of government expenditures of $50 billion (Fig. 9-1) raised the equilibrium level of national income from $550 billion to $700 billion, or by $150 billion? The answer we can now give is that the multiplier is 3, and the reason it is 3 is that the marginal propensity to consume shown in Fig. 9-1 is ⅔. (An exactly equivalent answer would be that the marginal propensity to save implied in Fig. 9-1 is ⅓.) This marginal propensity to consume can be determined by measuring the slope of the CC curve in Fig. 9-1.

Needless to say, the MPC need not always be ⅔. This is just what we assumed it to be in our hypothetical economy. What it is in any real-life modern economy at any particular period would, of course, have to be determined by careful empirical research.

The multiplier also allows us to say a further word about the effect

[2] We are dealing here with what is sometimes called the *instantaneous multiplier*. As every reader will recognize, it would normally take a considerable amount of time for all these successive stages of spending and income creation to occur. In more advanced treatments, the multiplier is often worked out over time in what is sometimes called *period analysis*.

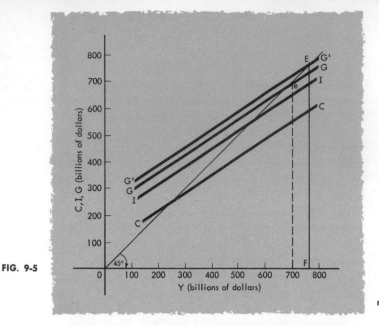

FIG. 9-5

In this diagram we have sufficiently raised government expenditures (G) to bring us to an equilibrium level of national income at full employment. (This assumes no change in tax revenues.)

of government expenditures. Suppose our economy is not yet at full employment and we wish to know by how much governmental expenditures would have to be increased (assuming no change in tax revenues) to bring us to the full employment level. The needed change in G can easily be shown graphically. Figure 9-5 is our original Fig. 9-1, except that we have added G'G' to represent the increased government expenditures necessary to bring us to full employment national income.

What the multiplier tells us in this case is how much the increase in governmental expenditures will have to be in numerical terms. Before G'G' was added, equilibrium national income was $700 billion. We wish to raise national income to the full employment level, which is $760 billion. The MPC in this figure, as before, is ⅔ and the multiplier is 3.

We can find our answer, then, simply by dividing the desired increase in national income, $60 billion, by 3. This gives us $20 billion, the amount by which we shall have to increase government expenditures if we wish to bring national income to the full employment level.

General Effects of Taxation: T

The preceding discussion has necessarily had an air of incompleteness. We have been discussing government expenditures without discussing government revenues. But we all know that the government taxes as well as spends. What can we say in a general way about the effects of tax policy on aggregate demand and equilibrium national income?

Now there are many different kinds of taxes, direct or indirect, taxes falling mainly on consumers or mainly on corporations, progressive or regressive taxes, and so on; each of these taxes will have different ultimate effects on the level of national income.[3] To bring out an important general point, however, let us suppose that the particular taxes that are levied fall entirely on the incomes of consumers. The government levies a tax of $30 billion on consumers in the economy. What effect will this have?

What we must do now is to reverse our field—or almost reverse it. G added demand, but T takes away income that might have added to demand. The effect of T, considered in isolation, then, is to reduce aggregate demand and hence to put a downward pressure on the economy.

The introduction of a $30 billion tax will lower equilibrium national income. Like government expenditures, taxation will have its effect magnified by the multiplier, but not in quite the same way. This is why I said we must "almost reverse" our field. There is a certain asymmetry in the effects of G and T. In particular, the multiplied downward effect of $1 of taxes is somewhat less than the multiplied upward effect of $1 of government expenditures.

To see why this is so, let us show how taxes affect the position of the consumption function in our case of a $30 billion levy. Figure 9-6 indicates, as we would expect, that the consumption schedule is shifted downward by the impact of taxes. At a national income of $500 billion, consumers now have at their disposal only the same amount of income that they previously had at a national income of $470 billion, the difference being the amount of the tax. Hence, their consumption demand at $500 billion will now be the same as it was previously at $470, or $397 billion. This is reflected graphically by moving horizontally to the right by the amount of T ($30 billion). (The reader should repeat this argument for other points on the consumption function; for example, the shift between $300 billion and $270 billion national incomes.) The after-tax consumption function ($C'C'$), then, is simply the original consumption function (CC) shifted horizontally to the right by $30 billion.

The effect of this shift on equilibrium national income is determined, however, not by rightward movements but by the *downward*

---

[3] For example, a tax that falls heavily on business corporations may have less direct effect on consumption than on business investment. In general, in order to bring out the central principles, our discussion is based on the simplest cases of taxation and also of government spending. In a more detailed analysis, we should have to classify the impact of G and T by their various components. Thus, an increase in G will usually increase not only personal income but also corporation income and, more or less automatically, tax revenues. Similarly, the effects of ordinary government expenditures are somewhat different from the effect of government transfer payments. The reader should keep these points in mind as qualifications to the very general conclusions we are attempting to present here.

shift of the schedule. It is the height of the $C + I + G$ line that ultimately determines where our equilibrium will be. Now this downward shift is not $30 billion, but $20 billion. More generally, it is equal to the MPC × T. This is easily seen in graphical terms, since the little triangles we have drawn at $500 and $300 billion represent the slope of the con-

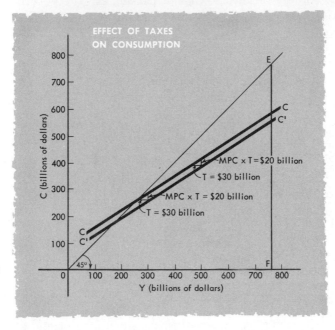

FIG. 9-6

A tax on consumers lowers the consumption function, but not by the full amount of the tax. If the MPC = 2/3 and the tax is $30 billion, the CC curve will shift downward by 2/3 × $30 billion = $20 billion.

sumption function—the MPC—and if the horizontal side of the triangle is $30 billion, the vertical side must be $20 billion. The vertical side, of course, tells us how much the function has shifted downward.

To determine the effect of T on national income, we take this $20 billion and then multiply it by the same factor we used in the case of G; i.e., 3. The downward effect of $30 billion of T, therefore, will be $60 billion. This would be in contrast to the upward effect of an equal $30 billion of G, which would lead to a *$90* billion increase in national income. We use the same factor (3) in each case, but we use a different starting point: $20 billion in the case of taxes, $30 billion in the case of an equivalent increase in government expenditures.

Why this asymmetry? The economic logic behind these differential effects can best be seen at the very first point of impact of G or T. When the government spends $1 to purchase some stationery for one of its offices, it has created in that very first step an added output (or income) of $1. This income then goes the rounds of consumption and saving, according to the multiplier principle. Now when the government taxes $1, it lowers consumption demand and income immediately, but not by the full $1. The consumer, had he not been taxed, would have *saved* part of this $1; in our case, he would have saved 33¢. This means that the initial impact of $1 taxes is to cut consumption demand not by $1 but by 67¢. And this explains why the total effect of a $30 billion tax increase is only ⅔ as great as an equivalent increase in government expenditures ($60 billion as opposed to $90 billion).[4]

$$MPC = \frac{\Delta C}{\Delta J}$$

G *and* T *Combined*
~*Different Routes to Macro-Stability*

We are now in a position to combine the effects of government expenditures and taxes and, even more important, to make some significant general comments about different kinds of fiscal policies.

Figure 9-7 represents a capsule summary of the points we have been making about the effects of government on the equilibrium level of national income. In Fig. 9-7, *a* shows the purely private economy of the previous chapter; *b* introduces $30 billion of G without taxes; *c* includes $30 billion of G and $30 billion of T. This third picture shows us the effects of government when there is a balanced budget.

Now there are four main fiscal approaches an economy can use when it faces problems of unemployment and below potential national income. We can now state some of the advantages and disadvantages of these different approaches.

1. *Laissez-faire.* The most ancient approach is for the government to do nothing (always assuming, of course, some modest—or not-so-modest—role of government in defense, education, and the like). The disadvantages of this approach are quite obvious; and after the Great Depression of the 1930's, these disadvantages seem decisive to most economists. For the laissez-faire approach runs the risk of leaving the economy, as in Fig. 9-7a, with substantial mass unemployment and unutilized productive capacity. The few economists who still support this view in anything like its pure form might argue either (*a*) that

---

[4] When G and T are equal, we have a balanced budget in the government. The principle according to which national income will expand when there are equal increases of G and T is sometimes called the *balanced budget multiplier*. The size of this multiplier will depend very much on the kinds of taxes levied and expenditures undertaken. In our simplified case, however, the *balanced budget multiplier* will be 1. That is, an equal increase of G and T (in our case $30 billion) will lead to an increase of national income of $30 billion. This is essentially because the effects of G and T are the same, except that G has one extra round of impact—the very first—and in this first round the full amount of the government expenditures ($30 billion) is added to national income. Afterwards, the process cancels out as the effects of G and T match each other exactly.

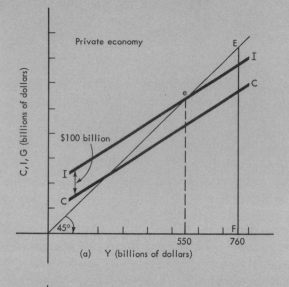

Private economy

(a) Y (billions of dollars)

In *a*, the problem is that, without government intervention, the private economy may not generate enough demand to produce full employment income.

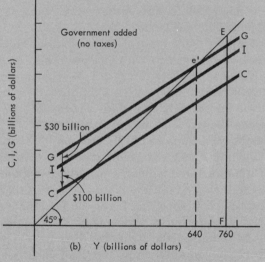

Government added (no taxes)

(b) Y (billions of dollars)

In *b*, added G has increased national income by $90 billion.

In *c*, the same amount of G, *but now matched by equal taxes*, has raised national income by a lesser amount, $30 billion. The fourth alternative—reducing taxes—can be assessed by comparing figures *b* and *c*. If $30 billion in taxes from *c* are removed, then we get *b*. This $30 billion tax reduction would raise national income from $580 to $640 billion, or $60 billion. (We use an MPC = 2/3, throughout.)

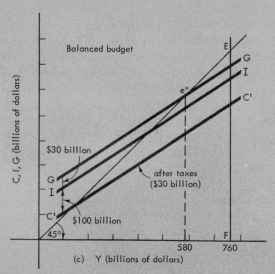

Balanced budget

after taxes ($30 billion)

(c) Y (billions of dollars)

FIG. 9-7

private recuperative forces are much stronger than might be imagined and that, consequently, recoveries will proceed fairly quickly along natural lines, or (b) that unemployment is not too high a price to pay to avoid the encroachments of government on the private sector, or (c) that government policies, either because of political pressures or lack of information or bad timing, will not be as effective as pure theory supposes them and, indeed, may often make things worse, rather than better.

As in the case of all the policies mentioned here, the reader should attempt to analyze these arguments from the point of view of discriminating between empirical differences (where matters of fact are at stake) and value differences (where it is more a question of political or moral judgments).

2. *Increase government expenditures.* The main macroeconomic advantage of an unmatched increase in government expenditures as a way of raising national income in a time of slump is that a dollar's worth of effort, so to speak, gives the maximum possible effect. In Fig. 9-7b, $30 billion of G alone raises national income by $90 billion. This is a greater impact than will result from any other policy. The disadvantages of this approach will be judged differently by different economists. The policy will ordinarily mean an expansion of the governmental national debt and will involve a greater impact of the government on the allocation of the resources of the economy. Some economists disapprove in varying degrees of both features. Other economists argue that the effects of an increased national debt may not be so harmful as generally supposed and that there are advantages in a greater public, as opposed to private, allocation of resources in an economy such as ours.

3. *Reduce taxes.* This policy also increases the national debt (assuming that the government continues its spending unchanged); and it has the disadvantage that for a given increase in the debt, it has slightly less impact on national income than an equivalent expansion of government spending. This is because of the asymmetrical effect of T and G that we have already discussed. A reduction of taxes of $30 billion in our hypothetical economy will raise national income by $60 billion instead of by $90 billion. Another way of putting this is to say that the size of the increase in the national public debt necessary to raise national income to the full employment level will be greater by this method than by the route of increased government spending. On the other hand, this method restores purchasing power to the private sector and therefore gives relatively greater private, as opposed to public, control over the allocation of resources in the economy.

4. *Increase G and T equally.* The final basic method of using fiscal policy to cure macroeconomic ills in a depression is to expand government expenditures and taxes by the same amount. Such an expansion

will lead to some expansion in the economy, although each step forward (increased government demand) is partially offset by a step backward (decreased private demand because of higher taxes). Figure 9-7c shows that a combined increase of $30 billion in both G and T will lead to an increase of $30 billion in national income. If we assume that the government has definitely been given the responsibility of maintaining full employment in the economy, then this approach maximizes the degree of public intervention in the economy. If the total required increase in national income is $180 billion, then the increase in governmental expenditures on this approach will have to be equal to that gap, or $180 billion. This would contrast with an increase in G unmatched by taxes, which would have to be only ⅓ of the gap, or $60 billion. Thus, a balanced budget approach involves, almost paradoxically, the highest level of governmental expenditure to achieve a given rise in national income. But then, of course, it involves no increase in the public debt.

These four approaches by no means exhaust all the steps the government might take (or not take) to deal with a problem of unemployment in the economy as a whole. We have not, for example, touched on the whole area of what is sometimes called *monetary policy*—government measures to influence the supply of money and interest rate in the economy. This will come in Chapter 11. There are also any number of different variants of tax and expenditure policies that can be tailored to specific situations. However, even this very basic grouping of approaches brings out a number of important points and also a number of significant questions.

One of these questions, clearly, has to do with the meaning and significance of the governmental national debt. How is one to make any kind of decision about approaches 2, 3, and 4, or even approach 1, unless one has given careful thought to the so-called burdens of the national debt. This important topic, therefore, will be our central focus of attention in the next chapter.

Summary

In this chapter we have expanded our treatment of national income determination to include some of the effects of government tax and expenditure policy (fiscal policy) on the economy in the aggregate.

To make headway with this analysis, we introduced an important general tool of macroeconomics: the *multiplier*. The multiplier tells us by how much an increase in any kind of spending (consumption, investment, government) will raise the equilibrium level of national income. The size of the multiplier in a simplified economy is determined by the *marginal propensity to consume,* or the fraction of an extra dollar of income that consumers will spend on consumption. (The *marginal propensity to save,* by contrast, is the fraction of that extra dollar that consumers will be willing to save, or MPS = 1 − MPC.) The formula for the multiplier is:

$$m = \frac{1}{1 - MPC}$$

or, alternatively,

$$m = \frac{1}{MPS}$$

The economic logic behind multiple expansions of national income as spending expands centers on the fact that each stage of spending creates further incomes which, in their turn, lead to further spending, further income creation, further spending, and so on. Each time, however, the amounts added to income are less because part of the income is leaked into extra savings.

With the multiplier concept, we were able to show more specifically what the effects of government expenditure and tax policies will be under certain simple circumstances. In general, the following conclusions were reached:

1. An expansion of government expenditures (G) unmatched by an expansion of taxes would lead to a fully multiplied increase in national income.

2. An increase of taxes (T) unmatched by G would lead to a multiplied decrease in national income, though the total effect would be somewhat less than under 1 because, in the first round, taxes cut down spending by less than the full amount of the tax. This, in turn, derives from the fact that part of the income taxed away would have been saved anyway.

3. An equal increase of G and T will lead to some expansion of national income, but less than under an equivalent expansion of G or reduction of T taken singly. Under certain simplified conditions, an equal expansion of G and T would lead to an expansion of national income by the same amount (i.e., the multiplier in this case is 1).

In approaching the problem of underemployment, or below potential GNP, in an economy, the government may decide on many different courses; e.g., doing nothing, raising expenditures, cutting taxes, or raising both expenditures and taxes. The judgment on which policy is best to pursue in any given circumstance will be influenced by a host of considerations including confidence in the recuperative power of the private sector, desire to expand or contract the area of public intervention in the allocation of resources, and, not least, one's views on the controversial subject of the public "national debt."

Questions for Discussion

1 • Imagine that there is a change in tastes resulting in an upward shift of the consumption function by $20 billion at each level of national income. Show how this could lead to an increase of $60 billion in national income if the MPC is ⅔. How much would the increase in national income be if the MPC were ⅘? ½? ⁹/₁₀?

2 • Our analysis in this chapter involved a number of simplifying assumptions. Some of the complications that may arise in reality are:

   a) The MPC falls as the level of national income rises.

   b) Investment is not a fixed amount but increases as the level of national income increases.

   c) Tax revenues of the federal government increase automatically (in the absence of any change in the tax structure) with any increase in national income.

   In each case, explain why these complications may arise. Then show what the general effect of each complication would be on the graphs we have been using in this chapter. Finally, indicate the ways in which we would have to modify our multiplier analysis to take these effects into account.

3 • *Discretionary fiscal policy* occurs when the government alters its tax and expenditure patterns to affect the over-all stability of the economy. But there are also certain *automatic stabilizers* that work in the right direction even in the absence of any discretionary policy moves. The fact that federal income tax receipts automatically rise and fall with rises and falls in national income (see question 2c) is one such stabilizer. Name a number of other government programs that would be likely to have the effect of stabilizing the economy in this automatic way.

4 • If the kind of government intervention discussed in this chapter leads to unfavorable effects on business confidence, then it could be at least partly self-defeating. In what ways do you think an active governmental fiscal policy might have an unfavorable impact on business confidence? Are there any ways in which the impact might be favorable? Is it your impression that the American business community is increasingly opposed to the "new economics"? Always was opposed to it and hasn't changed? Increasingly takes such governmental policies for granted?

Suggested Reading

Annual Reports of the Council of Economic Advisers published annually with the *Economic Report of the President.* Washington: U.S. Government Printing Office.

ECKSTEIN, OTTO, *Public Finance,* 2nd ed. Englewood Cliffs, N.J.: Prentice-Hall, Inc., 1967, Chap. 8.

HARRIS, SEYMOUR E., *The Economics of the Kennedy Years.* New York: Harper & Row, 1964, Chaps. 7-10.

LEWIS, WILFRED J., *Federal Fiscal Policy in the Postwar Recessions.* Washington: The Brookings Institution, 1962.

The national debt

10

The accepted view of most people in this
country for a long time was that the national
debt quite simply was a "bad thing." If you
had asked the man in the street how he felt
about the government, and especially the federal government, spending more than its tax
revenues and thus adding to the national
debt, he would likely have replied that it was
certainly unwise and probably immoral. Yet,
in Chapter 9 we spoke of increases in the public debt—"deficit financing" as it is sometimes
called—as though they were an ordinary and
not particularly alarming feature of a nation's
fiscal policy. Which attitude is correct? How
do we sort out the opposing views on this important question?

Differing Views on the National Debt

The question has to do ultimately not with occasional deficits in the federal budget but with differing over-all views as to the role of the federal budget in our national economic life. As far as specific deficits are concerned, every administration in the last thirty or forty years has faced circumstances that have required it to eat its words on the matter of the public debt. It is not often remembered now that Franklin Roosevelt campaigned in the early 1930's on a balance-the-budget platform, a platform quickly abandoned in the face of the tremendous pressures of the Great Depression. But Republicans are not exempt either. President Eisenhower's sincere desire to balance the federal budget is not in question, but it was in his administration in 1958 that this country ran the large peacetime deficit of $11 billion.

We are concerned, however, not so much with departures of practice from theory (though if departures are too frequent one must begin at least to question the theory), but with the basic theories themselves. Fundamentally, there are two different approaches (with variations) to the question of the public debt.

1. *The public debt as an instrument of a flexible fiscal policy.* The first approach takes up where we left off in the preceding chapter. It takes the premise that a private economy cannot guarantee full employment and price stability under all circumstances. It argues that government spending is expansionary and taxation is contractionary. If the economy is suffering major unemployment, then according to this approach, government spending should be increased and taxation decreased in one form or another with the consequence that the national debt will be increased. (In the opposite condition of inflationary pressures, the remedy, as we shall see in Chapter 12, would, of course, be the exact opposite.)

According to this view, a strict adherence to a balanced budget when there is unemployment would mean in effect that the government was exercising an *inhibiting* effect on the expansion of the economy. Why? Because if the economy were at full employment, its tax revenues would automatically be higher than when the economy was producing at below its full employment potential. Thus, the U.S. personal income tax, for example, automatically increases federal revenues when national income rises.[1] For a given level of federal spending, this increased tax revenue would imply a *full employment surplus* in the federal budget. Thus, a balanced budget when the economy was suf-

---

[1] This tendency of tax revenues to rise with every expansion of national income has been called *fiscal drag*, a term coined by Professor Walter Heller, former chairman of the President's Council of Economic Advisers.

fering unemployment would imply that the government's effective policy with respect to full employment was relatively contractionary. According to this view, such a policy would be poor medicine indeed for an economy that was suffering from a deficiency of aggregate demand.

2. *The principle of the balanced budget.* The opposite point of view regards it as very important in its own right that the federal budget be balanced. This view actually has many different variants. The simplest is the position that the government should attempt as a prime object of policy to balance its budget each and every year. A slightly more sophisticated version of this approach is that the government should attempt to balance its budget over somewhat longer periods of time, balancing deficits in the budget in periods of unemployment against surpluses in the budget during periods of inflation. A still more sophisticated version of this approach would argue that government spending and tax policy ought to be set so that at the full employment level the budget will be balanced. In other words, the *full employment surplus* we mentioned above would be removed (or at least substantially cut down). Like the variant of balancing the budget over the course of the business cycle, this approach would permit fairly substantial deficits in the federal budget in times of serious unemployment.

These variants obviously differ in the degree to which they accept or reject the teachings of the "new economics," but in each there is expressed the determination or at least hope that the balanced budget principle will not be lost sight of—that is, that there will be no long-run increase in the public debt. This principle, in turn, may be based on a variety of different grounds. Some people seem to feel that it is really impossible to proceed in any other way; i.e., that there is some essential contradiction in the notion of the federal government spending more than it taxes. Others would argue that the government might be able to get away with it in the short run, but that in the long run there will be a day of judgment in which the government will have to pay up, with ensuing economic chaos. Still others would not doubt the *possibility* of the government engaging in a long-run expansion of the debt but would claim that it was *unwise* to do so either because the long-run burdens of the debt, though sustainable, are too heavy, or because they feel that government spending should be held in check by the need to raise taxes to finance it, or because they feel that the economy does not need the element of stimulation which continuing deficits might be expected to give.

Now both these principles of policy have some elements of wisdom in them. It must be said, however, that on the whole the proponents of the balanced budget principle (especially in its rigid form) have been unduly alarmist both about the economic logic of an expanding national debt and about the actual facts of U.S. experience during the past thirty years. Let us take a moment to dispel a few of these alarms and then go on to analyze some of the actual costs and benefits of the public debt.

Arguments and Facts

One common concern about the expansion of the national debt may be put this way:

The federal government is no different from any private individual. Everyone knows that a private individual cannot keep accumulating indebtedness all the time. Consequently, the federal government should (or must) reduce the size of the public debt.

Now this argument is, in part, a throwback to the view that Adam Smith expressed in his famous declaration: "What is prudence in the conduct of every private family can scarce be folly in that of a great Kingdom." And, indeed, this is part of the problem with it, because Smith's statement is clearly untrue in a number of important circumstances. To take a couple of obvious examples: it is clearly prudent for a private individual to refrain from printing money, but does this mean that it is folly for the national government to print money? It is prudent for a private individual not to take the law into his own hands, but are we then to conclude that it is folly for the state to maintain a police force and legal system? And so on. The point is that the actions of the state and the actions of private individuals are often regulated by different principles and that the argument by analogy from one to the other is filled with pitfalls.

In the particular case of the public debt, moreover, there is at least one feature that distinguishes it from the debt of private individuals. When I owe a debt to you, I owe it to an external party. The proper analogy in the case of the nation as a whole would be a debt owed to some foreign country, or an *external debt*. The public debt, however, is not external, but internal, and, indeed, we could imagine hypothetical circumstances in which the holders of government bonds and the payers of taxes were identical individuals, in which case it would be literally true that we owe the debt to ourselves.

But even if the analogy were completely correct, there is another major flaw in this particular argument. And this is the incorrect assumption that private parties—individuals or business firms—do not increase their indebtedness in the aggregate over time. Figure 10-1 shows what has been happening to the public debt of the federal government in recent decades, compared to the debt of individuals and private corporations. Although the federal debt was growing substantially relative to private indebtedness in the period from the 1930's to the end of World War II, the last two decades have seen a complete reversal of form; private debt has been growing much more rapidly in this period and, at the present time, it is more than twice as great in total as the whole public debt. Nor is this surprising. We all know that businesses regularly issue bonds to finance new ventures and expansions; in a growing economy, we should expect this kind of indebtedness to increase over time. Similarly with households. We do pay back each debt as it comes due; but in the meanwhile, we incur new debts. While we are buying a car on credit, we are also taking out a mortgage on a new house and buying a washing machine and dryer on the installment plan. As the population grows and the average real income per capita rises, we should naturally expect a continuing expansion in outstanding mortgage loans and consumer credit. And this is exactly what we do have.

These facts should bring home the danger of loose analogies between the government and private parties. For if we were to take the analogy literally, then this would come perilously close to saying, "It's perfectly all right to expand the public debt indefinitely. After all, look at what consumers and businessmen are doing!"

In short, this first argument is fallacious on two fundamental counts and would not be worth spending time on, except that it is heard so frequently in everyday discussion.

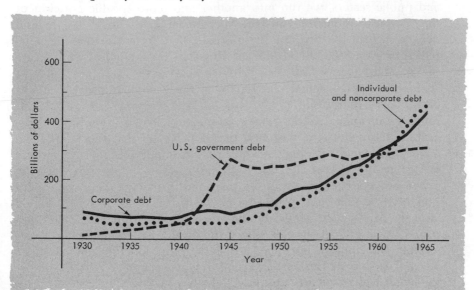

FIG. 10-1

Much the same can be said for a second common worry about the public debt that might be put this way:

All debts must ultimately be repaid, and so it is with the public debt. The U.S. federal debt now exceeds $320 billion. This sum is so huge that any attempt to repay it will cause huge burdens on the economy. Under these circumstances, any further increases in the public debt will ultimately lead us to national bankruptcy.

Like the earlier argument, this one also involves at least two major problems. The first of these problems—the assumption that all debts, including the federal debt, must in the aggregate be repaid—involves, indeed, difficulties similar to those we have already noticed. In the case of private debt, each particular loan does get paid back (unless someone goes bankrupt) but, in the aggregate, private indebtedness increases over time, as indicated by Fig. 10-1. Similarly, the government is regularly engaged in paying back its indebtedness to particular individuals as various government bonds come to maturity. But it then engages in issuing new bonds, with the result that although every individual can count on getting his money back at the proper time, the total of indebtedness can remain the same or increase for the government over time. In fact, it is inconceivable that the debt of the United States government ever will be repaid. It may be (and has been) reduced from time to time by surpluses in the federal budget, but the notion that we will ever get rid of the debt in total is ultimately fanciful. Nor is there any need to do so.

Moving away from these incomplete analogies between the private and public sectors, we run into another and more specific criticism of this alarmist argument. The real question of how "huge" the federal debt is cannot be decided by absolute figures in isolation. Is $300 billion or even $400 billion "huge"? How can we say unless we indicate the standard that we are using for comparisons? There are different standards that one might choose, but a fairly obvious one is the size of the debt in relation to the size of the economy as a whole, or roughly our annual GNP. Figure 10-2 shows this relationship in percentage terms over the past few decades. Notice that there has been a very substantial decline in the *relative* importance of the federal debt since World War II. This is significant when people start worrying about national bankruptcy. If we managed to survive the great expansion of debt that took place during World War II, it seems highly unlikely that we are seriously threatened by anything that has happened since. For all the talk about the "welfare state" and the "great society" and, indeed, the "new economics," the federal debt has been on the decline in this all-important relative sense. Which is simply to say that although the absolute debt has grown, the economy as a

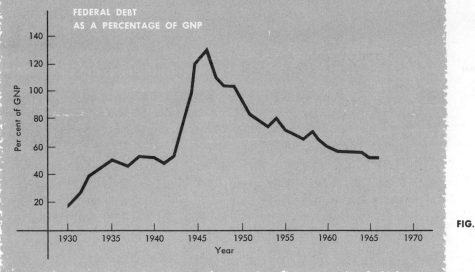

FIG. 10-2

whole has grown much more rapidly, reducing the weight of the debt in relation to our capacity for sustaining it.

Still another common concern is this:

By increasing the public debt, we are putting the burdens of the present generation off onto the shoulders of the future generations. We are saddling our children or our children's children with financial responsibilities that really ought to be borne by ourselves now.

This is a particularly interesting alarmist concern because it is always premised on the assumption that it would be a "bad thing" if we today were to put off any of our economic burdens to our children or to their children yet unborn. Yet would it be so unfair if we could manage it? After all, we do bequeath tremendous economic *assets* to our children's children. They have the whole stock of houses, buildings, factories, machinery, inventories of goods in stock—our national physical capital—that has been built up over the course of past generations simply handed over to them. Equally important, they have the enormous legacy of *intangible* capital: human knowledge, technological advances, skills, economic know-how. Would it then necessarily be so dreadful if we handed on a few "burdens"?

Quite apart from this, however, there is the question whether we *could* manage the shifting of burdens implied in this statement of concern. Admittedly, there are some future burdens to the public debt —we shall come to these in a moment—but in the sense in which this worry is usually conceived, the possible shifting is very limited. We know from figures 10-1 and 10-2 that our great modern increase in the national debt came during World War II. We ask then: Does this mean that the fundamental burdens of fighting World War II were passed on to later generations? Are we in fact "paying for" the war now?

Had the war been financed by external debt to other countries, so that the resources to produce the tanks and planes and ships had come from abroad, and were it true in the 1960's that we were sending equivalent resources back to these foreign countries, then it would also be true that we were "paying for" the war now in an economic sense. But we did not borrow from abroad; consequently, the resources required had to be our own, and they had to be put up *then*, not now. We are certainly not producing tanks, planes, and ships for World War II at the present time. Subject to a qualification we shall mention presently, the resources had to be used and were in fact used in the 1940's. Imagine a full employment economy operating on its transformation or production-possibility curve.[2] If it wants to produce more of one commodity (armaments), it must give up some of the other commodity (private production). When a war effort of the magnitude of our own in the 1940's is involved—50 per cent of our national income was given to defense purposes—then the basic costs must be sustained when they occur (by the current generation) and not in the future.

In sum, this source of alarm has little more fundamental foundation than the others we have discussed.

Costs and Benefits of the National Debt

Still, we must not go to the other extreme and assume that the size of the national debt is a complete irrelevance to our economic life. It clearly does involve certain burdens for the nation. It also may involve certain possible benefits. Without attempting to be all-inclusive, let

[2] See Chap. 1, p. 15. Of course, it may be said that when we entered World War II, we were far from a full employment economy. This, of course, is true, and it is further true that the economic sacrifices (not speaking, of course, of the tremendous human sacrifices involved) of the war in terms of actually "giving up things" were minimal. In a fundamental sense, we financed the war by taking up the tremendous slack in our economy—i.e., moving out to the production-possibility frontier—and also by pushing the curve outward. This, however, is not an argument against debt financing as opposed to the major alternative: total reliance on increased taxation. Indeed, it seems highly doubtful that without some debt financing we could have moved out so quickly to the production-possibility frontier. The huge burdens of taxation would have made mobilization on this scale very difficult. Hence while it is not right to say that the debt postponed the fundamental burdens of the war, it is fair to give debt-financing some credit for easing the pains of the war effort at the time it occurred.

us list a few features of the debt which may have real economic impact, primarily to get a sense of the scale of the problems involved.

1. *Interest charges on the national debt.* An important burden of the federal debt arises from the fact that we have to pay interest on it. Generally, these interest payments will have to be met by increased taxation, and taxes are not only personally unpleasant but may involve certain disincentive effects on effort and productivity in the economy.

This particular burden of the debt is somewhat offset by the fact that American citizens are (1) the taxpayers who finance the interest payments on the debt and (2) the bondholders who receive the interest payments. Even in the unlikely case that precisely the same individuals were involved, however, the net economic effect would still be some lessening of incentives, because the interest comes to us for doing nothing, but the taxes come out of our incomes produced by our hard efforts. If taxes rise high enough, then we may ask: Why put in the extra hour or two of effort if it will mostly go to the government anyway? The magnitude of this disincentive effect, however, must be judged in any given case by the magnitude of the interest charges in relation to our capacity to sustain them, or basically our GNP. Figure 10-3 shows that federal interest payments have been declining as a percentage of GNP since World War II (though not quite as rapidly as debt in relation to GNP, because interest rates have risen somewhat during this period).

Furthermore, it may be argued that these interest payments are to some degree simply payments for benefits being currently received. A portion of government expenditure goes into what in the private

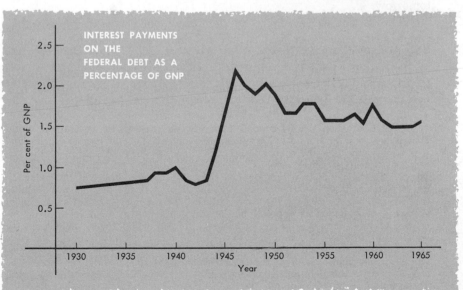

INTEREST PAYMENTS ON THE FEDERAL DEBT AS A PERCENTAGE OF GNP

FIG. 10-3

sector we would call capital formation, as it does when highways, schools, dams, etc., are built by the federal, state, and local governments. Insofar as these capital projects are financed by increases in the public debt, they are bringing us not only increased interest payments and taxes but also increased economic benefits.[3]

2. *Postponing burdens: the problem of investment.* We mentioned in our discussion of World War II that there was a qualification to the basic truth that the costs of the war were borne at the time of the war. This qualification arises from the fact that it is possible to postpone present burdens to the future to the degree that one "lives off" one's capital stock today and consequently bequeathes a smaller capital stock to the future generation. And, in fact, during World War II, we did limit the replacement and repair of a certain portion of our capital stock in order to achieve a maximum war effort.

To what degree debt financing was responsible for this postponement of burdens is, however, a different question. Even had the war been financed completely by current taxes, the same problem would have occurred, and it is doubtful that the solution would have been different in any fundamental way. Furthermore, it is possible to argue that an expansion of the national debt may in many circumstances effectively *increase* the capital stock available to a future generation. If an expansion of the debt is part of a successful fiscal policy that brings the economy closer to its full employment potential, then it has stimulated greater production today, part of which will go into greater consumption today, but *part* of which will also probably go into greater investment today and hence a greater capital stock tomorrow.

This is not to say that the debt may not have an unfavorable effect on investment or that it may not involve postponement to later generations. For example, insofar as the government, faced with the need to market large quantities of bonds, comes into competition with private investors for sources of financial capital, it may contribute to "tighter" money, and hence to some lowering of private investment.[4]

---

[3] Some countries in fact distinguish between the *current* expenditures of government (paying the mailman to deliver the mail) and *capital* expenditures (building a post office). Although one could argue that debt financing is especially appropriate for governmental capital expenditures, this in effect would imply a much too limited and inflexible role for a country's fiscal policy, which ultimately must be guided by the macroeconomic needs of the economy as a whole.

[4] It is also possible to argue that the debt involves some redistribution of income between generations on the grounds that the "younger generation" of today has to work to pay the taxes to pay the interest payments to the bondholding "older generation." Actually, it is doubtful that this qualification is of much practical importance.

What it does mean, however, is that the picture is quite mixed. Some effects of the debt may be in the direction of increasing future burdens, while others—as in the case of a successful fiscal policy—may actually benefit our children's children.

3. *National debt in relation to government activities.* Taxes are considered politically unpopular. If the government does not have to balance the budget, it may, some people fear, engage in "reckless" spending projects, thus increasing the sphere of government in our mixed economy and appropriating resources that might be more effectively used in the private sector.

One's judgment on the importance of this point depends upon one's general opinion about the desirability or undesirability of governmental spending in the economy and also on the more specific question of the degree to which the pressure for balancing the budget is an effective means of limiting government spending. Insofar as one is committed to reducing government expenditures at all costs, it is probably true that by insisting on a balanced budget one is at least creating a further argument against additional public spending. Thus, in the Vietnam war, spending on "great society" domestic programs is being curtailed in part by those who favor a balanced budget (or, realistically, keeping the deficit as low as possible). The opposite point of view might be expressed as follows: (1) the "great society" programs are desirable in their own right and should not be sacrificed to an arbitrary budget-balancing principle; and (2) the question of balancing or not balancing the budget should be determined on the general grounds of its effect on employment and price stability in the economy as a whole. In the particular circumstances of the economy in the Vietnam war, the proponents of this second point of view might actually be very much in favor of raising taxes and curtailing the budget deficit—not, however, to avoid the deficit, but rather because they see dark, inflationary clouds on the horizon.

Ultimately, this third point comes down to the question of whether or not this country needs the kind of financial discipline which the balance-the-budget principle requires. This, in turn, is really a question not about the burden of the debt, but rather about the burden of "reckless" spending. It is undoubtedly true historically and even today that some governments need every possible constraint imaginable to keep them from spending themselves into financial insolvency. Whether this is true of the United States in the 1960's, however, is a very different question.

In short, the picture with respect to this third point, as in the case of the other two points, is a mixed one. Somewhere between a total lack of concern for the debt and raising it to the level of mortal sin, the truth lies. If our general analysis is correct, there should be ample room in this intermediate range for the application of an effective fiscal policy in present-day America.

Summary

The national debt has been a subject of controversy in this country for many years. In the "new economics," the national debt is looked upon as an instrument of a flexible fiscal policy; increases in the debt may sometimes be considered not only tolerable but desirable if the nation is suffering from serious unemployment and inadequate aggregate demand. On the other hand, there are many who espouse the principle of a balanced budget either in a rigid form (annual balance) or in a more flexible form (surpluses in inflationary periods to offset deficits during depressions or recessions).

Many of the arguments for a rigidly balanced budget are based on unduly alarming arguments about the supposed ill effects of a substantial national debt. The argument that the government is just like a private party and that private parties cannot keep going into debt is refuted by the facts that (a) the government is not identical to a private party in many instances, and (b) individual and corporate debt in the United States has been growing more rapidly than the federal debt in recent years. The argument that the federal debt is so "huge" that its repayment will cause the country to go bankrupt is refuted by the facts that (a) the national debt will almost certainly never be repaid in total and (b) as far as size is concerned, the federal debt has been declining as a percentage of GNP ever since World War II. Finally, the argument that the debt is a way of foisting our burdens upon our grandchildren is seen, in its simplistic form, to ignore the fundamental facts about the way resources are mobilized and used in an economy such as ours, as exemplified by our experience in World War II.

The actual costs and benefits of the public debt are much more subtle than these alarmists' arguments would imply. The costs of the debt include, among other things, substantial interest payments which are financed by taxation, possible diminution of business investment under certain circumstances, and a possible loss of financial discipline if "reckless" government spending is encouraged by the absence of a balance-the-budget constraint.

All these points have comebacks: e.g., interest charges have been declining as a percentage of GNP, investment may be increased if an increase in the debt results in higher general employment and out-

put, government spending and deficits may be needed in many circumstances to promote the health of the economy.

   Although no one would deny the importance of keeping an eye
on the size of the national debt, it seems fairly safe to conclude that
the burdens of the debt in the present circumstances of the United
States do not in any way constitute a major obstacle to the application
of an effective modern fiscal policy.

Questions for Discussion

1 • Comment on the theoretical and factual issues involved in the following
   statements:
   a) "The trouble with the 'new economics' is that it does not play by its
       own rules. In theory, budget deficits in bad times should be balanced
       by budget surpluses in good times. But the proponents of the 'new
       economics' always seem to forget the latter. And this, of course, is the
       road to national bankruptcy."
   b) "When there is a balanced budget, the government is acting in a com-
       pletely neutral way as far as the over-all health of the economy is
       concerned."
   c) "A good general rule for modern fiscal policy is that the public debt
       should grow at the same over-all rate as national income."
   d) "The government should follow the following maxims in regulating its
       tax and expenditure policies: 1) pay for all current expenditures out of
       taxation; 2) finance the construction of all capital assets (highways,
       school buildings, etc.) by bond issues."
2 • Argue the pros and cons of the present Congressional policy of having a
   specific limitation on the size of the federal debt.
3 • Since private indebtedness has been growing more rapidly than public
   indebtedness in recent decades, should there be some attempt to limit the
   increase of private indebtedness in the economy? What might be some of
   the issues involved?
4 • In the late 1930's and 1940's, a group of American economists called the
   "stagnationists" predicted that there would be a tendency for saving to
   outrun investment in the American economy and, consequently, that there
   would be increasing unemployment unless the government stepped up its
   intervention. Considering what has been said in the last few chapters
   about the performance of the American economy and the changing role of
   the government since World War II, do you feel that these predictions
   have been verified or refuted by our experience? Explain your answer.

Suggested Reading

BOWEN, W. G., R. G. DAVIS, and D. H. KOPF, "The Public Debt," *American Economic Review*, L (Sept., 1960).

BUCHANAN, J. M., *Public Principles of Public Debt*. Homewood, Ill.: Richard D. Irwin, Inc., 1958.

ECKSTEIN, OTTO, *Public Finance*, 2nd ed. Englewood Cliffs, N.J.: Prentice-Hall, Inc., 1967, Chap. 7.

HARRIS, SEYMOUR E., *Economics of the Kennedy Years*. New York: Harper & Row, 1964, Chap. 11.

SAMUELSON, PAUL A., JOHN R. COLEMAN, ROBERT L. BISHOP, and PHILLIP SAUNDERS, *Readings in Economics*, 4th ed. New York: McGraw-Hill, Inc., 1964, Chaps. 24-26.

Money and
monetary policy

11

In the preceding five chapters, we have been setting out the basic structure of national income analysis and the relationship of this analysis to public policy. Our presentation so far has three main limitations: (1) it has omitted any explicit discussion of the role of "money" in the national economy; (2) it has been centered almost wholly on the problem of unemployment to the exclusion of the problem of inflation; and (3) it has been limited to the analysis of a "closed" economy and hence has not dealt with the interesting problems of international trade.

In the next three chapters, we shall take up each of these problems in order. In this chapter, our focus will be on "money" in relationship to the theory of national income

determination and on the great issues of governmental policy that
handling the nation's money supply involves.[1]

The Role of Money—a Synopsis

The omission of the role of money in our analysis so far is a particularly
serious one. Economists always have been concerned with this topic,
and, indeed, it was in connection with speculations about the impact
of "treasure" on the national economy that many of the first steps in
the field were taken.[2] Furthermore, the development of the modern
theory of national income determination is specifically related to certain developments in the theory of money. We mentioned when we
were discussing the work of John Maynard Keynes that one of the
main things he did was to try to provide a synthesis of *real* and
monetary analysis—attempting to show the impact of financial mechanisms and institutions on *real* things like output and employment. And,
finally, we know from our reading of the newspapers that the management of our country's money supply is considered of vital importance
to our over-all economic health. *Monetary policy* is concerned with
action designed to affect both the level of the interest rate and the
size and availability of the money supply in the national economy.
Monetary policy must be put next to *fiscal policy* (the government
tax and expenditure programs we have just been discussing) as one
of the main avenues by which the government can influence the over-
all level of employment, output, and prices in the nation.

So money is important in the economy, but it is also difficult to
analyze. How are we to capture the essence of its role in a few pages?

The best approach is to sketch out the picture as a whole very
quickly, and then to come back and look at the details. Let us put the
question this way:

How is the monetary policy of a government like that of the United States
supposed in theory to affect the level of prices, output, and employment in the

[1] It might be added also that the analysis in the whole of Part II is limited by
the fact that it concentrates on the short run and does not focus on the factors behind long-run growth. As we have said earlier, however, the entire theory of national income determination from its original conception to the present time has been
oriented to short-run problems and solutions. This special focus has probably helped
make this part of economics one of its most successful parts in actual practice. By
contrast, long-run growth theory (which will be our general area of interest in
Part III) is as yet much less well-developed.

[2] The so-called *mercantilist* writers of the sixteenth and seventeenth centuries,
who antedated the classical school, devoted great attention to the problem of money
—especially in the form of the precious metals. They also devoted great attention to
problems of international trade, as we shall notice below (p. 200).

economy as a whole? By what chain of logic does government action affecting the money supply reach down into the economy and influence such important variables as the number of jobs available or the number of tons of steel produced or the cost-of-living index?

The chain of logic connecting these different variables can then be set out in four basic propositions. These are:

1. An increase in the quantity of money, *cet. par.*, will generally cause a fall in the interest rate.
2. A fall in the interest rate, *cet. par.*, will generally cause an expansion of business investment.
3. An expansion of business investment, *cet. par.*, will generally cause an expansion of GNP and employment.

These first three points indicate that the basic direction of monetary policy in a depression or recession should be expansionary. According to these points, an expanded money supply will lead through changes in the interest rate and business investment to a higher level of GNP and employment in a previously depressed economy. A fourth point deals with the opposite problem of inflation—i.e., when there is not too little but too much aggregate demand.

4. When the quantity of money is decreased, the opposite effects will generally occur; that is, a decrease in the money supply will cause a rise in the rate of interest, which will cause a fall in business investment, which, in turn, will cause a fall in GNP and employment or, if the problem is inflation, a reduction of inflationary pressures.

Since one would normally follow a contractionary monetary policy in an inflation and since the problem of inflation will be the subject of our next chapter, we shall concentrate for the moment solely on the first three points.

Each of these points represents one important link in the chain of logic connecting the money supply with national income and employment. As far as our understanding is concerned, these links are of very different degrees of difficulty, particularly in view of what we have already accomplished in earlier chapters. To make things as clear as possible, let us take up these links in the order of less to greater difficulty of understanding; this will mean taking them up in the reverse order, beginning with point 3 and ending with point 1.

The Investment–GNP Link

The easiest link for us to understand is clearly that expressed in point 3:

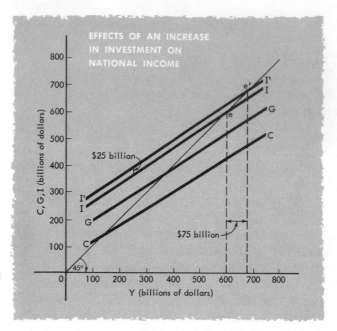

FIG. 11-1

An expansion of business investment, *cet. par.*, will generally cause an expansion of GNP and employment.

This is nothing but our theory of national income determination again. Figure 11-1 is a duplicate of diagrams we have used many times before, the only difference being that we have put investment on the top, so that we could show more clearly the effects of an increase of investment (from *I I* to *I' I'*). If investment goes up by whatever amount, national income will rise by a multiplied amount, the multiplier being determined in the simplest case by the formula:

$$m = \frac{1}{1 - \text{MPC}}$$

In this particular diagram, MPC = $\frac{2}{3}$, and m = 3, the increase in investment is $25 billion and the resulting increase of equilibrium national income is $75 billion. This should be completely familiar to us from our previous work.

The Interest Rate–Investment Link

The next easiest link, though one we shall want to say a few words about, is that expressed in point 2:

A fall in the interest rate, *cet. par.*, will generally cause an expansion of business investment.

Point 3 was about the *effects* of an increase in investment; this point is about the *causes* of an increase in investment. What is the logic behind the interest rate–investment link?

Actually, we have already discussed this matter briefly (Chapter 8), but there are two further comments, one a clarification, the other a qualification, that we should add here.

The clarification has to do with ascertaining the *direction* in which changing interest rates move the level of investment. There is a potential possibility of misunderstanding here, largely because of the different ways we use the term "investment" in everyday discourse. Nowhere is it more important than now to remember our earlier distinction between "financial" investment (buying a stock or a bond) and ordinary business investment (building a new factory, adding to one's inventories of goods in stock, etc.). The reason for this special caution is that the effect of changes in the rate of interest will be very different; in fact, ordinarily in opposite directions, depending on which kind of investment one has in mind.

To make this point clear, let us consider "financial" investment first. Now from the point of view of the "financial investor" a high rate of interest is a good thing. The issue before him is not whether or not to build a factory, but whether or not to buy a bond. If the interest rate is high, this will not discourage him from buying the bond; on the contrary, it will ordinarily make him eager to do so. At 4 per cent interest, he gets $4 a year by putting $100 into a bond. At 6 per cent, he gets $6 a year from the same $100. In certain circumstances, this difference may induce him to buy an extra bond or two. The point is that for the "financial investor," the interest rate appears as a *payment* for the use of the money he has lent.

It is just the reverse when we come to investment in the ordinary sense in which we have been using the term—i.e., the actual adding of new productive capacity to our economy. For when we talk about this kind of investment we are approaching everything from the point of view not of the lender but of the borrower. The businessman wishes to borrow money to expand his productive capacity. To say that the interest rate has gone up is nothing but to say that the *costs* of borrowing have gone up. As a businessman, you wish, say, to invest in a new machine that costs $1,000. You go to the bank to finance this purchase with a loan. If the bank charges you 4 per cent on the loan, then you have to pay out interest charges of $40 per year on the machine. If the rate is 6 per cent, you have to pay out $60 a year. It may be the case that the machine will be just profitable to you at 4 per cent, but not profitable at 6 per cent, and decidedly unprofitable at 7 per cent or 8 per cent. A high interest rate then is not an encouragement but a definite *dis*couragement as far as ordinary business investment is concerned.

This clarification should make it apparent that the direction of changes in investment in this second sense will be in the opposite direction from changes in the rate of interest. A high interest rate will tend to discourage investment. A low interest rate—meaning that the costs of borrowing are low—will tend to foster higher levels of investment. And this, in fact, is precisely what our point 2 states.

We now ask: How *great* an effect on investment will these changes in the interest rate have? And this leads us to a certain qualification that should be made in connection with point 2. For although the *direction* of this effect is now perfectly clear, it is much less certain how *large* that effect will be.

The problem, essentially, is that there are many different factors that influence business investment, and the interest rate is only one— in many circumstances not the most important one. We have mentioned some of these factors before: business expectations, technological progress, amount of retained profits, and, of course, the interest rate. If, say, business expectations are sufficiently pessimistic, then it may be that investment will stay small no matter how enticingly low the interest rate may be. Conversely, if there are certain remarkable new products or processes available for investment, businessmen may be difficult to discourage, no matter what (within limits) are the costs of borrowing.

A technical way of describing this is to say that investment demand may, for wide ranges of different interest rates, be *interest-inelastic;* i.e., the percentage change in investment for a given percentage change in the interest rate may be quite small.[3]

---

[3] We have come upon the concept of *elasticity* before (p. 62). In the case of investment and the interest rate, we might imagine a diagram such as this one. We measure the amount businessmen are willing to invest along the x-axis, and the rate of interest on the y-axis. This investment demand curve shows us that businessmen will invest more at lower rates of interest. However, this particular curve has been drawn relatively *interest-inelastic,* meaning that it takes a big change in the interest rate to produce even a small change in investment.

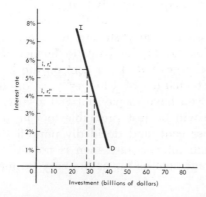

THE INVESTMENT DEMAND SCHEDULE

This does not mean that our point 2 is incorrect. It simply means that the strength of this link is not great. If under particular circumstances a fall in the rate of interest produces only a modest increase in investment, then this will clearly limit the results we can hope for when we are trying to cure unemployment by interest rate changes. We shall come back to this difficulty presently.

Money Supply–Interest Rate Link

With points 3 and 2 in hand, we are now ready to turn to point 1. And here we shall have to linger a moment. For it is at this juncture that the role of money at last enters explicitly into our picture. Point 1 states:

An increase in the quantity of money, *cet. par.*, will generally cause a fall in the interest rate.

If we can establish this point in a general way, then we shall have succeeded in building our logical chain from money, on the one side, to national income, employment, and prices, on the other.

Now the way we shall analyze the effects of an increase in the quantity of money in the economy is by considering the manner in which such an increase might actually take place in the present-day American economy. The responsible agency for managing the money supply in the United States is not the President, nor Congress, nor even the Treasury Department, but rather the *Federal Reserve System*. The Federal Reserve Banks were established in this country in 1913. They are ultimately responsible to Congress, and they usually work in cooperation with the President and the Secretary of the Treasury, although there have been times when there has been disagreement among these parties concerning what monetary policy should be followed. The Federal Reserve Board, or the Fed as it is commonly called, is the institution through which an increase in our money supply would normally be initiated.

To understand the leverage that the Federal Reserve Board has over our money supply, we must first be clear on two important points. The first point has to do with the nature of the instruments we call "money" in our economy. *Money* can be defined as any instrument (whether beads, cattle, or dollar bills) that we will generally accept in exchange for commodities or services or for the payment of debts. We all know certain obvious forms of money in the United States: coins and bills.

The most common form of money in this country, however, is not cash or currency but something called *demand deposits. Demand deposits* are really nothing but our checking accounts at the bank—they are payable by check "on demand." A moment's reflection will convince anyone that these deposits are as generally acceptable as hard cash for settling financial transactions in this country at the present time.[4] And the important point for us to notice here is that these demand deposits are the most common form of money in the United States—about 80 per cent of our total money supply in 1965.

The second preliminary point to notice is that banks are legally required to hold certain *reserves* against their demand deposits. In 1966, city banks were required to have reserves equal to 16½ per cent of their demand deposits, and country banks had to have 12 per cent. The need for some reserves is fairly obvious. Although deposits and withdrawals may often cancel out, nevertheless there are periods when particular banks face an excess of withdrawals or, indeed, when the banking system as a whole is faced with a run on the system. The required reserves of the commercial banks that are members of the Federal Reserve System are a defense against such occasional (but historically often serious) problems. What we must notice particularly, however, is the composition of these reserves. In the case of a member bank, the basic form of these reserves is not cash or currency (although most banks do, in fact, keep some "vault cash" on hand) but deposits of the member bank with the Federal Reserve Bank in its district. The Federal Reserve Bank serves as a bank's bank. The member bank makes deposits in the Federal Reserve Bank (just as you or I make deposits in the member bank), and these deposits then form the backbone of the bank's required reserves.

These two points—the importance of demand deposits as our typical form of money, and the nature of the required reserves held in the Federal Reserve Bank by the member banks—already bring us fairly close to the process by which the money supply in the United States may be expanded. Essentially, the Federal Reserve can bring about an expansion in the money supply either by making more reserves available to the commercial banks or by changing the legal reserve requirement. When either of these steps is taken, the commercial banks are then collectively able to expand the volume of demand deposits—money—in the economy.

The three main tools the Federal Reserve Board has for achieving this effect are: (1) simply lowering the legal reserve requirement

---

[4] It is true, of course, that if a stranger comes into town we may not accept his check. However, this is usually a case not of doubting the acceptability of demand deposits but of doubting whether the stranger actually has demand deposits in the bank to make his check good. When we are sure he does have the "money" in the bank, we will usually accept his check.

from, say, 16½ per cent to 15½ per cent; (2) lowering the interest rate at which the member banks may borrow from the Federal Reserve Bank to replenish or augment their reserves (this particular interest rate is called the *discount rate*); and (3) by engaging in open-market purchases of government securities. This third method—"open market operations" as it is often called—is a particularly important one, and also somewhat complicated to understand. Let us therefore follow it through in a step-by-step fashion. In this way, we shall be able to show (*a*) how the Federal Reserve can expand the money supply and (*b*) how the effect of this expansion will be to lower interest rates in the economy generally.

Very well then. The Fed is interested in expanding the money supply, and it attempts to do this through open-market purchases of government securities. Let us suppose it buys a $100 government bond directly from one of the commercial banks in the system. The effect of this action will be to increase the reserves of the commercial banks in the system and, consequently, permit them to expand their loans to the public. As they expand their loans, the money supply in the economy will increase and the interest rate will fall.

To follow the process through, it is necessary to look at the balance sheets of the member bank in the system.

SIMPLIFIED BALANCE SHEETS OF A MEMBER BANK

Before Open-market operation		After Federal Reserve Bank purchases $100 government bond	
Assets	Liabilities	Assets	Liabilities
$200 Reserves in the Federal Reserve Bank	$1,000 Demand deposits	$300 Reserves in the Federal Reserve Bank	$1,000 Demand deposits
$800 Loans, investments, bonds		$700 Loans, investments, bonds	

Our stripped-down examples represent the situation of the member bank *before* and *after* the Federal Reserve Bank has purchased the government bond. Three items are to be noticed before the purchase:

1. The bank has $200 listed as deposits in the Federal Reserve Bank. These are the legally required reserves we have been speaking of. We are assuming that the legal reserve requirement in our hypothetical system is 20 per cent of demand deposits.
2. The second asset item represents loans, investments, and government bonds. Here the bank is engaged in lending out money or buying bonds or other securities in order to make money in the form of interest. These are the

interest-earning assets of the bank, and they are, of course, an essential feature of the commercial banking system.

3. On the liability side, we have $1,000 worth of demand deposits. In the real world, there are other forms of deposits as well, but we are concentrating on the fundamentals of the system only. These deposits are called liabilities because they are owed by the bank to its depositors. They are also the principal form of money in the American economy.[5]

This, as we have said, is the member bank's balance sheet *before* the Federal Reserve purchases a $100 government bond from the member bank. What happens immediately *after* this purchase is shown in the balance sheet on the right. The loans, investments, etc., category has gone down by $100 through the sale of the bond. At the same time the Federal Reserve Bank has credited the member bank with an additional $100 in its reserves with that Federal Reserve Bank. This is the way in which the Federal Reserve Bank pays for the bond. The new totals are recorded: $300 in reserves; $700 in loans, investments, and bonds; $1,000 in demand deposits.

So far, we notice, there has been no change in the money supply. That is, we still have $1,000 in demand deposits. However, the stage has now been set for an expansion of the money supply, because this bank (and, consequently, member banks as a whole) now has $100 more in reserves. This means that this bank can now lend out money to businesses and individuals, because it has reserves in excess of its legal requirements. When it lends out money, it does so by creating demand deposits for those who are borrowing from it. But this is not all; the process goes beyond an additional $100 of demand deposits. And the reason is that it is the *reserves* that have been increased by $100, and a $100 increase in reserves can ultimately sustain a fivefold (assuming a 20 per cent reserve requirement) increase in demand deposits in the system as a whole. In other words, if the member banks are willing to lend out all their excess reserves, then ultimately the $100 open-market operation will lead to a $500 expansion in the money supply.

This process cannot be accomplished by one small bank alone. All it can do is to lend out the $100. But this $100 will then be deposited in some other bank, which will then find that *its* demand deposits and reserves have both been increased by $100. This second bank, in turn, will have excess reserves of $80 (it must keep $20 against its new demand deposits of $100) which it can then lend out. This, in turn,

---

[5] An actual bank balance sheet would, of course, be much more complicated than this. So also would the concept of "money." For example, banks carry not only demand deposits but also time deposits or savings deposits. One cannot write checks on these deposits, but they can be easily turned into cash. Are these deposits "money"? The answer is almost, but not quite. Most economists would call them "near-money."

will create $80 of new reserves and demand deposits in still a third bank, which will find that *it* now has excess reserves of $64, and so on. The next group of balance sheets follow the process through a few rounds. Actually, this process looks formally very much like the national income multiplier of Chapter 9, with the role of the MPS being played by the legal reserve requirement. Formally, in fact, it is identical—though, of course, the substance is completely different.

THE PROCESS OF MULTIPLE CREDIT EXPANSION

After our original bank has loaned out its $100 in excess reserves, this $100 will be deposited in Bank A. If Bank A's original balance sheet was identical to our original bank's, the change will be reflected as follows:

1.

Bank A	Assets	Liabilities
(*Before* $100 is deposited)	$200 Reserves	$1,000 Demand deposits
	$800 Loans and investments	

Investments

Bank A	Assets	Liabilities
(*After* $100 is deposited)	$300 Reserves	$1,100 Demand deposits
	$800 Loans and investments	

Bank A now lends out $80 and its balance sheet becomes:

Assets	Liabilities
$220 Reserves	$1,100 Demand deposits
$880 Loans and investments	

Addition to money supply in first round = $100

2. The $80 loaned out by Bank A is now deposited in Bank B.

Bank B	Assets	Liabilities
(*Before* $80 deposit)	$200 Reserves	$1,000 Demand deposits
	$800 Loans and investments	

Bank B	Assets	Liabilities
(*After* $80 deposit)	$280 Reserves	$1,080 Demand deposits
	$800 Loans and investments	

Bank B now lends out $64 and its balance sheet becomes:

Assets	Liabilities
$216 Reserves	$1,080 Demand deposits
$864 Loans and investments	

Addition to money supply in second round = $80

3. The $64 loaned out by Bank B is now deposited in Bank C.

Bank C	Assets	Liabilities
(Before $64 deposit)	$200 Reserves $800 Loans and investments	$1,000 Demand deposits

Bank C	Assets	Liabilities
(After $64 deposit)	$264 Reserves $800 Loans and investments	$1,064 Demand deposits

Bank C now lends out $51.20 and its balance sheet becomes:

Assets	Liabilities
$212.80 Reserves $851.20 Loans and investments	$1,064 Demand deposits

Addition to money supply in third round = $64

In the next round, Bank D will be able to lend out 80 per cent of $51.20 or $40.96; in the next round, Bank E will be able to lend out 80 per cent of $40.96, or $32.77; and so on. The *total* addition to the money supply (ΔM) when all the rounds are completed will be:

$$\Delta M = \$100 + \$80 + \$64 + \$51.20 + \$40.96 + \$32.77 + \ldots$$

$$\Delta M = \$100 \, (1 + .80 + (.80)^2 + (.80)^3 + (.80)^4 + \ldots + (.80)^n + \ldots)$$

$$\Delta M = \$100 \left(\frac{1}{1 - .80} \right)$$

$$\Delta M = \$100 \, (5) = \$500$$

If we consolidated all these balance sheets and looked at the process before, during, and after the expansion had taken place, it would look like the situation described in the final example. The total reserves of the member banks have gone up from $2,000 to $2,100. As a consequence, and on the assumption that each bank at each stage of the game lends out any excess reserves that come its way, the demand deposits in the system have gone up from $10,000 to $10,500— i.e., for the Federal Reserve purchase of a $100 government bond, there has been a $500 expansion of the money supply.

CONSOLIDATED MEMBER BANK BALANCE SHEETS

If we assume that there are 10 banks in the system, each with a balance sheet identical to those we have been describing, then we have:

1. Consolidated balance sheet before Federal Reserve open-market operation:

Assets	Liabilities
$2,000 Reserves in Federal Reserve Bank $8,000 Loans and investments	$10,000 Demand deposits

2. Consolidated balance sheet immediately after Federal Reserve purchase of a $100 government bond:

Assets	Liabilities
$2,100 Reserve in Federal Reserve Bank	$10,000 Demand deposits
$7,900 Loans and investments	

3. Consolidated balance sheet after multiple expansion of credit has taken place:

Assets	Liabilities
$2,100 Reserves in Federal Reserve Bank	$10,500 Demand deposits
$8,400 Loans and investments	

Now at the same time that one is learning to understand this expansionary process, one is actually also learning to understand why an expansion of the money supply tends to bring the interest rate down—and this, of course, is the main point we are trying to demonstrate here.

To see this, all one needs to do is to visualize what is happening in the case of each of the banks in the system as it receives its share of excess reserves. Each bank, being a commercial institution, is now eager to make money by lending out this excess; there is a generally increased willingness on the part of lenders in the economy to lend. This is really analogous to the kind of supply-and-demand analysis for goods and services that we described in Chapter 2. In this case the good is "loans" and the "price" is the interest rate. There has been no change in the position of the borrowers (i.e., business investors) but there has been developed an increased willingness on the part of the banking system to supply more loans. The consequence, as we would expect, is that the price—i.e., the interest rate—will fall.

This is the essence of the process by which Federal Reserve open-market purchases of government securities can lead both to an expansion in the money supply and an easing of the terms on which banks are ready to lend to businesses, and especially a fall in the interest rate. (To test his understanding of the process, the reader should follow through the opposite policy, showing how Federal Reserve sales of government bonds to the member banks can lead to a contraction of reserves, multiplied contraction of demand deposits, or money, and a raising of the interest rate.) The banks find themselves with excess reserves. Whereas previously they would lend to businesses —or, for that matter, to home-builders or state and local governments— only at 6 per cent interest, now they are willing to lend at 5½ per cent or 5 per cent.

Thus, our point 1—the link between the money supply and the rate of interest—has been demonstrated, and the chain connecting the money supply with the level of national income and employment is now complete.

A Recapitulation
and Some Qualifications

Rather, it is "complete" subject to a number of qualifications. Let us first go over the whole process from beginning to end, and then notice a few problems.

To recapitulate: The Federal Reserve Board finds the economy suffering from unemployment and below-potential national income. It can use *monetary policy* to combat this situation in many ways; e.g., changing the reserve requirement, lowering the discount rate, or engaging in open-market operations. Let us suppose it decides to combat the recession by open-market purchases of government securities. Let us suppose further that it purchases these securities directly from its member banks:

As a consequence of these open-market purchases, the member banks will find their reserves in excess of the legal requirements. They will be ready and eager to lend more to businesses. In this process of lending more, the money supply will be increased, and the banks will find themselves offering better terms—lower interest rates—to businessmen. Businessmen, in their turn, will find the lower interest rates attractive, an inducement to expand their investments. They will now be willing to undertake expansions of their plant and equipment and machinery that heretofore would not have been profitable. The same also will be true of people who wish to borrow money to build homes, or of state and local governments who may need to float loans for new schools. In general, then, the lowered interest rates and the increased availability of money will cause an expansion of investment and other spending in the economy. This expansion of investment and other spending will, by virtue of the national income multiplier, lead to an expansion of national income and employment in the economy as a whole. Thus, monetary policy, like fiscal policy, is shown to be a tool by which the government can influence the level of spending and, consequently, the level of national income and employment in the economy.

This, in capsule form, is the fundamental way by which the nation's monetary policy reaches down into the economy to affect the major economic aggregates of output, employment, and prices.

One factor we have not mentioned—though in all logic it should have been part of the chain that we have been attempting to construct—is sometimes called the *transactions demand for money*. One of the reasons we hold any of our wealth in the form of money (as opposed, say, to stocks or bonds or other assets) is quite simply that we need money to carry on the ordinary business of life. We need a certain amount of money to handle our normal day-to-day or month-to-month financial transactions. Now the *amount* of money we need for these transactions purposes will, on the whole, be determined by the amount of business we do or, for the national economy, by the level of national income in money terms. At a national income of $300 billion annually, we need considerably less transaction money than at a national income of, say, $800 billion. The point is this: in our capsule summary we spoke of the end product of monetary policy as being a certain expansion of national income. What we did *not* do was to take account of the extra transaction demand for money that such an expansion brings. What this factor means, in essence, is that only *part* of the expanded money supply can, so to speak, go into financing a lower rate of interest; another part of it must be made available to finance the expanded transactions required by the increased national income.

But there are other qualifications as well. We have already mentioned that the interest rate–investment link may be weak. It may be particularly weak when the object is to *increase* investment. If interest rates are very high, the monetary authorities may be able to choke off a certain amount of investment, but how does one lure businessmen to invest when their expectations are pessimistic? Imagine a situation in which business firms are already operating under conditions of excess capacity. They are already producing less output than could easily be handled by their existing plant and machinery capacity. Will a change in the interest rate from 5 per cent to 4 per cent be likely to induce them to expand their currently redundant stock of plant and machinery? Will any change in the interest rate be sufficient to offset the other negative factors operating on their demand for investment?

But if the interest rate–investment link may be weak, so also may be the link relating Federal Reserve action affecting reserves to the expansion of the money supply and the lowering of interest rates. If interest rates are low and business conditions look poor, then the member banks may not lend out all their excess reserves as we have imagined. They may decide to hold excess reserves, thus frustrating the multiple credit expansion that the Fed is attempting to promote. More generally, when interest rates are low, people in the economy as a whole may find that their desire to hold money as opposed to other assets is quite strong. For businesses and individuals want money not simply for the transaction purposes we have just mentioned, but also for what is sometimes called *liquidity* purposes. If you are holding a stock or a bond, its price may fall (say from $80 a share to $60 a share), and you will have sustained a monetary loss. In the case of money, the price of a dollar remains forever a dollar. If interest rates are low (in which case the opportunity cost of holding money is low), you may decide to hold perfectly *liquid* money rather than take a risk that your stocks or bonds may fall in money value.[6] What this means is that even when the money supply is substantially increased, it may not have a very great effect on bringing down interest rates. As these rates get lower and lower, people may simply decide to hold all the additional money *as money*, for these liquidity reasons. After a certain point is reached, people may refuse to buy bonds and other securities, with the consequence that even if more money is pumped into the economy, it will not bring a lowered interest rate and hence will have little or no effect on business investment.

These are not the only qualifications that one might make about the effectiveness of monetary policy. We shall mention further specific difficulties in our next chapter in connection with the problem of controlling inflation. These general points, however, should make it clear that although the logical chain we have constructed between monetary policy and national income is essentially valid, the *impact* of monetary policy may be very different under many different circumstances. If business expectations are very pessimistic, if the banks are cautious about lending out their excess reserves, if a strong preference for liquidity pervades the economy, then it may be that even an extremely vigorous easy-money policy may have only a marginal impact.

What this means is that in ordinary circumstances the economy should not rely on monetary policy alone to do the job. It is an important tool for promoting the economic well-being of the economy, but it will usually be desirable to employ it in connection with fiscal policy and the various other tools available to the government when the problem of depression or inflation is a really serious one.

Summary

In this chapter, we have brought the role of money explicitly into our analysis of national income, attempting to show how the monetary policy of the government may affect the levels of national income and employment in the economy.

[6] A *liquid* asset is one readily turned into money. Since money *is* money, it is perfectly *liquid*. When interest rates are low, this is the same thing as saying that bond prices are high: $5 a year on a bond that sells for $200 is an interest rate of 2½ per cent; $5 a year on a bond that sells for $100 is 5 per cent. When bond prices are high, people generally may fear that they are due for a fall. This is an important reason for preferring money to bonds when interest rates are low.

The reader should be clear that perfect liquidity does not imply a constant purchasing power. Although a dollar is always worth a dollar, it may be worth less in terms of real goods when there is a general inflation. Indeed, when prices in general are rising, the costs of holding perfectly liquid money are increased, since that money will be worth less (in real terms) in the future.

The basic links in the logical chain connecting money with national income, employment, and prices are as follows:

1. *An increase in the money supply will generally lower the interest rate.* The agency responsible for handling the money supply of the United States is the Federal Reserve Board. The Fed has various instruments available for increasing the money supply, including: changing the reserve requirements of its member banks; lowering the interest rate (*discount rate*) at which the member banks may borrow from the Federal Reserve Bank in their district; and making open-market purchases of government securities.

We followed through a Federal Reserve purchase of a government bond from one of its member banks. We showed that this purchase would (*a*) increase the reserves of the member banks; (*b*) lead to a multiple expansion of demand deposits in the economy; (*c*) bring about generally lowered interest rates and easier availability of credit to business investors. In understanding this process, it is necessary to remember that demand deposits are the most common form of money in the United States.

2. *A fall in the interest rate will generally lead to an increase in business investment.* To understand this point, we should recall that we are talking about "investment" in the sense of adding machinery and plant to the productive capacity of the economy (not "financial investment," i.e., buying a stock or a bond). To the businessman who is thinking of buying a new machine or expanding his factory, a low interest rate will mean lowered costs of borrowing money. Hence, it will generally encourage *investment,* in our sense of the word.

3. *An increase in business investment will generally lead to an expansion of national income and employment.* This is simply our old friend the national income multiplier from earlier chapters.

(A *fourth* point relating decreases in the money supply to higher interest rates, lowered investment, and a contraction of aggregate demand was postponed until the next chapter, which deals with inflation.)

In evaluating this logical chain, one has to remember some important qualifications:

a) A certain proportion of our money supply is used for *transactions* purposes. If national income expands, there will generally be an increased demand for money for transactions, with the consequence that not all of any given increase in the money supply will go into bringing lowered interest rates.

b) A low interest rate may have fairly little impact on raising the level of investment if other factors affecting investment are strongly negative; e.g., the existence of excess capacity, pessimistic business expectations, and so on.

c) If the banks are cautious about lending out their excess reserves and if there is a strong *liquidity* demand for money in the economy as a whole, then the Fed may be largely frustrated in its efforts to being interest rates down.

These various points make it clear that, although monetary policy is a very important tool for correcting imbalances in the economy in the aggregate, it is a tool that will usually have to be employed in conjunction with other tools, like fiscal policy, when the macroeconomic problems facing the country are serious ones.

Questions for Discussion

1 • Define *money*. What are some other forms, besides money, in which people might hold their wealth? Rank the various assets you have listed according to their degree of liquidity.

2 • What is meant by the phrase "a synthesis of real and monetary economics"? Is this synthesis achieved in the analysis presented in this chapter? If so, explain how.

3 • Suppose an individual, having come to distrust the banking system, withdraws his $1,000 demand deposit from a commercial bank and buries the $1,000 in a hole in his backyard. Will this have any effect on the money supply of the economy? Follow through the steps involved.

4 • It sometimes happens that the Treasury, unable to market government securities to the public on acceptable terms, sells them to the Federal Reserve System. The balance sheet of the Federal Reserve Bank is thereby altered as follows for a $1 million sale:

Stage I: The Treasury is credited with a $1 million deposit at the Federal Reserve Bank:

FEDERAL RESERVE BANK BALANCE SHEET

Assets	Liabilities
+ $1 million government bonds	+ $1 million U.S. Treasury deposits

Stage II: The Treasury spends the money, and the individuals who receive it deposit it in their commercial banks. The commercial banks thereby increase their reserves at the Federal Reserve Bank:

FEDERAL RESERVE BANK BALANCE SHEET

Assets	Liabilities
+ $1 million government bonds	+ $1 million Member bank reserves

What effect will this transaction be likely to have on the money supply of the country?

It has been said that this way of financing the federal debt is very much like "printing money." Do you agree?

Suppose the Treasury, instead of selling its bonds to the Federal Reserve System, sells them to private individuals who pay for them by check on their demand deposit accounts at their commercial banks? Will this have a similar or different effect on the money supply of the country? Explain.

5 · Explain (a) the money supply–interest rate link; (b) the interest rate–investment link, (c) the investment–GNP link. Indicate the main weaknesses in these links if our objective happens to be to "cure" a depression by monetary policy.

Suggested Reading

BOARD OF GOVERNORS OF THE FEDERAL RESERVE SYSTEM, *The Federal Reserve System: Its Structure and Function,* 4th ed. Washington, D.C., 1961.

DAVENPORT, JOHN, "The Strain Is on the Banks," *Fortune,* July, 1966.

DUESENBERRY, JAMES S., *Money and Credit: Impact and Control,* 2nd ed. Englewood Cliffs, N.J.: Prentice-Hall, Inc., 1967.

FRIEDMAN, MILTON, *Program for Monetary Stability.* New York: Fordham University Press, 1959.

MUELLER, M. G., *Readings in Macroeconomics.* New York: Holt, Rinehart and Winston, Inc., 1966, Chaps. 10-14; 24.

SLESINGER, REUBEN E., MARK PERLMAN, and ASHER ISAACS, *Contemporary Economics,* 2nd ed. Boston: Allyn and Bacon, Inc., 1967, Chaps. 43-45.

Inflation

12

Except for occasional references to inflation, our analysis of the economy in the aggregate has so far been primarily concerned with the problems of depression and unemployment. This approach can be justified on several grounds: national income analysis was originally developed mainly as a theory of unemployment; the problem of below-capacity output has been a more serious one than inflation for the United States, historically; finally, many of the tools we have presented in connection with the analysis of recessions and depressions can be applied with suitable adjustment to the question of inflation. Still, inflation is an important problem in its own right, and it is time now to redress the balance a bit. This chapter will consider the meaning, causes, and possible cures for inflation in an economy like ours.

Inflation and the Public Interest

What exactly is inflation? And what is its impact on the public at large?

By *inflation*, we mean any general increase in the price level of the economy in the aggregate. In Part I of this book, when we were concerned with microeconomic supply-and-demand analysis, we spoke of a rise in the price of one commodity relative to other commodities. Inflation, however, is a macroeconomic concept. It means that there is a rise in the prices of all commodities, or of most commodities, or, most commonly, of some *index* that measures the average of various prices taken together.

This definition, however, is still a bit general. For one thing, we might wish to know exactly *what* prices are being included in any particular index of inflation. In the United States, for example, there are three main indices of inflation in common use: (1) the Index of Consumer Prices; (2) the Wholesale Price Index; and (3) the GNP Price Deflator. The third index, which reflects the distinction between changes in *real* GNP and changes merely in money GNP, is the most general of these indices, but for particular purposes, we may be more interested in one of the other two. As consumers, we may have a special concern about the consumer price index since this attempts to estimate the cost of living as it affects the average American family.

Even more important, however, is the fact that this definition of inflation fails to distinguish between different *kinds* of inflation. In the very first chapter of this book, we mentioned the German hyperinflation of the 1920's when the price index soared into the trillions. Now this kind of runaway inflation, with its enormously destructive effects on the whole fabric of the society, has to be distinguished from the kind of inflation that the United States suffered from 1955 to 1965, when the cost-of-living index was rising at an average of perhaps one or two per cent per year.

Indeed, when we look at the world today, we find quite striking differences in the degree of inflationary pressures in different countries. In the less developed countries, and especially in certain Latin-American countries, rapid month-to-month, or even week-to-week, inflation is a fairly common occurrence. Brazil's price level rose 5 or 6 times between 1958 and 1963. Chile in the 1950's saw price increases of 60 per cent to 80 per cent per year. In Bolivia, the cost-of-living index rose 25 times between 1953 and 1958. By contrast, even the 3 per cent to 4 per cent increase in the cost-of-living index in the United States in 1966 seems quite modest.

The distinction between rapid or runaway inflation and this much more moderate general rise in prices is important when it comes to determining the impact of inflation on the well-being of the economy. Runaway inflation may have seriously destructive effects on a country's domestic economy and its economic relations with other nations. Moderate inflation—which will be our main concern here—is much more limited in its effects and, indeed, not all of these effects must be considered harmful. Most economists would consider completely stable prices to be the ideal, but it is not unthinkable to take the position that a "little inflation" can be a "good thing." Or, at least, that it is not so bad a thing as is commonly supposed.

Why then has there been such an outcry against inflation in the United States in recent years? Why do some people seem to consider it an evil to be ranked with, if not worse than, unemployment? Part of the answer, it seems, lies in a failure to look beyond immediate and apparent effects. Another part lies in the fact that inflation, even moderate inflation, does have certain clearly unfortunate consequences.

The misunderstanding stems from the fact that people often fail to connect the process that raises prices and the process that raises their earnings, with which they will meet these increased costs. They sometimes talk as if every rise in prices impoverishes them by exactly that amount, since they can buy that much less with a given income. Or they may speak disparagingly about how little a dollar is worth now, failing to ask at the same time how many more dollars per week or per year they and other people now earn. Such an approach is clearly inadequate. We know from our earlier discussion of the concept of gross national product that a rise in the money value of output will necessarily be a rise also in the money value of national income. They are two different ways of looking at the same thing. To speak of the harmful effects of a general rise in prices on the assumption that all money incomes in the society remain unchanged is very nearly a contradiction in terms. The interesting and much more relevant question is: What are the effects of inflation when prices and wages, salaries, and other incomes are all rising at the same time?

These effects might generally include the following:

1. CHANGES IN THE DISTRIBUTION OF INCOME.   Although all incomes may be rising to some degree in an inflation, some income-receivers will be gaining much more rapidly than others. The people who will be hurt will be those who are living on fixed pensions or on the interest from government or other bonds; or salaried individuals employed by institutions, like churches, that may find it difficult to adjust their pay-scales to rapid increases in the cost of living. Although there are not many people in the economy whose incomes are strictly "fixed"—i.e., do not adjust at all to inflation—the rate of adjustment is different in different groups, and the ones who are left behind really will be "impoverished" by the rise in prices.

2. CHANGES IN THE POSITION OF CREDITOR, DEBTOR, SAVER. Inflation undermines the value of past savings if these savings are held in a form that represents a fixed claim on money (i.e., savings accounts, government bonds, life insurance policies, etc.). More generally, it alters the creditor–debtor relationship. Creditors suffer because the real value of their credits falls while debtors benefit, since their debts are also falling in real value. Thus inflation involves not only a redistribution of income but also a redistribution of the stock of wealth in the community.

3. PRODUCTION AND THE USE OF RESOURCES. Inflation may cause productive resources to be devoted to speculative or other uneconomic uses. This problem is really serious only when the inflation is rapid, but it may exist to some degree even when prices are rising moderately. In general, inflation puts most business firms in a quite favorable profit position somewhat irrespective of their performance. It diminishes the penalties for mistakes and dulls the sharp incentive to maximum effort. Also, again especially if the inflation is fairly rapid, planning for the future may be more difficult if tomorrow's prices are substantially different from today's.

4. EFFECTS ON THE INTERNATIONAL BALANCE OF PAYMENTS. Most countries, as we shall see in the next chapter, are concerned about preventing their imports from exceeding their exports. Inflation at home may generally go with high demand for imports from abroad. At the same time, our high domestic prices may discourage foreign countries from buying our exports. This can lead to difficult balance of payments problems. It should be noted, however, that this is not so much an argument against inflation, per se, as it is an argument against inflation that is more rapid than that of the countries with which one trades.

5. FORCED SAVINGS, INVESTMENT, AND GROWTH. Under certain circumstances, inflation can lead to a redistribution of output at the expense of consumption and in favor of investment and future growth. This is one of the reasons inflation is sometimes favored in less-developed countries where the desire for growth is particularly intense. Suppose that all consumers are wage earners and that all wage earners wish to spend all their income on consumption. If it happens that prices rise more rapidly than wages, then the *real* incomes, and hence total consumption of the wage earners, will be less than they would have been under stable prices. The gain in a private economy will accrue to business firms that will have higher profits and will be able to invest more than they would be able to otherwise. The process is sometimes called *forced saving*, since the society as a whole is saving more, even though the wage earners themselves would have preferred to consume more.

It should be apparent from this list that inflation can and does have certain definitely harmful effects. The classic case of misfortune is represented by the widow or elderly couple living on a fixed pension with a small savings account and a few government bonds. For such people, prolonged inflation even of the moderate sort means a continual reduction in the purchasing power of their already small incomes and the value of their past savings. On the other hand, it is also apparent that many of the harmful effects of inflation really become serious only when the inflation is either very rapid or at least more rapid than that of other nations. Furthermore, it is apparent that there are some cases at least where a mild inflation may divert production away from consumption and into areas that are considered more important. This may be true in the case of investment and growth; it also may be true when a country is attempting to launch a major war effort and finds it politically or economically infeasible to levy taxes to the full amount required. It is no accident that the periods of major price increases in our history have all been fairly closely associated with the various wars in which the United States was engaged.

In short, the picture is a mixed one. Stable prices remain the ideal. Yet it is also clear that people often overstate the dire consequences of moderate inflation.

Causes of Inflation

We have been speaking of effects; now let us turn to the question of causes. The best way to begin is to return to our earlier analysis of national income determination. What we might think of as the "classic" case of inflation is caused by an aggregate demand for goods and services that exceeds national income at the full employment level.[1]

Such a situation is depicted in Fig. 12-1. This diagram is the same as those we have used before, except that the sum of consumption, investment, and government demand $(C + I + G)$ exceeds the level of national income at FE, or full employment. This means that we cannot follow our previous course, which has always been to say that the level of national income will be determined by the intersection of the $C + I + G$ curve with the 45° line. There is, of course, some flexibility in the concept of "full employment national income." We can always work a little harder; more potential wage earners (e.g., housewives, young people) may enter the labor force; and so

---

[1] This "classic" case is really the Keynesian case, not that of the nineteenth century "classical economists" we mentioned earlier (Chapter 2). These early economists thought inflation was characteristically due to an increase in the quantity of money in the economy. Indeed, in general, they thought that the price level in the economy would always be proportional to the quantity of money in the economy. There has been some modern interest in a sophisticated version of this so-called *quantity theory of money,* though most modern economists think it better to analyze inflation in terms of the aggregate demand theory that we are presenting here. But even this theory has definite limitations, as we shall point out in a moment. All modern economists now recognize that it is possible to have a degree of inflation and unemployment at the same time.

on. Still, there is some upper limit beyond which our total output cannot be increased in the short run. In Fig. 12-1 we are assuming that the total demand of consumers, businessmen, and the government exceeds this upper limit. What happens in this case?

The answer is that something has to give. And what is likely to give is the general price level.

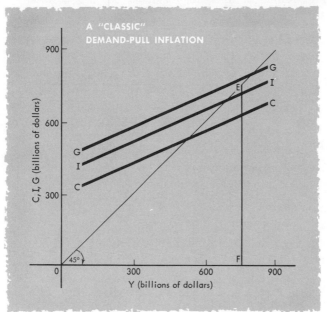

A "CLASSIC" DEMAND-PULL INFLATION

FIG. 12-1

When the sum of $C+G+I$ exceeds full employment income at *FE*, then there will be a natural tendency for prices to rise. Price rises, in turn, will be accompanied by wage increases, further price rises, further wage increases, and so on, in a continuing inflationary spiral.

We cannot actually picture this process in the terms used in Fig. 12-1, since this diagram depicts national income in *real* terms; i.e., as measured in "constant prices." We can easily imagine the inflationary process however. The situation at full employment is that not just one industry but all industries in the economy are faced with more demand for their products than they can supply.

When businessmen are confronted by a situation in which demand exceeds supply, our earlier analysis tells us that there will be a rise in the prices of their products. This, however, is not the only effect. Businessmen in such circumstances will also be trying to expand production. To do this, they will try to hire more laborers. But the economy, as we know, is already at full employment. Consequently, the main effect of businesses bidding for laborers will be to raise the price of labor—i.e., the general level of wages throughout the economy. This rise in wages, however, will only *add fuel to the inflationary fire*. The rise in wages means that wage earners will have higher money incomes than before, and this will increase the money value of their demand for goods. This rise in demand will mean that aggregate demand still exceeds aggregate supply, even at the new and higher level of prices. Therefore, the whole process is likely to repeat itself. Businessmen will raise prices and attempt to expand production once again. Wages and consequently the money value of the wage earners' demand for goods and services will rise a second time. And again businessmen will find themselves with a situation in which the demand for their products exceeds the available supply. And so on to a third round, fourth round, and so on. A continuing inflationary process is now under way.

We have here then the classic case of what is often called *demand-pull* inflation. We can relate it to our earlier discussion of national income analysis as follows: When the economy is suffering unemployment, increases in aggregate demand will ordinarily lead to increases in output and employment up to the point where full employment is reached. *After* this point, however, the effect of further increases in aggregate demand will be felt not in increased output, but inflation. Wages and prices will spiral upward in the fashion we have just described. The rapidity of the inflation will be determined in a very general way by how great the excess of aggregate demand is at the full employment level.

Two questions arise immediately: (1) What could cause such an excess of demand to arise? (2) Is this classic case the only or even the typical inflationary situation encountered in a modern industrial economy?

The general answer to the first question is, of course, that any factors which tend to bring consumption, business investment, or government spending to unusually high levels will be likely to result in an excess of $C + I + G$ at full employment. Historically, as we have said, the major factor in our own experience has been wartime circumstances which have led to extraordinary expansions of G not fully balanced by taxes. However, excess demand can also originate in the private sector. Schumpeter [2] emphasized the role of innovation and private investment in his analysis of inflation. Suppose there is some major technological breakthrough like the railroads in the mid-nineteenth century. The introduction of this new technology may require substantial investment, which may raise aggregate demand sufficiently to get the inflation started. But then the inflation itself may be a stimulus to further innovations. Prices are rising, profits are high; other innovators may come along wishing to invest in the railroads or in subsidiary industries or even in unrelated industries whose prospects have been improved by the generally buoyant state of demand in the economy as a whole. Sudden changes in private consumption

[2] We have mentioned Schumpeter before in connection with his stress on the importance of innovation. See p. 124.

demand could also in theory give rise to inflationary pressures, although this case is probably somewhat less common in actual fact.

The second question requires a somewhat fuller answer. Most economists would agree that on two related grounds, our classic description of inflation is inadequate as a rendering of present-day American experience. First, it assumes that inflationary pressures arise completely from the demand side. Second, it describes inflation as occurring only when the economy is at full employment. But we know that there are forces on the "supply" side that can also lead to inflationary pressures, and we also know that prices in general often rise even when there is some unemployment in the economy.

The ultimate explanation of these facts lies in the structure of labor and business organization in the American economy which, as we know, is far from that implied by the theory of pure competition.[3] If labor unions throughout the economy or in certain major industries are particularly strong, they may be able to get wage increases that are excessive even when aggregate demand is not pressing against the full employment barrier. By "excessive" here we do not mean *any* general rise in wages, for labor productivity is increasing annually, and the laborers would ordinarily expect to share in that productivity increase even in the most purely competitive economy. But suppose the wage increase exceeds the productivity increase. Laborers, say, are producing 3 per cent more output this year because of technological progress, but they demand and receive a wage increase of, say, 10 per cent. Such a wage increase is clearly inflationary. It will be sustainable by industry only if industry raises its prices. But a general rise in prices may stimulate further wage demands. The wage–price spiral is on. This upward movement of wages and prices would look very similar to that occurring in a demand-pull inflation (in fact, the two cases are not always easy to distinguish in practice), but it differs from it in that its origins have been inflationary wage increases, not the pressures of excess aggregate demand. And the main test of this fact is that such wage increases can and do take place when there is unemployment and other evidence of "slack" in the economy as a whole. This type of inflation is usually called *cost-push* inflation.

Such supply-originating inflations reflect the structure of American business as well as American labor. The ability of industry to absorb inflationary wage increases and to pass them on to the consumers through price increases is to some degree a testimony to the existence of substantial market power such as we would expect in

[3] Our case of classic inflation really assumes something like pure competition in the labor and product markets. Indeed, it is one of the limitations of Keynesian analysis in general that it tends to ignore market imperfections of various kinds. For our comments on the actual structure of American industrial and labor organization, see Chap. 5.

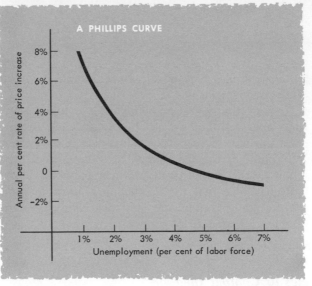

A PHILLIPS CURVE

FIG. 12-2

This curve shows the relationship between unemployment and inflation. At low levels of unemployment, the hypothetical economy shown here would suffer substantial inflation. The exact shape and position of the Phillips curve must be determined empirically for any particular country at any particular time.

oligopolistic industries. More generally, there is a considerable resistance to downward changes in prices in much of American business. This means that a fall in demand for an industry's products may be reflected in lowered output, employment, and excess capacity, rather than in lowered prices. An increase in demand, however, will ordinarily bring a rise in prices. When price changes take place only on a one-way street—rigid downward, but flexible upward—then inflationary situations can arise even when there is no excess of aggregate demand in total. A shift in demand from one industry to another may bring rising prices in one industry while leaving prices in another unchanged. The effect in total is inflationary although there is no over-all excess in demand.

Such institutional factors as these help explain why inflation may arise in a non-"classic" situation. They also help explain why inflation may sometimes be more difficult to cure than it would be in a classic situation. For if inflation can get started even when there is considerable slack in the economy, then it may be impossible to control except at the expense of considerable unemployment.

The general relationship between inflation and unemployment is sometimes set out in terms of what is called a *Phillips curve*, after the economist A. W. Phillips, who originated it. The actual shape of this curve for a given country at a given time would have to be determined empirically, but its typical shape would be like that shown in Figure 12-2. The economy shown in this figure would be able to get stable prices (0 rate of price increase) only if it was prepared to suffer a 5 per cent rate of unemployment. At this level the institutional and other factors exerting inflationary pressures on the supply-side are exactly counterbalanced by the downward pressures of inadequate aggregate demand. At lower levels of unemployment, however, price rises begin to occur, even though the economy is still short of full employment.

Now the degree to which this conflict between full employment and price stability is a problem will clearly depend on the actual shape and position of this curve. (For example, if the curve passed through the point of 0 price change at a level of 2 per cent unemployment, there would be no great problem to worry about.) Still, most economists believe that the conflict does exist to some degree and that it substantially complicates the measures one must take to remove or reduce inflationary pressures.

Policies to Combat Inflation

We have spoken about effects and causes. Now what about cures?

Insofar as there is a strong demand-pull element in any given inflation, the obvious remedies consist of using fiscal policy or monetary policy or both to restrain aggregate demand and hence to reduce the inflationary pressures.

In the case of fiscal policy, the measures to be taken would be some variant of increasing taxes or reducing government spending. An increase in taxes would lower the $C + I + G$ curve either by reducing personal consumption or, if the taxes were directed primarily at business corporations, by reducing business investment. A reduction of government spending would, of course, lower G directly. The choice between the reduced spending or the increased tax approach, and also the choice between different variants of these approaches, would reflect a number of other considerations. Are government spending programs essential or are they expendable? Is the allocation of output between consumption and investment too heavily weighted to the consumer or the investor? And so on.

In the case of monetary policy, the approach would be the reverse of that used in the case of a depression. The Federal Reserve system could increase reserve requirements, raise the discount rate, or engage in open-market sales of government securities. These open-market sales of securities would have the effect of lowering the reserves of the commercial member banks. If the banks in the system were fully "loaned up," there would be a curtailment of loans and investments to business. The money supply would fall, businesses would find it harder to obtain credit, the interest rate would rise. The effect would be to curtail areas of spending that are most sensitive to changes in the interest rate—certain kinds of business investment, construction, state and local government spending which is dependent on bond issues, and so on. This curtailment, in turn, would mean a reduction of aggregate demand and of the inflationary pressures arising from the demand side.

In the last chapter, we noticed that monetary policy had certain weaknesses when it came to curing problems of depression and unemployment. Used to combat inflation, it is undoubtedly a somewhat stronger tool. Indeed, it is difficult to imagine an inflation of any substantial magnitude continuing very long unless there is an increase in the money supply to feed it. As the money value of national income rises, the amount of money necessary to support the transactions demand for money increases. If there is a continuing inflation and *no* increase in the money supply, there will be very little money left over for liquidity purposes. Ultimately this leads to such a "tight money" situation and to such a rise in interest rates that investment, and other interest-dependent spending, is almost certain to fall.

In ordinary circumstances, then, monetary policy is likely to be more effective in inflationary then in depressed situations. However, if monetary policy alone is used—i.e., without accompanying fiscal restraint—it may have to be applied so strenuously that it causes serious problems in certain areas of the economy. The United States faced a situation rather like this in 1966. The price level, which had been fairly stable up to this point, began rising more rapidly in 1966. Many voices were raised advocating fiscal restraint, and especially a rise in taxes, but on the whole these voices were not heeded; except for one or two measures, government spending and tax policies were unchanged. Thus, monetary policy was given the whole burden of restraining the inflationary pressures. It was applied quite vigorously. The money supply which had heretofore been expanding with the general expansion of the economy at about 5 per cent or 6 per cent a year was actually reduced, falling, in the second half of 1966, from about $172 billion to $167 billion.[4]

And costs in terms of certain specific activities were quite high. Tight credit hurt local governments, who had to put off plans for needed schools, parks, and highways. The residential home-buyer was particularly hard hit. As mortgage rates climbed to 6½ per cent, housing starts fell to a postwar low, and the construction industry was in tight straits. The financial world went into something close to a psychological collapse. As *The New York Times* commented shortly after-

[4] Even a *constant* money supply would be considered something of a "restraint" in an economy that grows every year and consequently always needs more money for transactions purposes. An actual *reduction* of the money supply, therefore, is fairly strong medicine.

ward, the "credit markets were close to panic," and only timely fiscal action by the President, suspending the investment tax credit, helped save the day. The point is that the restrictive effects of monetary policy are felt keenly in certain particular areas of the economy; if general inflationary pressures are to be curbed by monetary measures alone, the result is likely to be very destructive to those specific areas.

Furthermore, monetary policy is unable to solve inflationary problems adequately when they originate from *cost-push* factors. This limitation applies also to fiscal policy and, indeed, to any set of measures that attempts to work through changes in the level of aggregate demand. For a given Phillips curve, these policies can be successful in curbing inflation only to the degree that they depress the economy sufficiently to create substantial unemployment.

In the modern economy, therefore, even fiscal and monetary policy taken together may not be adequate to curb inflation, and direct attention may have to be given to altering the shape and the position of the Phillips curve. And, indeed, this is just what the federal government has been attempting to do in recent years. The most important example is probably the so-called *guideposts* for wages and prices which are indicated each year by the President's Council of Economic Advisers. The principle behind the *guideposts* is that wage increases should be no greater in general than the nation's increase in productivity and that industry's prices should on the average be stable. (Industries where productivity increase is lower than the national average might raise prices under this policy, but this should be counterbalanced by reduced prices in industries with higher than average productivity increase.)

The *guidepost* policy is no cure-all. It is difficult to make such a policy effective without very substantial governmental intervention in the marketplace, and it is not clear that government wage- and price-setting is what the economy needs or the country wants. (We recall that many "command economies" now seem to be introducing more decentralized price policies because of the complications of central decision-making in this area.) Thus, the *guideposts* are likely to remain hortatory rather than regulatory, and this will to some degree limit their effectiveness. Still, they should not be cast aside, nor should any other policy that may help even in a limited way in reducing the conflict between price stability and full employment. For such policies do not stem from an unbounded desire to increase the degree of government intervention in the economy; rather, they arise from a desire to achieve two goals, both of which are in the interest of every American citizen.

Inflation is the economist's term for a general rise in prices, though there are many different kinds of inflation, some very rapid, others—like that of the United States in recent years—quite moderate.

The harmful effects of a moderate inflation are sometimes overstated by those who fail to realize that rising prices and rising incomes (wages, salaries, profits, etc.) are not wholly separable phenomena. In general, a moderate inflation will have the following effects (some harmful, some less so) on an economy: (1) redistribution of income at the expense of groups whose incomes rise less rapidly than prices; (2) improvement in the position of debtors relative to creditors; (3) possible uneconomic use of resources; (4) harmful effects on the international balance of payments when inflation is more rapid than that of other countries; (5) possible forced saving as investment (or, say, in wartime, government spending) increases at the expense of consumption.

In the "classic" case, inflation arises because of an excess of aggregate demand at the level of full employment national income. However, inflation is not necessarily of the *demand-pull* type. It may result from structural features on the supply-side, as in the case of *cost-push* inflation. Labor may succeed in reaching wage settlements that exceed the increase in labor productivity. Businesses may be resistant to downward adjustments of prices but may be able and willing to increase prices when there are shifts in demand or increases in wage costs. Because of these structural features, inflation may occur even when there is fairly substantial unemployment in the economy. The Phillips curve (to be derived empirically for any given country at any given time) shows the relationship between price changes and unemployment.

When inflation is of the demand-pull variety, fiscal and monetary policy can both be used to curtail aggregate demand. On the whole, monetary policy is probably better suited to "curing" inflation than it is to halting recessions; but if employed without fiscal restraint, it may lead to serious difficulties in certain areas of the economy. Both fiscal and monetary policy, moreover, are limited when the inflation originates in part from the supply-side, because they may be able to halt the rise in prices only by lowering aggregate demand to the point where there is unemployment in the economy. The President's *guideposts* for price and wage behavior are one attempt to reconcile the problems involved in seeking to achieve price stability and full employment simultaneously.

Questions for Discussion

1 • Distinguish between the harmful effects of a runaway inflation and those of a moderate inflation. Can you see any way in which inflation might be cumulative, i.e., moderate price increases might lead to behavior on the part of businesses or individuals that would lead to more rapid price increases? Why is it said that a runaway inflation can never occur unless it is fed by a fairly substantial increase in the money supply?

2 • "Inflation is an even worse threat to our economic well-being than depression: for whereas depression impoverishes only some of us, inflation impoverishes us all." Discuss.

3 • Distinguish between *demand-pull* and *cost-push* inflation. Why might this distinction be difficult to ascertain in an actual empirical situation? What structural features of American business and labor markets might contribute to inflationary pressures from the supply side?

4 • Draw two possible Phillips' curves, one showing a severe, the other a less severe, conflict between full employment and price stability. How would your recommendations for governmental policy be different depending upon which curve was descriptive of the situation the nation actually faced?

Suggested Reading

BOWEN, WILLIAM, *The Wage-Price Issue*. Princeton: Princeton University Press, 1960.

HARLAN, H. C., ed., *Readings in Economics and Politics*. New York: Oxford University Press, 1961, Chap. VIII.

PHELPS, EDMUND S., ed., *Problems of the Modern Economy*. New York: W. W. Norton & Company, Inc., 1966, pp. 63-105.

SAMUELSON, PAUL A., JOHN R. COLEMAN, ROBERT L. BISHOP, and PHILLIP SAUNDERS, eds., *Readings in Economics*, 4th ed. New York: McGraw-Hill, Inc., 1964, Chaps. 14-16.

SCHULTZE, CHARLES L., *National Income Analysis*, 2nd ed. Englewood Cliffs, N.J.: Prentice-Hall, Inc., 1967, Chap. 5.

————, "Recent Inflation in the United States," Study Paper No. 1, U.S. Congress Joint Economic Committee, *Study of Employment, Growth and Price Levels*, 1959.

International trade

13

No man is an island unto himself. Certainly no nation is. In this chapter, we shall "open" our heretofore "closed" economy and consider some of the implications of the fact that nations do trade with one another and that this trade can be the source both of major benefits and of major problems. With this application to the area of international trade, our survey of the main branches of short-run macroeconomics will be complete. What will remain for us then will be to consider some of the problems of long-run growth; and this will be our focus in Part III.

Historic Controversies

International trade, like the subject of money, is one of those areas of economics that has been of interest to economists since the dawning of the field. It has also been a particularly controversial subject perhaps because it involves national self-interest, and nationalism, for good or ill, has been a major force shaping the modern world.

In the sixteenth and seventeenth centuries, much of the economic writing of Europe was dominated by the so-called mercantilists, who were passionately interested in trade, commerce, and other mercantile activities. These writers (who were a varied lot of public officials, merchants, and pamphleteers, and who gave only part of their time to economics) tended to see international trade as an instrument in the growing commercial and political rivalries among the then emerging nation-states. One of their characteristic doctrines was that each nation should strive to secure a *favorable balance of trade*—roughly an excess of exports over imports. This would bring precious metals into the country, providing revenues for the sovereign and also stimulating the domestic economy. They saw trade as competitive: my nation's gain is your nation's loss. And in this competition they wanted to see their own nation benefit at the expense of others.

The mercantilist view gathered strength in the seventeenth century, but in the eighteenth century it ran headlong into the "classical" economists. Adam Smith devoted a whole long section of *The Wealth of Nations* to an attack on the mercantile system. David Ricardo, and also a lesser known classical writer by the name of Robert Torrens, tried to show that trade was not necessarily a rivalry; i.c., that *all* countries could benefit from trade. The mercantilists had favored regulating trade, but the hallmark of classical thought was the cry for free trade, a battle climaxed by the repeal of the Corn Laws in 1846.[1]

This victory of the classical economists, however, by no means ended controversy in the trade field. Indeed, the issues the mercantilists raised—whether about the need to regulate trade or about the desirability of a favorable balance of trade—have been with us ever since. Consider our own experience. The question of regulating trade through various forms of protective tariffs has been central throughout the history of the United States. Fifteen years after *The Wealth of Nations* was published, Alexander Hamilton was defending protection for infant industries in his famous *Report on Manufactures*. In the period

---

[1] The Corn Laws involved duties on imported wheat. The issues at stake in the Corn Laws involved not only free versus regulated trade in general, but also a specific conflict between the interests of the English landowner (who wanted to keep food and raw materials out, so that there would be a great demand and high price for land) and the English manufacturer (who needed cheap food, to keep wages low, and cheap raw materials for his factories). The repeal of the Corn Laws thus became a kind of symbol of Britain's full emergence as an industrial, as opposed to agrarian, economy.

between the War of 1812 and the Civil War there was great strife between the North and the South on the tariff question. When the so-called Tariff of Abominations was passed in 1828, South Carolina responded by proclaiming the doctrine of "nullification." The tariff history of the United States is one of great upswings and downswings in tariff rates as one or the other side of the controversy has held the upper hand. After World War I, there was a sharp rise in tariffs around the world, including the United States, but since the mid-1930's, the trend of American tariffs has been decidedly downward, the latest step being the so-called "Kennedy round" of tariff reductions pursuant to the Trade Expansion Act of 1962.

Similarly, the problem of our balance of payments has been a significant one, particularly in very recent years. In the immediate aftermath of World War II, everyone spoke of a dollar shortage in the world. Our European allies and former enemies were badly in need of our exports and yet lacked the productive capacity to send us their exports in sufficient quantity to pay for them. This dollar shortage produced the Marshall Plan and also a tendency for most people to assume that America's balance of international payments was immune to any major difficulties. Thus it was with something of a shock that economists and the general public awoke in the late 1950's and the 1960's to realize that this country was running a regular and substantial deficit in its balance of payments and furthermore that we were losing gold to other countries (about a third of our entire gold supply in the decade 1955-1965). Suddenly, old mercantilist fears began to arise again. We were losing gold. Would this bankrupt the nation? What would happen to our credit abroad? What would the effects on the domestic economy be? And so on.

Thus the ancient problems are still with us today, though always, of course, in a somewhat new and therefore challenging way. Two questions are particularly central: (1) What exactly *are* the benefits from trade? If trade raises so many problems, we might be tempted to forbid it (to follow a policy of autarky) [2] or at least to surround it by so many protective tariffs that its effects would be limited. Our willingness to permit trade depends on our assessment of the benefits that trade brings. (2) What is the meaning of our international balance of payments and what significance does it have when this balance of payments gets out of kilter? A related question is: What does it mean

[2] *Autarky* is a term meaning "economic independence of other nations." It is, by the way, a policy that some countries have actually followed historically. A good example is Russia in the 1930's who cut her international trade to a tiny fraction of its normal level, so that she would not be economically (or militarily) dependent upon what she felt was a hostile world.

when a country begins losing gold and what should be done about it?
Let us make a few points about each of these two central questions in the international trade field.

Benefits from Trade

The credit for first showing that international trade could be mutually beneficial to all nations involved goes to the classical economists. Their reasoning on this point remains basically convincing today; indeed, it underlies the preference for free trade (or at least freer trade) shared by most modern economists.

Now in a certain sense it seems easy to show that international trade can benefit all parties to the trade. Suppose, for example, that one country has large deposits of iron and coal and has a cold climate. Another country has no iron or coal but has a perfect climate for growing bananas. It does not take any very sophisticated reasoning to suggest that both these countries will be happier if they trade steel for bananas. Otherwise, in fact, they might have to do without one or other of these commodities. Since natural resources are scattered unevenly over the world and since soil conditions and climate also vary considerably, there will be many examples to show the desirability of trade for all participants just for these reasons alone.

Trade in the real world, however, is by no means confined to commodities that are nonexistent or extremely difficult to produce in particular countries. The United States, for example, produces automobiles, but also imports automobiles. India produces wheat but also imports wheat. It may be said that India imports food simply because she cannot produce enough food for herself. But how about the United States, a country with a varied climate, rich natural resources, an advanced technology, an abundance of capital, and a highly educated labor force? The United States, it seems, can produce almost every product more easily than most other countries, and yet we, too, are engaged in trade.

In other words, trade is a much more widespread phenomenon than could be accounted for by the fact that it is hard to produce bananas in Iceland. And, indeed, the classical economists tried to explain this phenomenon by showing that trade could be mutually beneficial even in the most difficult case—i.e., the case where one country could produce *all* commodities more easily than a second country.

Their theory is sometimes called the *doctrine of comparative advantage*. It states that mutually beneficial trade does not depend on any country having an *absolute* advantage in the production of a commodity; it is relative or *comparative* advantage that is crucial. A definition of *comparative advantage* is:

A country has a *comparative advantage* in the production of a given commodity when it must give up less of other commodities to produce a unit of this given commodity than some other country.[3]

This definition, and its relevance to our problem, is somewhat difficult to understand in the abstract. Let us therefore illustrate the operation of the principle through a numerical example.

TABLE 13 – 1 / PRINCIPLE OF COMPARATIVE ADVANTAGE

Country	Wine	Cloth
	Man-hours required to produce 1 unit	
England	100	100
Portugal	150	300

A possible exchange rate: 1 unit of cloth for 1.5 units of wine.

Table 13-1 shows two countries, England and Portugal (these were the countries David Ricardo used in a comparable example in 1817), both of which can produce two commodities, wine and cloth. England has an absolute advantage in the production of both commodities, in that it takes her less labor to produce each than it does in Portugal. England, however, has a *comparative advantage* only in the production of cloth. The comparative advantage in wine production is Portugal's.

(Portugal's comparative advantage in wine production can easily be seen. If she were producing both wine and cloth domestically, she would have to

---

[3] The reader should sense the presence in this definition of our production-possibility or transformation curve of Chapter 1. The slope of this production-possibility curve tells us, for any given point, how much of one commodity we must give up to produce a unit of the other commodity. The curve "bows out" because of the increased difficulty of producing more of any given commodity, the more of that commodity we are producing (see pp. 12-13, above). In our illustration of comparative advantage, however, we are taking a simpler case where the production-possibility curve for each country is a straight line. After reading the numerical example, the reader should try to draw possible production-possibility curves for both England and Portugal.

give up ½ unit of cloth to produce a unit of wine. This is because it takes 300 man-hours to produce a unit of cloth in Portugal and only 150 man-hours to produce a unit of wine. England, however, must give up a full unit of cloth to produce a unit of wine. Thus Portugal meets our definition of comparative advantage with respect to wine. She must give up less of other commodities (½ unit of cloth) to produce a unit of wine than some other country (England must give up 1 unit of cloth). It is this *relative* efficiency that is important when it comes to trade, as we shall now see.)

To show that trade can be mutually beneficial under these circumstances, let us imagine someone establishing an artificial exchange rate of 1 unit of cloth for 1½ units of wine. Given this exchange rate, it can readily be proved that England will benefit by concentrating on cloth production and trading for wine, while Portugal concentrates on wine production and imports her cloth from England. Thus, from the English side: if we put our domestic resources in wine production, we shall have to give up 1 unit of cloth (100 man-hours) to get a unit of wine (also 100 man-hours). Instead of doing this, however, suppose we produce only cloth and trade for our wine. This way we shall get 1½ units of wine for each unit of cloth we trade. Thus, it is clearly beneficial from the English side to produce cloth and trade for wine.

Since it is also possible to prove that Portugal can benefit at this exchange rate by trading wine for cloth (the reader should demonstrate this for himself), it becomes clear that mutually beneficial trade can, in fact, take place at the supposed exchange rate. And this despite the fact that England can produce both commodities with less labor than Portugal.

This demonstration of the theory of comparative advantage is somewhat incomplete. Thus, someone might wish to ask immediately: How do we know where the exchange rate really will be? Actually, we have not given sufficient information in our example to determine where the exchange rate will be. What we *can* say, however, is that the exchange rate between cloth and wine will have to be somewhere within the range of 1:1 to 1:2. (Our hypothetical exchange-rate of 1:1.5 clearly falls within this range.) If we get less than 1 unit of wine for a unit of cloth, then both countries will start concentrating on wine production, and no one will be offering cloth in exchange for it. By contrast, if we offer more than 2 units of wine for a unit of cloth, then both countries will concentrate on cloth production, and no one will have the wine to trade for it. Where the actual exchange rate will be in any given case will depend upon the relative strengths of supply and demand for the two commodities in the two countries. What we have done here is simply to show that a possible range of exchange rates exist and that within this range both countries gain from the trade if they concentrate on producing that commodity in which they have a comparative advantage.

Now this conclusion is a highly significant one. It is not the only thing that can be said pro and con about the benefits of international trade.[4] But it is one of the most fundamental things that can be said, for it shows that the benefits of trade are not due to highly special or unique circumstances but, in fact, arise under the most general conditions. This, in turn, puts a heavy burden of proof on those who wish to institute measures that interfere with the freest and fullest possible flow of goods among different countries.

Nowhere is this clearer than when it comes to the question of tariff policy. For essentially what tariffs do is to limit the potential gains that all countries can enjoy through international trade. Where a tariff is sufficiently high, so that all trade in a commodity ceases, then the country that has imposed the duty has thereby cut itself off from the benefits that it could otherwise have gained. If England in our example had placed a sufficiently high tariff on wine, to keep all Portuguese wine out (a 100 per cent tariff would do the trick), then England would simply have that much less wine and cloth *in total*. Her wine producers would be protected and saved the inconvenience of shifting over into unfamiliar lines of work (cloth production) but at the expense of the welfare of the community as a whole. Even if tariffs do not cut off trade altogether, they are likely to reduce it and, in so doing, to reduce simultaneously the positive benefits that can be expected from trade.

Since there are other aspects of trade that may prove troublesome, the doctrine of comparative advantage does not serve as an ironclad guarantee that totally "free" trade will benefit every country in every circumstance. But it does suggest that the number of valid arguments for interference in the trade process, at least in the developed industrial countries, is fairly small. It also suggests why economists, with a rare degree of unanimity, regard the "Kennedy round" of tariff reductions in the mid-1960's as evidence of genuine economic progress at the international level.

Balance of Payments Problems

One of the limitations of our presentation of the doctrine of comparative advantage is that it was cast wholly in *real* terms—wine and cloth—

---

[4] Thus, proponents of the benefits of trade would also point out that there may be further gains as countries specialize in the production of certain commodities and therefore become more and more efficient in producing them. Also, they might point out the benefits of foreign competition in stimulating greater efficiency among our own domestic producers. As against this, the opposition might bring out the "infant industry argument"—we must protect our manufacturers against the more experienced producers abroad (an argument clearly irrelevant to the United States, though possibly still relevant to some underdeveloped countries) and also arguments about balance of payments problems and their effects on the domestic economy. The latter we shall be taking up in a moment.

whereas international trade also involves money payments and in different currencies: dollars, pounds, francs, and so on. When we move out of the barter, wine-for-cloth world, we enter into the world of *balance of payments* problems, and life immediately becomes much more complicated.

A table showing a nation's balance of payments in full detail is a very complex affair including many different kinds of items. We shall mention some of these different items presently, but first, let us imagine the simplest possible situation. Let us suppose that we have a hypothetical nation whose balance of payments can be represented by three items, as in Table 13-2: commodity exports, commodity imports,

TABLE / A SIMPLIFIED HYPOTHETICAL
13 – 2 / BALANCE OF PAYMENTS (in millions)

Credit	Debit
$500 Commodity exports	$300 Commodity imports
	$200 Gold imports

This hypothetical balance of payments table is simply a point of departure for studying trade problems. In reality, a country's balance of payments includes many different items. The classification of these items, however, is made easier if we remember the central principle that a *credit* item is any item that creates a demand for your currency, while a *debit* item is one that creates a supply of your currency demanding other currencies.

and gold exports or imports. Table 13-2 tells us that this nation has exported commodities to foreign countries to the value of $500 million, while importing $300 million worth of commodities from these countries. This leaves a $200 million excess of exports above imports. How are these paid for by the foreign countries? By shipping $200 million in gold to our hypothetical country. We have here then the simplest possible case of a nation with a favorable balance of trade *à la* the mercantilists. And the mercantilists would have been delighted with the country's position, since it is receiving "treasure" from abroad.

Now even this highly simplified situation can serve as a useful point of departure for understanding more complex matters. For one thing, we notice that the table is arranged in two columns: credit and debit. What makes one item a credit item and another a debit in international trade accounting?

Perhaps the simplest way to look at this matter is to recognize the fact that every transaction in international trade is essentially two-sided. Every good that we import from abroad must be paid for in one way or another. If we import an automobile from a European country we must pay for it either by exporting goods of equivalent value or by exporting gold abroad or by transferring dollars to a foreign account or by sending an IOU to the foreign country (in which case the foreign country is increasing its investment in the United States). Since every transaction is two-sided in this way, there is a certain accounting sense in which the balance of payments is always in "balance."

Now as far as the classification of items is concerned, the fundamental rule is that any transaction that creates a demand for your currency—say, dollars—is a credit item. By contrast, any transaction that creates a supply of your currency seeking other currencies—say, dollars being offered in exchange for francs or pounds—is a debit item. Our commodity exports create a demand for dollars in terms of other currencies. The German who wants to buy an American good must ultimately pay the American producer in dollars. Hence he uses his marks to buy dollars to pay us for the export. This is a credit item in the U.S. balance of payments because it represents an increase in the demand for dollars. When Americans import commodities from abroad, however, they must pay the foreigner in *his* currency. In this case, we use the dollars we have to buy marks to pay for the import. The supply of dollars offered in exchange for other currencies has increased; consequently, our imports are a debit item. Gold imports are a bit more complicated to see, but, essentially, we can treat them as any other import. When a foreign country ships gold to us, it receives dollars in exchange, and thus the supply of dollars has been increased. (These dollars may then be used to pay for the extra exports the country has taken from us.) Thus gold imports are a debit item, and gold exports are a credit item.

Once these general principles are clear, it becomes possible to apply them to the many more complex items that make up a country's actual balance of payments; e.g., tourist expenditures of Americans abroad, our military expenditures abroad, interest and dividend payments to American owners of foreign securities, U.S. private business investment abroad, and so on. Take the last for example: a long-term investment by an American firm, say, in a factory in France. Does this create a demand for dollars or a supply of dollars? The American puts up the dollars which are then exchanged for francs to pay workmen in France to build the factory. Hence, the answer is that the supply of dollars has been increased and that U.S. investment abroad is to be treated as a debit item.

In an accounting sense, as we have said, the balance of payments is always in balance. What then do we mean by a *surplus* or *deficit* in a country's balance of payments? Actually, there are many specific definitions involved, but the central characteristic is that the surplus or deficit is intended to measure the change in the country's reserve assets. A deficit in the balance of payments means that the country in question is either losing gold to other countries or that other countries are increasing their holdings of liquid claims against that country (claims that could ultimately be translated into a loss of gold). A surplus occurs when a country is accumulating additional gold reserves or liquid claims against foreign nations. In our simplified example in Table 13-2, the country in question is enjoying a surplus in its balance of payments since it has acquired a $200 million addition to its gold stock in the period in question.

We have been speaking mainly about accounting principles, but now let us look more deeply at the economics of Table 13-2. Exports of our hypothetical country exceed imports. Does this fact have any economic significance? In what way?

There is definite significance to this excess of exports over imports, and it relates to our earlier discussion of national income analysis, which now must be modified to take into account international effects.

Consider exports first. When we bring foreign nations into the picture, we have to recognize that the demand for the products of our country is no longer limited to domestic consumption, investment, and government expenditures. We also have a foreign demand for our products. When a foreign firm puts in an order for a certain number of our machines, its effects on production are the same as if it came from a business firm in the United States or from the U.S. government. Aggregate demand, therefore, must include an allowance for demand originating from abroad.

But there is also the import side to look at. As a consumer, say I have an income of $10,000 a year. I decide to save $1,000 of this, to buy $8,000 worth of American goods, and to buy $1,000 of goods imported from abroad. Now as far as *American* industry is concerned, it is not my total of $9,000 consumer demand that is relevant but only the $8,000 that I shall be spending on American goods. The $1,000 I spend on goods abroad has no more direct effect on American industry than does the $1,000 I decided to put in my savings account. This is to say, then, that our import spending must be *subtracted* from our total spending to give us the aggregate demand that will be effective in creating jobs and income in this country.

If we use X to stand for exports, M for imports, and Y for national income, we can contrast the equilibrium situation in a "closed" and in an "open" economy as follows:

CLOSED ECONOMY.   We have equilibrium when national income equals the sum of intended consumption, investment, and government spending:

$$Y = C + I + G$$

OPEN ECONOMY.   We have equilibrium when national income equals the sum
of intended consumption, investment, and government spending, *plus* exports
minus imports:

$$Y = C + I + G + (X - M)$$

In the case of our particular hypothetical economy of Table 13-2, we
could conclude that its balance of payments was definitely having an
expansionary effect on the economy, since its net exports $(X - M)$ was
positive ($200 million).

This conclusion, incidentally, suggests why some modern writers
have shown more tolerance for the mercantilist desire for a favorable
balance of trade than did the Classical Economists. If a country's exports are buoyant and its imports are restrained, then the effect on a
depressed economy will be just like a little dose of expansionary
fiscal policy. The only problem with using the balance of payments as
an instrument of domestic policy is that not every country can be doing
it at once. If one country is exporting more than it imports, some other
country will be importing more than it exports. A policy to curtail imports and expand exports is rather like trying to export one's depression
abroad. And it is likely to be met by countervailing action by other
countries, so that no one's position is improved (though all countries
are likely to suffer the losses that occur when trade is subjected to detailed national regulation).

One last point about our simplified balance of payments is the significance of the $200 million gold inflow. Although the mercantilists
would have stressed this greatly, modern analysis suggests that the
gold inflow would have real importance for the country only if it were
running short on its international reserves. Gold is a universally accepted medium of international payments (so also are certain "key
currencies," especially dollars and pounds) and all countries must maintain gold or other reserves to protect themselves against cyclical or
other fluctuations in their trading position. If our hypothetical country
was short on such reserves, the $200 million inflow would be most wel-
come; otherwise it would be of relatively little significance.

Very little can be said in a general way about the direct effect on
domestic economy when $200 million is added to its gold stock. If the
nation's money supply were directly and mechanically tied to its stock
of gold, the effect would be expansionary in the same way as an expansionary monetary policy. In the United States, however, the Federal
Reserve system can nullify any effects of increasing gold on the money
supply through its open-market operations. Thus, in the two years before we entered World War II, our gold stock rose by over $5 billion,
but the greater part of this was neutralized by the Federal Reserve's
open-market operations during that period. In general, most countries

will try to keep their money supply in line with their aggregate economic needs rather than in a fixed and automatic relationship to their gold supply. Thus, the direct effects of a gold inflow, in and of itself, are not likely to be decisive on the domestic economies of most nations.

A Note on American
Balance of Payments Difficulties

The leap from our simplified balance of payments example to the complex international position of the United States in the 1960's is a large one. However, let us make just a few brief comments on recent American difficulties in this area, indicating thereby how domestic and international policies interact in an "open" economy.

The basic facts are these: The United States has been running a deficit in its over-all balance of payments since the early 1950's. This deficit has averaged between $2.5 billion and $3 billion a year since 1958 and, even in 1966, after various attempts were made to correct the situation, it was still well over $1 billion. Since World War II, there has been a decline of about $9 billion in our stock of gold. Paradoxically, this deficit has been accompanied by a substantial surplus of U.S. commodity exports over commodity imports. This surplus, however, has been more than offset by a number of other debit items. A list of the major items would include our foreign aid program, our military expenditures abroad, our large tourist expenditures in foreign countries, and the substantial amount of U.S. private business investment abroad during the past few years.

Nearly everyone is agreed that this balance of payments deficit cannot be allowed to continue forever. In one sense, we are in a favorable position in that dollars, being a "key currency," are held by many countries as a reserve in very much the same way as gold is held as a reserve. As long as no one feels any lack of confidence in the dollar (and therefore does not attempt to turn the dollars into gold) the situation in which foreign banks and individuals accumulate dollar holdings is perfectly tenable. However, as our obligations increase and as our gold stock dwindles, there is the inevitable danger that confidence in the dollar will weaken. If this should happen on a large scale, the potentialities for damage to the whole international payments scheme are virtually unlimited.

So the balance of payments deficit should be corrected. Yet how to do so is a most complicated problem. For one thing, there may be a conflict between this objective and important domestic objectives. If

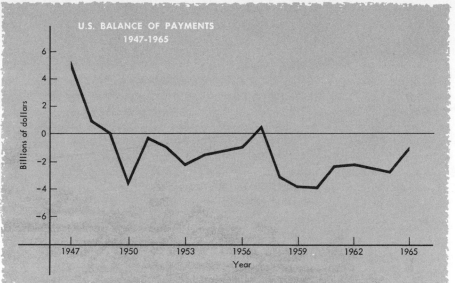

U.S. BALANCE OF PAYMENTS
1947-1965

Billions of dollars

FIG. 13-1

we rule out devaluation of the dollar,[5] the standard remedy would be to apply restrictive monetary and fiscal policies at home. By reducing aggregate demand through such policies, we would reduce the demand for imports, lower the rate of inflation (making our exports cheaper for foreign countries) and, with the higher interest rates involved, attract more foreign investment to this country. A restrictive policy might also convince the world that we were serious in our determination to defend the dollar, which might increase confidence in the dollar and thus reduce the likelihood that its reliability would be tested.

But are these the policies that we would want to follow on other grounds? In earlier chapters, when dealing with a "closed" economy, we were able to argue that restrictive monetary and fiscal policies should be used only when the problem was one of inflation. In periods of recession, expansionary fiscal and monetary policies were called for. But can we be sure that a balance of payments deficit and a less-than-full-employment domestic economy will not occur simultaneously? The answer is no. The American economy has been operating at something

[5] Devaluation of the dollar would, in theory, help remove the deficit by raising the prices of foreign goods in terms of dollars (thus discouraging imports) and lowering the prices of American goods in terms of foreign currencies (thus encouraging exports). Some economists have urged that this was the proper solution to our deficit problem. However, the government has officially rejected this alternative, and it is at least doubtful that it would work, since other nations might devalue along with us. The result might be no great improvement in our balance of payments position and considerable damage to the stability of the world monetary system. Whether the British devaluation of the pound (1967) from $2.80 to $2.40 will have an effect strong enough to overcome these arguments against devaluing the dollar is doubtful, but remains to be seen.

less than full capacity during much of the period of our balance of payments problems. Indeed, we face a difficulty here of the same general nature as that involved in the conflict between full employment and stable prices. We worried that an attempt to bring the economy to full employment production might result in rising prices. Now we must also be aware of the possibility that the attempt to achieve this kind of domestic expansion may lead to a worsening of our already serious balance of payments deficit.

As in the case of the earlier conflict, there is no simple answer to the problem. It might seem that an easy solution would be to reduce or eliminate the deficit items that have offset our surplus of commodity exports above imports. Cut military spending abroad, slash foreign aid, limit tourist expenditures, curtail private business investment abroad—all these "solutions" have been proposed at one time or another. But they are not as uncomplicated as it might seem. Do we want our military expenditures abroad dictated by foreign policy considerations or by balance of payments considerations? Similarly for foreign aid. Also, we should be aware that foreign aid expenditures are largely spent for U.S. goods, so that a $1 cut in foreign aid would produce only a fractional improvement in our balance of payments deficit. Nor is the problem much easier when it comes to regulating tourist spending, or limiting private investment abroad when that investment is profitable to private citizens and also to the countries who receive it.

In actual fact, our policies have been a little bit of this and a little bit of that. We have tried to attract tourism to this country, we have raised short-term interest rates, we have tied aid to purchases of American goods, we have developed a program of voluntary "guidelines" to limit private business investment and bank lending abroad, and so on. Whether such selective measures will succeed in solving the long-run problem is for the future to determine. That they have been tried, however, should come as no surprise, for the alternative of drastically curtailing the flexibility of our domestic monetary and fiscal policies is one not to be entered into lightly. As in the case of the wage–price guideposts of Chapter 12, the means may be somewhat crude, but they do represent attempts to permit the achievement of several different objectives at once—objectives which are rightly considered necessary and desirable.

Summary

International trade is an ancient and controversial area of concern to economists. Mercantilist writers in the sixteenth and seventeenth centuries saw trade as a rivalry between nations and argued that it should be heavily regulated. The Classical Economists stressed the mutual benefits to be derived from trade and urged a free trade policy. In one form or another, these controversies have survived to the present day.

One major conclusion, first derived by the classical writers, is that trade can be beneficial to all trading parties under a wide variety of general conditions. The doctrine of comparative advantage shows that it is not the absolute but the relative efficiency of a country which determines its trading capabilities. Even in the case where one country can produce all commodities with less labor than a second country, mutually beneficial trade can take place when these countries concentrate on goods in which they have a comparative advantage. This doctrine provides a major argument against tariffs and other interferences with the free flow of international trade.

International trade involves not only the exchange of commodities, but payments in different currencies. When analyzing a country's balance of payments position, it is important to remember the general rule that any transaction that creates a demand for a country's currency is a credit item, while any transaction that creates a supply of that currency in exchange for other currencies is a debit item.

The domestic economic effects of trade are important. Foreign demand for our exports is similar in effect to domestic consumption, investment, or government demand. Conversely, our demand for imports from abroad must be subtracted from our over-all demand for goods and services. The total aggregate demand of an economy therefore will be represented by domestic consumption, investment, and government spending, plus an item representing *net exports* $(X - M)$.

The United States' balance of payments has been in substantial deficit for several years now, causing, among other things, a considerable outflow of monetary gold. Although there is general agreement that this deficit must be cured, the means for doing so are not completely clear. One reason for this is a conflict between the measures we might want to use to solve the balance of payments problem (restrictive fiscal and especially monetary policy) and the requirements of our domestic economy (that is, when we are producing a less-than-full-employment national income at home). Another reason is the difficulty of curtailing deficit items—like foreign aid, military spending, tourist expenditures abroad, U.S. private foreign investment—that have contributed to the problem.

The general approach of the government has been to adopt a wide variety of selective measures in the hope of avoiding a general contraction of the domestic economy which, it is felt, would be a harsh price to pay to improve our international position.

Questions for Discussion

1 • Suppose that we have country A and country B each capable of producing commodity X and commodity Y according to the following table:

Country	X	Y
	Man-hours required to produce 1 unit	
A	5	50
B	12	40

   a) Which country has a comparative advantage in producing commodity X? Commodity Y?

   What is the range of possible exchange rates of X for Y under which mutually beneficial trade between A and B could take place?

   b) Fill in the blank in the following table so that neither country has a comparative advantage in either commodity:

Country	X	Y
	Man-hours required to produce 1 unit	
A	5	50
B	12	?

   c) How might our analysis of comparative advantage be altered if we took into account the fact that as countries produce more and more of a given commodity, the costs of producing that commodity (in terms of other commodities) may tend to increase?

2 • "The fairest tariff policy is that which puts our domestic producers on equal terms with their foreign competitors." Discuss.

3 • Imagine a country that has the following situation:
   a) a constant level of commodity exports;
   b) a level of commodity imports that increases with the level of national income;
   c) commodity exports exceed commodity imports at all levels of national income.

   How would you display this general information in the familiar 45°-line diagrams we have used in the theory of income determination?

4 • Explain what is meant by a *credit* or *debit* item and by a *surplus* or *deficit* in the balance of payments in international trade accounting. The United States currently enjoys an excess of commodity exports above imports but still suffers from a deficit in her balance of payments. How is this possible?

Suggested Reading

HABERLER, GOTTFRIED, *A Survey of International Trade Theory*. Princeton: International Finance Section, 1961.

KENEN, PETER B., *International Economics*, 2nd ed. Englewood Cliffs, N.J.: Prentice-Hall, Inc., 1967.

MEADE, JAMES E., *The Balance of Payments*. London: Oxford University Press, 1951.

MEIER, GERALD M., *International Trade and Development*. New York: Harper & Row, 1963.

RICARDO, DAVID, *Principles of Political Economy and Taxation*, ed. P. Sraffa. Cambridge: Cambridge University Press, 1951, Chaps. VII, XXII.

SLESINGER, REUBEN E., MARK PERLMAN, and ASHER ISAACS, *Contemporary Economics*, 2nd ed. Boston: Allyn and Bacon, Inc., 1967, pp. 511-39.

III

PROBLEMS OF GROWTH,
DEVELOPMENT, AND AFFLUENCE

Modern
economic growth

14

In Part II, we have been discussing the factors that determine a society's aggregate output and income in the short run. We have assumed that the nation's basic productive capacity was given, and we have asked: Where will a society's *actual* level of national income be in relation to this given productive *potential* in any particular period? In this analysis we have put special emphasis on the factors that contribute to the aggregate demand for the nation's output: consumption, investment, government spending, and the net foreign demand for our exports.

In Part III, we shall shift our focus to the problems of *long-run economic growth*. In this setting, our primary interest will be precisely in those long-run factors that determine the size of a society's productive potential at any given time and the growth of that potential over time. The productive capacity of the nation will no longer be a "given"; it will be the main variable to be explained.

Now these two areas of economics are by no means completely independent. If, for example, short-run aggregate demand is weak, so that national income is far below its full employment potential, then this will have at least some effect in slowing down the growth of the economy's productive capacity. If national income is low, there will be less output available for investment in future productive capacity. For that matter, who will want to invest if current demand is so slack? We recall that in the Great Depression of the 1930's, net investment was actually negative at one point.

Despite the interdependence of these short-run and long-run factors, however, there is a definite shift of emphasis as we move into this new area of economic growth. Whereas earlier the demand side was given paramount (though not exclusive) attention, now our focus moves primarily (though again, not exclusively) to the supply side. We can even put the issue this way: Suppose the problem of aggregate demand takes care of itself. Suppose that whether through natural forces or through a very sophisticated application of monetary and fiscal policies there is no difficulty of a gap between actual and potential output. What factors, under these admittedly special circumstances, will determine the nation's long-run rate of growth? This way of putting the problem has the virtue of making it clear that some of the territory we are about to enter has not been explored in our earlier analysis.

We shall consider the growth problem in three main connections. In this chapter, we shall look at the growth process in the economically advanced countries and try to draw what general conclusions we can from their experience.

In Chapter 15, we shall turn to the related, but still quite distinguishable, problem of growth in the modern underdeveloped countries of Asia, Africa, and Latin America.

In our final chapter, we shall look at what we might think of as the "consequences" of growth. Growth has created the so-called affluent society. What problems distinguish this kind of society from others we have known in the past? This final chapter will take us to the heart of many of the issues debated in the United States in the 1960's. And it will be an appropriate note on which to end this study of "economics and the public interest."

A Brief History of Modern Economic Growth

"Modern economic growth" in the title of this chapter suggests that what we are dealing with is a relatively new phenomenon. In a country like the United States, we are likely to take the process for granted, because rapid growth has been a constant feature of our personal experience. In a broader historical perspective, such rapid growth is decidedly "modern" and indeed unprecedented.

The beginnings of the process are usually dated in terms of the English industrial revolution of the late eighteenth century. This dating is necessarily somewhat arbitrary. England had been making substantial economic progress for at least two centuries before the revolution occurred. Furthermore, even this earlier progress was dependent upon the general expansion of the European economy that had its roots back at least as far as the tenth or eleventh century. Historians, eager to prove the essential continuity of the British experience, are easily able to find antecedents for virtually every change that took place in the economic structure of late eighteenth century England.

Still, the concept of a genuine revolution is not altogether arbitrary. For it was only in late eighteenth century Britain that certain distinctive features of what we think of as "modern growth" appeared unequivocally on the scene. For the first time in the history of mankind, a nation began to produce an output of goods and services that was regularly expanding at a rate far in excess of its rate of population growth. We can put this even more strongly. The industrial revolution in England was accompanied by a marked acceleration in the rate of population growth. To have *matched* this growth of population with an equal growth of production would have been achievement enough by any previous historical standard. To have *exceeded* it so that output *per capita* was also growing rapidly was something basically new in historical experience.

And this is what we mean by "modern economic growth":

MODERN ECONOMIC GROWTH is a sustained, relatively regular and rapid increase in a nation's GNP, and especially in its GNP per capita.

It is this kind of growth that was born in Britain in the late eighteenth century.

This birth process had many different aspects. Some of them were clearly favorable and were so regarded by the more perceptive observers of the time. This was particularly true of the rapid development of new technologies of production. Economically useful inventions were being developed and applied at what earlier would have been considered an astonishing rate. There were improvements in virtually all branches of industry—in cotton textile production, in iron and steel, in pottery making, even in agriculture. The greatest single invention of the period was probably James Watt's steam engine (1769). This invention came to affect many different branches of industry and was important in giving durability to the growth process as it continued on into the nineteenth century. It was not, however, the "cause" of the industrial revolution, since the process of technological change was general and pervasive, and, indeed, the revolution was well under way before the steam engine made its impact felt.

Some other aspects of the birth process were not so favorable. This period saw the development and spread of the factory system and, in consequence, a substantial dislocation of the traditional British way of life. It was a period that witnessed great distress among certain groups in society—children employed in the new cotton mills, craftsmen displaced by new techniques of production, rural villagers and squatters dispossessed of their lands. Indeed, these unpleasant features of the transformation of English society were so pronounced that the leading economists of the early nineteenth century (especially Malthus and Ricardo) took a very pessimistic view of the future. They convinced themselves that society was heading towards a dismal "stationary state" in which the great mass of people would be buried in poverty.

As it turned out, they couldn't have been more wrong.[1] As a consequence of the industrial revolution, Britain jumped economically far ahead of all her rivals. By the middle of the nineteenth century, she was far and away the outstanding industrial nation in Europe. She was called, and indeed was, the "workshop of the world."

This was the beginning, but then, as our map indicates, the process spread far beyond the British Isles. The United States was already very much embarked upon the growth race before the Civil War. Germany began making major strides in the second half of the nineteenth century. Russia was a very "backward" economy through most of the nineteenth century, but then, in the 1890's, she began to make her move. It is an interesting fact of history that the Russian Revolution of 1917 came not when the Russian economy was deteriorating, but after two decades of quite substantial economic progress under the Czars.[2]

The process went beyond the boundaries of Europe and the United States—to Canada, Australia, and, rather remarkably, to Japan. The astonishing rate of growth of the Japanese economy since World War II was made possible ultimately by the groundwork that Japan laid in the late nineteenth and early twentieth centuries. Indeed, this early achievement is really more astonishing than the later one. Japan had to face

[1] "Wrong," that is, about the future prospects of an industrializing economy like that of Britain. But Malthusian-Ricardian fears still have relevance to some underdeveloped countries of today, as we shall see (pp. 252-54).

[2] Though, of course, Russia was still very far behind the economically advanced countries of Europe and North America. Even in 1928, when she began her first Five Year Plan, Russia's per capita industrial output was probably only 5 to 10 per cent of that of Britain.

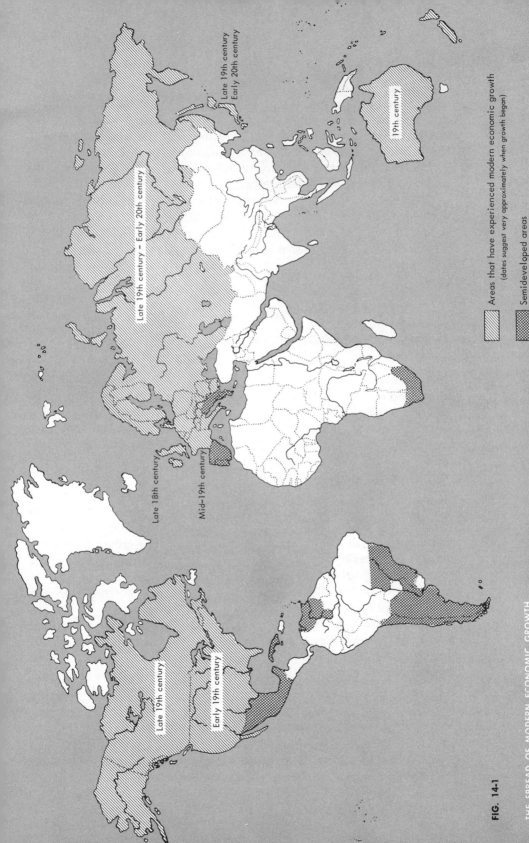

Late 19th century
Early 20th century

Late 19th century – Early 20th century

19th century

Late 18th century

Mid–19th century

Late 19th century

Early 19th century

Areas that have experienced modern economic growth
(dates suggest very approximately when growth began)

Semideveloped areas

FIG. 14-1

THE SPREAD OF MODERN ECONOMIC GROWTH

all kinds of obstacles—poor natural resources, heavy density of population, a culture largely isolated from the industrial world of Europe, relatively meager assistance through foreign investment—and yet she still managed to have an industrial revolution of her own beginning in the 1870's and 1880's. The Japanese experience, to this day, remains a particularly fascinating one for those who wish to understand the underlying causes of modern growth.

The process spread, but not everywhere. Large areas of the map—most of Asia, Africa, Latin America—are either blank or ambiguously shaded. These areas will occupy us in the next chapter. But wherever the process did spread—Europe, North America, Australasia, Japan—the countries involved began to experience a new and dramatic expansion of their GNP and their GNP per capita.

Growth Trends in the United States

The expansion of output per capita in these various countries was accompanied by a transformation of their entire pattern of economic life. Before examining some of the causes of this phenomenon, let us sketch out a few of the elements of this transformation, using the American economy as our example. The trends we will now describe, though differing in detail from one country to another, are fairly typical of the modern growth process in general.[3]

1. *Population growth.* Figure 14-2 shows the massive increase in American population over the past 160 years, from 5 million or 6 million to nearly 200 million in 1966 and still growing. Population increase was more rapid in the United States than in most of the industrial nations during this period (because of special circumstances, including, of course, heavy immigration from Europe) but an increasing population is a characteristic feature of a growing economy, especially in the earlier stages of growth.

2. *Increase in life expectancy.* One of the causes of our substantial population increase was a sharp increase in life expectancy during this period, as Table 14-1 shows. In the economically advanced countries, increases in life expectancies have been reflective of the over-all growth process in the dual sense that growth brings higher standards of living and material comfort and that growth has also been accompanied by considerable improvement in our medical technology.

[3] For a somewhat more detailed study of growth in the United States, see my *Economic Development: Past and Present,* 2nd ed. (Englewood Cliffs, N.J.: Prentice-Hall, Inc., 1967), Chap. 4.

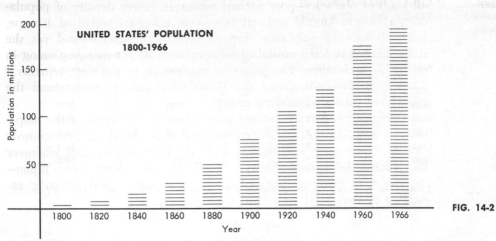

FIG. 14-2

Source: Bureau of the Census, U.S. Dept. of Commerce

3. *Urbanization.* The growth process has transformed the United States from a largely rural to a predominantly urban society. Increasing urbanization is a characteristic feature of modern economic growth.

4. *Changing occupations.* In 1800, the characteristic American male was a farmer. Over the course of the century-and-a-half since,

TABLE / INCREASING LIFE EXPECTANCY
14 – 1 / IN THE UNITED STATES

Year	Average of male and female life expectancies at birth, years *
1850	39.4
1878-1882	42.6
1890	43.5
1900-1902	49.24
1909-1911	51.49
1919-1921	56.40
1929-1931	59.20
1939-1941	63.62
1949-1951	68.07
1954	69.6
1963	69.6

* For years 1850, 1878-1882, and 1890, life expectancies are for Massachusetts only.
Source: Gilboy and Hoover, op. cit.; Statistical Abstract of the U.S., 1965.

TABLE / URBANIZATION IN
14 – 2 / THE UNITED STATES

Year	Percentage of population in urban areas	Year	Percentage of population in urban areas
1800	5.6	1900	39.7
1820	7.3	1920	51.3
1840	10.5	1930	56.2
1860	19.7	1940	56.5
1880	28.1	1950	59.0

Source: Peter B. Kenen, "Statistical Survey of Basic Trends," in Harris (ed.), American Economic History, op. cit.

the occupational structure of the American labor force has changed drastically. There has been an enormous decline in the number of farm families and farm workers. This has been accompanied by a substantial rise in the percentage of the labor force in manufacturing

TABLE / PERCENTAGE DISTRIBUTION OF EMPLOYMENT
14 – 3 / OF THE U.S. LABOR FORCE *

Year	Agriculture, Fishing & Forestry	Mining	Manufacture, Construction †	Transport, Communications, Commerce & Finance	Professions, Government, Other Services ‡
1820	72.0	—	—	—	—
1860	59.9	1.6	18.5	7.5	12.5
1870	50.8	1.6	23.5	11.5	12.8
1880	50.5	1.8	23.2	12.1	12.2
1890	43.1	2.0	26.3	14.9	13.5
1900	38.0	2.6	28.0	16.9	14.4
1910	32.0	2.9	29.2	19.6	16.3
1920	27.6	3.0	31.7	22.0	15.7
1930	22.6	2.3	29.5	25.9	19.5
1940	18.3	2.2	30.9	25.8	22.8
1950	11.6	1.7	35.7	27.0	23.8

* Excluding parts of the labor force whose industry is unknown.
† Includes also labor force in Electricity and Gas.
‡ Covers the following categories: Professions and Entertainment; Forces; Other Government Services; Private Domestic Service; Other Services.

Source: Adapted from Colin Clark, Conditions of Economic Progress, 3rd ed. (London: Macmillan, 1957), pp. 519-520.

and construction and an even more dramatic increase in the percentage of the labor force in the professions, commerce and finance, government service, and other so-called service occupations. Within industry as a whole there has been a steady movement away from "blue-collar" to "white-collar" positions.

5. *More leisure time.* The standard workweek has been falling steadily over the past century. In the 1870's, the average was about 67 hours per week. By 1920, it had fallen to 46 hours; by 1958, to 39 hours. Individuals enter the work force later now and, with increasing life expectancies, they also have more leisure after retirement.

6. *Increasing education.* Today the average American—man or woman—has far more formal education than he did in 1900. Table 14-4 indicates the order of magnitude of some of the important changes. It shows, for example, that the number of years of schooling per member of the population over fourteen and per member of the labor force both increased by roughly 40 per cent between 1900 and 1957. It also shows that the total years of schooling "embodied in" the entire labor force more than tripled between 1900 and 1957. Actually, these numbers are a substantial understatement because, for one thing, an average school year was more than twice as long in 1957 as it was in 1900. Another way of making the general point is by looking at enrollment in universities and colleges. Around 1900, only about 7 per cent of all children attended college. By the late 1940's, the figure had already risen to approximately 20 per cent; and in the next decade or so the higher education "industry" grew dramatically, so that in 1962-1963 the enrollment in institutions of higher learning was nearly 40 per cent of the eighteen through twenty-one-year-old population. Today that figure is in the vicinity of 50 per cent, and the time when it will cease to grow is nowhere in sight. (From R. Freeman Butts and Lawrence A. Cremin, *History of Education in American Culture.* New York: Holt, Rinehart, & Winston, 1953.)

7. *Growth in output per capita.* Finally, we come to the trend in output per capita itself. Figure 14-3 shows the course of output per capita in the United States from 1839 to 1959 in "constant 1929 prices," as estimated by Professor Raymond Goldsmith. The earlier figures are necessarily somewhat conjectural, but they are perhaps sufficient to indicate the general drift of things. The numerical table below the diagram tells us that while population was growing quite rapidly during this period (about 2 per cent per year), GNP was growing so much more rapidly that output per capita was increasing by the healthy rate of 1.64 per cent per year.

Is this a rapid rate? By present-day American and European standards it is nothing very remarkable. By any past historical standard—that

TABLE 14 – 4 / YEARS OF SCHOOLING COMPLETED BY THE POPULATION 14 YEARS AND OLDER AND BY THE LABOR FORCE 18-64 YEARS OF AGE, U.S., 1900-1957

Year and index 1957	Population			Labor force		
	Number (millions)	Yrs. of schooling completed per person	Total yrs. schooling completed (millions)	Number (millions)	Yrs. of schooling completed per person	Total yrs. schooling completed (millions)
1900	51.2	7.64	391	28.1	7.70	216
1910	64.3	7.86	505	35.8	7.91	283
1920	74.5	8.05	600	41.4	8.12	336
1930	89.0	8.32	741	48.7	8.41	410
1940	101.1	8.85	895	52.8	9.02	476
1950	112.4	9.95	1,118	60.1	10.10	607
1957	117.1	10.70	1,253	70.8	10.96	776
Index 1957 (1900 = 100)	229	140	320	252	142	359

Source: Theodore Schultz's article in Selma J. Mushkin (ed.), *Economics of Higher Education* :alth, Education and Welfare), p. 96.

is, prior to the industrial revolution—it is, however, a very extraordinary rate indeed. To see this, all one has to do is to get out a compound interest table and observe that a 1.64 per cent annual increase implies a fivefold increase every 100 years. The present level of family income in the United States is about $7,000 a year. If we actually succeed in continuing at a 1.64 per cent annual expansion for the next two centuries, then in the year 2170, average family income in the United States would be $175,000, and this in terms of *today's prices and purchasing power*. It is this extraordinary multiplicative power of apparently modest annual increases in output per capita that makes it clear that modern economic growth is a fairly recent historical phenomenon. Had it been going on long at these rates, we would be far richer than we are now.

This then is the story of modern growth as exemplified in the American experience. We live longer now, we are a much bigger nation, we live in cities instead of on the farm, we work at manufacturing and the professions rather than agriculture, we are much better educated, we enjoy an increased productive power that dwarfs anything in past history, and at the same time our leisure has been significantly increased. And all this is directly attributable to, or in large part a re-

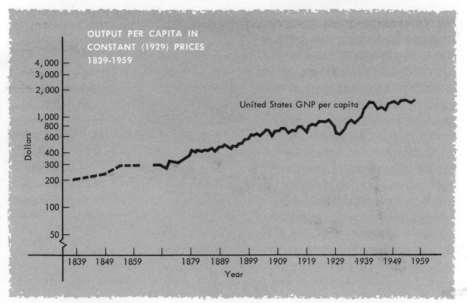

FIG. 14-3

Source: Material presented by Professor Raymond Goldsmith to Joint Economic Committee,
U.S. Congress, published in *Staff Report on Employment, Growth, and Price Levels*, 1959.

INCREASE IN GROSS NATIONAL PRODUCT, POPULATION,
AND OUTPUT PER CAPITA, UNITED STATES, 1839-1959
(Percentage increase per year)

	Entire-period 1839-1959	40-year sub-periods 1839-1879	1879-1919	1919-1959
Gross national product	3.66	4.31	3.72	2.97
Population	1.97	2.71	1.91	1.30
Output per capita	1.64	1.55	1.76	1.64

flection of, the phenomenon of modern economic growth. This is not
to say that we are happier now—the affluent society also has its problems, as we shall see—but it does mean that our entire way of life has
been transformed in what, historically speaking, is a very short period
of time.

Major Factors in Modern Growth

Technically speaking, the growth process involves a continual shifting
outward of our production-possibility curve. In year 1, we have to

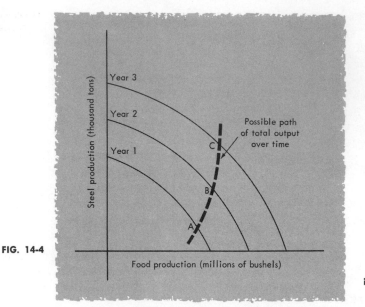

FIG. 14-4

Steel production (thousand tons)

Year 3

Year 2

Year 1

C

B

A

Possible path
of total output
over time

Food production (millions of bushels)

Growth shifts the
production-possibility
curve outward. A society
may follow the path
indicated by line *ABC*.
Food production is
increasing absolutely,
but steel production is
increasing much more rapidly.

choose between various determinate amounts of food and steel. In year 2, we can have more of both commodities. In year 3, still more. A possible path of choices is indicated in Figure 14-4, where our hypothetical society is seen to be choosing relatively more steel and relatively less food as it becomes richer. This reflects the relative shift toward industry and away from agriculture which we observe in all economically advancing societies.

But the matter is a bit more complicated than this, because some of the choices we make today may affect the rate at which the production-possibility curve shifts outward. If we consume all our income today in the form of luxuries and "riotous living," then we shall not be accumulating additional productive capacity for tomorrow. If instead of consuming champagne and caviar we use part of our output to build a factory, we shall have a higher potential output next year. If instead of spending our nights dancing, we study how to become engineers, we shall be more productive workers next year. As a consequence of such choices, our production-possibility curve will shift outward more rapidly, meaning that we may have more consumption (champagne and caviar) and more leisure (for dancing) in the future.

This brings us then to the question of the *causes* of modern economic growth. This question is a very large one, because growth is such a pervasive phenomenon that virtually no aspect of our social organization is irrelevant to it. For example, one can readily see that a society's political structure may have a decided impact on its rate of growth.

Even in a pure market economy there is an underlying assumption that the State is strong enough to guarantee the rights of property and the orderly administration of justice. In many societies, past and present, however, such an assumption is unjustified: property is destroyed, lawlessness is unchecked, civil strife is the order of the day. In such a society, it may be necessary to build up the political preconditions for stability and order before modern economic growth can even begin.

Faced with such a wide range of influences, the economist must be somewhat selective. In general, the economic analysis of growth has centered around three main variables:

1. Population growth
2. Capital accumulation
3. Technological (or sometimes "technical") change

This is clearly not an exhaustive list of the factors that influence a country's rate of growth; on the other hand, it is not quite so narrow as one might suppose. For many of the political, social, and other elements that affect the growth rate may make their impact felt through changes in one or another of these three factors. Thus, the structure of family life in a society will have an influence on its rate of population growth. The role of government in the society may affect its rate of capital accumulation.[4] And so on.

This list then forms a useful starting-point for organizing the analysis of the many forces influencing modern growth. Let us say just a word or two about each of these factors.

Population Growth

The effects of population growth on modern economic growth are not easy to predict in all circumstances. In general, an increase in population will bring about an outward shift in a society's production-possibility curve, for the simple reason that it will bring more laborers into the economy and hence a greater productive capacity. But modern economic growth involves an increase in output *per capita*. Will the increase in population bring about a proportionately larger or smaller

---

[4] Thus, for example, in our discussion of the command economy in Chap. 3, we pointed out that such economies, if oriented to rapid growth, might accumulate capital at a more rapid rate than the more consumer-oriented market economy. This is one of the ways in which a society's political structure may operate on the growth rate through one of our three factors: population growth, capital accumulation, and technological change.

increase in total output? If the increase in total output is proportionately larger than the increase in population, we will have an increase in output per capita. If the increase in total output is proportionately smaller than the increase in population, we will have a decline in output per capita.

The simplest view might seem to be that an increase in population, everything else unchanged, would bring about an equivalent expansion of total output and, consequently, would leave output per capita unchanged. Double the number of laborers, and you double the productive potential of the economy. This simple view, however, ignores certain aspects of the picture that may either inhibit or enhance the output-creating effects of population increase.

One of the major factors that has been ignored is the famous *law of diminishing returns*. We have already mentioned this law in connection with the analysis of the supply curve in Chapter 2. To repeat our earlier definition:

The law of diminishing returns states that in the production of any commodity, as we add more units of one factor of production to a fixed quantity of another factor (or factors), the addition to total product with each subsequent unit of the variable factor will eventually begin to diminish.

The operation of this law with respect to population growth is shown in Figure 14-5. Our commodity in this case is "total output" and our

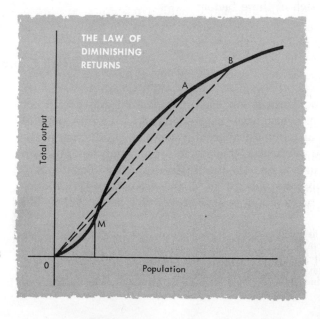

THE LAW OF DIMINISHING RETURNS

Total output

Population

FIG. 14-5

A graphical representation shows that as we increase population (holding natural resources and capital stock constant), total output eventually begins to increase at a diminishing rate. As we move out from point A to point B, there is a fall in output per capita.

variable factor is population. What is the "fixed" factor (or factors)? Essentially, it is the whole group of other means of production, natural or man-made, that cooperate with labor in the production of total output. If population increases while the society's natural resources and stock of capital remain fixed, each laborer will, on the average, have less land, minerals, etc., and fewer tools, machines, etc., to work with than he had before. The law of diminishing returns says that this will eventually lead to a declining rate of increase of total output. This happens in our diagram after point M, where it can be seen that the total output curve, while still rising, is rising at a diminishing rate. Sooner or later, this is likely to lead to a decline in output per capita. In our diagram, for example, output per capita declines as we move out from point A to point B. (Why? Because the slope of the line OA or line OB is measured by total output divided by population. As these lines become less steep, it means that output per capita is falling).

Now the *significance* of the phenomenon of diminishing returns in the real world is likely to be great or small depending upon a number of other factors. The worst possible situation is this: a very rapid rate of population increase combined with a very slow rate of capital accumulation and a heavy density of population in relation to land and other natural resources. In this case, each laborer has markedly less capital and land to work with and is likely to add very little to total output. The best possible situation is: plenty of land and other natural resources, a rapidly growing stock of machinery and other capital goods, and a relatively less rapid growth of population. Here there is very little pressure on our "fixed" natural resources, and each laborer has more machines and tools to help him do his work.

To complicate the matter further, however, we must now add that there may also be certain *offsets* to the law of diminishing returns. This is why we put the adverb *eventually* in our statement of the law. For as an economy expands, there may be certain *economies of scale* that develop.[5] Large-scale production may in many instances be more efficient than small-scale production. A larger economy as a whole may permit an increased specialization of economic functions or *division of labor*, as it is sometimes called. This is a matter that was greatly stressed by Adam Smith nearly two centuries ago. The point is that while an increase in population may be putting pressure on the other factors of production, it is also to some degree increasing the "scale"

[5] Technically speaking, *economies of scale* may be said to exist when, having increased all the factors of production in a certain proportion, total output increases in a *greater* proportion. If you double both the quantity of labor and the quantity of machines and thereby get more than double the previous output, you have *economies of scale*.

of the economy as a whole. In an economy with a fairly abundant supply of natural resources, this scale effect may actually dominate over the diminishing returns effect for long periods of time.

What this discussion brings out is that the effect of population growth in contributing to, or inhibiting, modern economic growth will depend very much on how, when, and where it occurs. In the history of the United States, our rapid population growth was much less of an obstacle to achieving an increase in per capita output than it might have been in other countries, because we were a very sparsely settled nation throughout the whole of the nineteenth century. On the whole, it probably contributed to an *increase* in our output per capita during this period. By contrast, even a slower rate of population growth was a serious problem for late nineteenth and twentieth century Japan and, indeed, the Japanese have been very vigorous and effective in bringing their rate of population growth down. When we come to modern underdeveloped countries in the next chapter, we shall see another evidence of the importance of the context in which population growth occurs. In some of these countries, the rapid increase of population probably constitutes the major single obstacle to achieving modern economic growth.

Capital Accumulation

It is evident from what we have been saying about population growth that the accumulation of machines, tools, factories, etc., is also an important factor in a nation's economic growth.

In speaking of *capital accumulation* we are really speaking of the same phenomenon as we were in Part II, when we referred to *real investment*. These are equivalent terms, and they both mean adding to the society's stock of physical means of production over a given period of time. The shift in emphasis when we move from short-run to long-run problems is particularly evident in our point of view toward investment. For one thing, our earlier short-run analysis was largely concerned with the *demand-creating* effects of investment. In Part II, we pointed out that when businessmen invested, they were creating more aggregate demand, which might lead to more jobs and higher levels of output in the short run. When our interest is in long-run growth, however, we become especially interested in the *supply-creating* effects of investment. We emphasize the fact that investment represents an increase in our productive capacity. Short-run analysis can afford to pay little attention to this aspect of investment, because the addition to our total capital stock in a period of a year or two is quite small in comparison to that whole stock. In the *long run*, however, these capacity-creating effects of investment are of the essence. It is the small accretions to our capital stock, undertaken year after year, that gradually build up the kind of massive productive capacity we have in an industrialized economy like that of the present-day United States.

This shift in emphasis is also apparent in our view of the relative roles of consumption and investment. In a demand-creating sense, consumption demand and investment demand are equally good. When it comes to capacity-creation, however, they more often stand in opposition to one another. In the short run, one is likely to say: "Let's get everyone to consume more and save less, in order to raise aggregate demand." In the long run, one is more likely to say: "How can we cut consumption, so that the society will save more and thus be able to increase its investment in more machines, buildings, factories, and so on?" Now this opposition between consumption and investment is not usually complete even in the long run,[6] but the fact is that whereas saving (nonconsuming) tends to be the villain of the piece in the short run, it is usually regarded as the hero of the piece (or, at least, one of the heroes) in the long run. And the change in roles is explained by the different nature of the problems to be solved.

The effects of capital accumulation on economic growth can be analyzed in much the same general terms as the effects of population growth. If natural resources and population in the society remain constant while the capital stock continually increases, then we should expect "diminishing returns" to capital, except insofar as they are offset in the early stages by whatever economies of "scale" the increased capital stock makes possible. There is one significant difference, however. When population growth is attended by diminishing returns, we face a decline in output per capita (in Fig. 14-5, as we move from A to B). In the case of capital, however, diminishing returns means not that output per capita is declining, but only that it is increasing at a slower rate for any given amount of investment. Insofar as additional capital is still increasing total output, then, for a given population, the effect will be *some* (even though a diminishing) *increase* in output per capita. (This follows simply from the fact that output per capita is defined as total output divided by population.) Unlike population growth, then, the increased accumulation of capital will

---

[6] If a society has a great deal of unemployment, then it may be the case that an increase in consumption through its multiplied effects on national income may lead businessmen to raise their investment as well. It is, strictly speaking, only in a full employment economy that consumption and investment become completely competitive.

always have at least some favorable effect on the growth of output per capita.

Until 10 or 15 years ago, most economists gave capital accumulation pride of place among the factors producing economic growth. And, indeed, every economically advanced country in the world has witnessed an extraordinary expansion of its capital stock since the industrial revolution. This expansion has been far more rapid than the expansion of population, with the result that workers in these countries have regularly had more machines and tools to assist them in producing increasingly high levels of output. In the United States, for example, the capital-to-labor ratio nearly tripled between 1879 and 1944. This has clearly been a major factor in promoting our continuing high rate of growth.

Still, the constant increase of capital relative to population, without changes in any other factor, would doubtless have encountered diminished returns by now, with the result that our output per capita might be expected to increase ever more slowly as time went on. That this has *not* happened seems to be attributable to the fact that the growth in our capital stock has regularly been accompanied by a process of technological change. It is this third major factor that has, indeed, occupied the lion's share of attention in growth analysis in the past decade or so.

Technological Progress

Population growth and capital accumulation both involve increases in the supplies of our factors of production; by contrast, *technological progress* is concerned with the new and different ways in which we utilize our basic factors of production. Briefly,

We attribute to *technological progress* in the broadest sense those increases in output that cannot be accounted for by the increase in our inputs alone. Technological progress involves new knowledge and the application of this new knowledge to economically useful ends. It may occur through the development of new kinds of machinery, an increase in the skills of the labor force, a reorganization of the productive process, or through the development of new products hitherto unknown. In any case, the emphasis is on doing things in new and different ways as compared to times past.

Technological progress, in this broad sense, has been a characteristic feature of the growth process since the British industrial revolution. From the spinning jenny and steam engine of the eighteenth century to electricity, synthetics, atomic energy, and computer technology in our own there has been a virtually unbroken line of major innovations in our methods of production.

In very recent years, economists have been attempting to separate out the effects of technological progress on growth from the effects due to the increases in factor inputs (labor and capital). In practice, this is very difficult to do. For one thing, new techniques of production may become effective only when they are embodied in new productive capacity. To develop the technology of the railroad is one thing; to make railroads economically effective is something else again, requiring large investments of capital. In general, the expansion of our capital stock and the expansion of our technological knowledge have gone hand in hand, and difficult interpretive problems arise when one tries to separate them. For another thing, there are some "investments" that are intended precisely to expand the technological know-how of the society and the ability of the society to absorb technological advance. Consider education, for example. If a person or firm devotes time and money to education or research, they are making an investment that may lead to the development of new technology or to an increased ability to operate the new technologies as they come into being. This process is very similar to ordinary capital accumulation, except that we are dealing not with physical capital but with what we might call "intangible" capital. We are saving and investing not in new machines, but in new knowledge. Again, the borderline between capital accumulation and technological progress may become blurred.

These points are well worth keeping in mind because they are important qualifications to a general conclusion of some significance that economists have developed in recent years. The conclusion is this: If we try to evaluate the effect of technological progress as opposed to capital accumulation on the rise in output per capita in the American economy, we find (at least in our experience over the past 50 to 75 years) that technological progress is by far the more important factor. Estimates are that technological progress may account for as much as 80 per cent of our rise in output per capita, leaving only 20 per cent or so to be explained by the fact that each worker has more capital to work with. This general conclusion is confirmed by studies of various industrial economies in the post-World War II period. These studies suggest that even when we look at *total* output (as opposed to output per capita), the combined effects of capital accumulation and growth of the labor force together may account for little more than *half* of the growth of total output in these countries.[7]

[7] See, for example, E. Domar, S. M. Eddie, P. Hohenberg, M. Intriligator, and I. Miyamoto, "Economic Growth and Productivity in the United States, Canada, United Kingdom, Germany and Japan in the Post-War Period," *The Review of Economics and Statistics*, XLVI, No. 1 (Feb., 1964).

The rest is attributable to a "residual" item which, in the very broad sense we are using the term, is closely related to technological progress.

Now this conclusion—or perhaps hypothesis is the better description—has many implications. One point it suggests is that the growth process is best understood as a continuing development into new areas rather than as a simple quantitative expansion of what we already have. And this, I believe, makes sense intuitively. Consider the products we buy today. How many of them were in existence or even had equivalents one hundred years ago? The automobile, telephone, television, household appliances, electric lights, synthetics, plastics, and so on. And this is quite apart from the technological progress involved in finding new methods for producing "old" products. Think of the agricultural revolution in this country over the past century. Now 7 per cent or 8 per cent of our population not only feeds us but sustains major exports to the outside world and (as we saw in Chapter 4) often creates surpluses to be taken off the market by the government. Growth, in other words, is not just more tools or more people to use the tools: it is new products, new methods, new approaches—nothing less than a continuing revolution in our day-to-day lives.

Another important implication is that the factors that stimulate technological progress may be particularly important in maintaining a country's rate of growth. Education and research, the acquisition of new skills, general literacy, on-the-job training, all these ways by which a society prepares its members to discover, develop, and apply new knowledge may have economic implications of the first magnitude.

In a sense, American society has already paid tribute to this fact by its increasing emphasis on education over the past century. This emphasis has grown sharply in the past two decades. The increasing number of students finishing secondary schools and entering colleges has been a major phenomenon of the postwar period. Further, expenditures on research in the United States are now many times above their prewar levels.

Not all education, of course, has an economic purpose. Nor are its effects only economic in nature. The philosopher and political scientist have long stressed the importance of education for the general life of society. The humanist will properly stress the fact that education is a good thing in and of itself for those individuals who strive to acquire it. Still, it does no harm to add the economist's blessing as well. For as far as our present understanding of the matter is concerned, the continual improvement in the education of our citizens is perhaps the best single warrant there is for expecting a continuation of the process of modern growth into the indefinite future.

In this chapter, we shift our attention from short-run national income analysis to the problems of long-run growth. We are interested now less in departures of actual from potential output than in the growth of potential output and productive capacity over time.

Modern economic growth involves a continuing, relatively regular, and rapid increase in GNP per capita. It is a decidedly new phenomenon from the historical point of view. The great breakthrough was the English industrial revolution of the eighteenth century, when new techniques and the reorganization of production produced (*a*) considerable social dislocation and (*b*) the beginnings of an expansion of production that substantially exceeded the increasing rate of population growth of the period. Britain was for a time the "workshop of the world," but soon the United States, Continental Europe, Russia, Japan, Australia, and other countries joined in.

The experience of the United States, though special in a number of ways, nevertheless indicates some general features that are associated with the modern growth process. These features include: population growth, increased life expectancies, urbanization, the decline of agriculture in national income and employment relative to manufacturing and especially to the service industries, increased leisure time, higher levels of education, and, of course, a continuing expansion of output per capita. Simple arithmetic shows that apparently small annual increases in output per capita—of the order, say, of 1 per cent or 2 per cent per year—lead over time to surprisingly massive increases in family incomes.

Of the many factors that produce modern economic growth, economists tend to focus attention on three major variables: population growth, capital accumulation, and technological progress. All three of these factors will shift out the production-possibility curve over time, but their effects may be quite different.

Population growth may have either positive or negative effects on the level of the society's output per capita, depending on whether the law of diminishing returns is offset by other effects such as "economies of scale." In general, population growth will be an obstacle to the achievement of modern economic growth if it is very rapid, is accompanied by relatively little capital accumulation, and takes place in an already densely populated society. By contrast, in the United States, where our problem in the nineteenth century was the sparsely settled nature of the country, population growth may have had a favorable effect on the growth of output per capita.

Capital accumulation. By "capital accumulation," we mean what we earlier referred to as "real investment," except that now our attention is focused less on the demand-creating side than on the supply-creating (capacity-creating) side. Capital accumulation is clearly a factor favorable to the rise in output per capita, though this rise in output per capita may be at a diminishing rate if the capital stock is growing in relation to population and natural resources and if no other elements in the picture change.

Technological progress. Technological progress involves changes in the quality and in the utilization of our basic factor inputs. It involves new things: new skills, new methods of production, new products, and so on. Recent studies have suggested that technological progress is a particularly important factor in modern economic growth, accounting for considerably more of our increased output per capita in recent decades than the accumulation of more capital per worker. These studies have to be qualified in a number of important ways, but they do make sense intuitively as we think of the novelties that modern growth has brought in the past century or so. Also, they confirm the widespread feeling in this and other countries that education, besides being of value in and of itself, may have important economic consequences.

Questions for Discussion

1 • Define *modern economic growth*. Indicate some of the changes in the structure of a society that usually accompany the growth process.

2 • Discuss various possible favorable and unfavorable effects of population growth on the rate of growth of output per capita.

3 • "The problem with standard national income analysis is that it focuses completely on the demand-creating side of investment and neglects the capacity-creating side." Discuss.

4 • It has been said that an industrial revolution is nothing more nor less than the process by which a country that has been saving and investing 5 per cent or less of its GNP begins to save and invest 10 per cent or 12 per cent of its GNP. What arguments do you think could be made for and against this proposition?

5 • In the early twentieth century, the Austrian-American economist Joseph Schumpeter gave a central role to *innovation*—the introduction of new methods of production and new products into the economy—in the growth process. How has modern analysis tended to verify Schumpeter's basic intuition? Schumpeter also characterized the growth process as one of "creative destruction." Does this term seem apt to you?

6 • Economists sometimes use the term *marginal capital-output ratio* to refer

to investment in a given year divided by the increase in output during that
year. If I = investment and ΔY = the increase in output during a given
year, then:

$$\text{marginal capital–output ratio} = \frac{I}{\Delta Y}$$

Suppose this term is constant and equal to 3. Can you show that, with a
3 per cent rate of population growth, investment will have to equal 9
per cent of national income to insure a constant per capita income? Suppose that with the same rate of population growth and marginal capital-output ratio, investment is equal to 18 per cent of national income. What
will the rate of growth of total output be? Of output per capita?

Suggested Reading

GUTMANN, PETER M., ed., *Economic Growth—An American Problem*. Englewood Cliffs, N.J.: Prentice-Hall, Inc., 1964.

KUZNETS, SIMON, "Notes on the Take-Off" in Theodore Morgan, George W.
Betz, N. K. Choudhry, eds., *Readings in Economic Development*. Belmont,
Calif.: Wadsworth Publishing Company, Inc., 1963.

KUZNETS, SIMON, *Six Lectures on Economic Growth*. New York: The Free
Press, 1959.

MANTOUX, PAUL, *The Industrial Revolution of the Eighteenth Century*. New
York: Harper & Row, 1962.

NORTH, DOUGLASS C., *Growth and Welfare in the American Past: A New Economic History*. Englewood Cliffs, N.J.: Prentice-Hall, Inc., 1966.

ROSTOW, W. W., *The Stages of Economic Growth*. London: Cambridge University Press, 1960.

The underdeveloped countries

15

The process of modern economic growth which we described in the last chapter has spread to many countries throughout the world—but not everywhere. Indeed, one of the most striking facts of the world's economic landscape in the mid-twentieth century is the enormous gap in living standards and economic well-being that separates the richer nations from the poorer. These poorer nations have been called at various times "the developing nations," "the less developed nations," "the underdeveloped nations," or even "the economically backward nations." Whatever the name, they include most of the countries of Asia, Africa, some in Latin America, and even a few in Europe. They total anywhere from one-half to two-thirds of the world's population. And they are still faced with the ancient problems of food, clothing, shelter, the need for protection from famine, flood, drought and epidemic, the basic bare-bones struggle for survival—problems that have long since disappeared, except in very special and limited cases, in the West.

It is with these nations and their efforts to achieve modern economic growth that we shall be concerned in this chapter.

Meaning of
Economic Underdevelopment

The depth of poverty that exists in many of these countries can be attested to by any traveler who has seen the conditions in which the mass of their people live. It can also be confirmed by any of a great variety of statistical measures. One might look at figures on life expectancy, calories in the diet, number of teachers or doctors per head of population, steel output or electrical power output per capita, percentage of the population living in rural areas or working in the agricultural sector, number of automobiles, miles of road, movie theaters, household appliances, plumbing facilities, and so on. In each case, one would find a striking contrast between the extraordinary material comforts of the industrialized world and the harsh facts of subsistence in their poorer neighbors.

Since modern economic growth is defined in terms of a continually rising output per capita, economists usually use this index as a general measure of the degree of poverty or "underdevelopment" in any particular country. Actually, this measure is not a completely satisfactory one, for a number of reasons. One simple reason is that the necessary information often is lacking. Statistical collections in many poor countries are often either nonexistent or little better than not-so-educated guesswork. Another reason is that in many of these nations there is a great deal of production that never enters explicitly into the marketplace. A small village in India or in some African country may produce mainly for its own needs, with the result that only a small part of its total production would appear in formal statistics, even if we had them. There is also a fundamental difficulty involved in any attempt to make comparisons among societies that differ radically in their economic structure. If country A produces exactly the same goods as country B, and in the same proportions, but has ten times more of each good, then we can say fairly unequivocally that country A has ten times the total output of country B. But if country A is a rich country and country B is a poor country, they will not in general be consuming the same goods and in the same proportions. Rice may be the most important product in country B, while in country A it may be automobiles, or washing machines, or vacuum cleaners. For that matter, what exactly would the significance of a vacuum cleaner be to country B if its villagers lived in huts with earthen floors? The point is that comparisons between countries with drastically different standards of living involve not only practical problems but also difficult philosophic problems. To a certain degree, these comparisons must be taken with a grain of salt.[1]

Still, the gap in levels of output per capita between the rich and the poor countries of the world is so great that even the very rough statistics we are able to gather tell a meaningful and dramatic story. Table 15-1 shows how great this gap is. Half the world's population has an annual per capita output of below $100; another sixth of the world's population has a per capita output between $100 and $300. Even if we correct these figures upward (as we probably should), we still have a very large fraction of the people of the world who live on perhaps a tenth of the income we are accustomed to enjoying in the present-day United States.

Such a huge gap did not exist two centuries ago or even one century ago. There were differences, of course. Some countries were richer than others, as has been the case throughout history. But the salient fact of the past 100 or 200 years is that the gap has been widening, not just absolutely, but in percentage terms, and not slowly but rapidly. The fundamental reason, of course, is that the nations of Europe and North America were engaged in the modern growth process we described in the last chapter, but these poorer countries were not. Economically they stood still—in some cases, they may even have lost ground—while the advanced countries shot ahead at theretofore inconceivably rapid rates. Stagnation in one area of the world, rapid modern growth in the other brought about the great disparities in standards of living in the 1960's, some of them, unfortunately, increasing.

Historical versus
Modern Development

The past 20 years have seen a sharp awakening, in both East and West, to the facts we have just been describing. We are living in the so-

---

[1] The same problems are also present when we try to measure the growth of a single country over very long periods of time. For as we indicated in the last chapter when discussing various trends in U.S. history, modern economic growth involves a large-scale transformation in the pattern of a country's economic life. Thus, the comparison between a "late" and "early" stage in any one country's experience is similar in difficulty to a comparison between a "rich" country and a "poor" country at a given moment of time. Such comparisons are extremely useful, but they also must be treated with a certain amount of caution.

TABLE / ANNUAL PER-CAPITA OUTPUT IN 1957
15 – 1 / (Converted to U.S. dollars by means of foreign exchange rates)

$0–$100 (includes 49.7% of the world's population)

America	Asia and Middle East	Africa
Falkland Islands	Pakistan	Ruandi-Urundi
and Bolivia	Sarawak	Somaliland
Greenland	Thailand	South West Africa
	Truncial Oman	Span. Guinea
Asia and Middle East	Vietnam (North and South)	Sudan
Afghanistan	Yemen	Tanganyika
Bhutan		Togoland
Brunei	Africa	Uganda
Burma	Angola	Others
Cambodia	Belgian Congo	
China	Br. Cameroons	Oceania
Gaza Strip	Eritrea and Ethiopia	Australian Oceania
India	Fr. Equatorial Africa	Br. Oceania
Maldive Islands	Fr. West Africa	Fr. Oceania
Mongolian People's	Gambia	New Zealand Oceania
Republic	Kenya	U.S. Oceania
Muscat and Oman	Liberia	Naura
Nepal	Libya	New Hebrides
Neth. New Guinea	Madagascar	New Guinea
North Borneo	Mozambique	Pacific Islands (U.S.)
North Korea	Nigeria	Western Samoa (N.Z.)

$101–$300 (includes 17.1% of the world's population)

Latin America	Latin America	Asia and Middle East
Brazil	Virgin Islands	Jordan
British Guiana	West Indies (other)	Korea (South)
Br. Honduras		Macao
Colombia	Europe	Philippines
Dominican Republic	Albania	Port. India
Ecuador	Andorra	Port. Timor
El Salvador	Faeroe Islands	Ryukyu Islands
Fr. Guiana	Portugal	Saudi Arabia
Guadeloupe	Spain	Turkey
Guatemala	Yugoslavia	U. A. R.
Haiti		
Honduras	Asia and Middle East	Africa
Martinique	Aden	Algeria
Mexico	Bahrein	Fr. Cameroons
Neth. Antilles	Ceylon	Ghana
Nicaragua	China (Taiwan)	Mauritius
Paraguay	Hong Kong	Morocco
Peru	Indonesia	Rhodesia and Nyasaland
St. Pierre and Miquelon	Iran	Tunisia
Surinam	Iraq	

TABLE
15 – 1   (Cont.)

$301–$600 *(includes 18% of the world's population)*

Latin America	*Asia and Middle East*	*Europe*
Argentina	Japan	Greece
Canal Zone	Malaya	Hungary
Chile	Singapore	Iceland
Costa Rica	Lebanon	Ireland
Cuba	Cyprus	Italy
Federation of West Indies		Malta
Panama	*Europe*	Poland
Puerto Rico	Bulgaria	Rumania
Uruguay	E. Germany	San Marino
	Gibraltar	U. S. S. R.

Africa
Union of South Africa

$601–$1,200 *(includes 7.5% of the world's population)*

Latin America	*Europe*	*Europe*
Venezuela	Belgium	Monaco
	Czechoslovakia	Netherlands
Asia and the Middle East	Denmark	Norway
Israel	Finland	United Kingdom
	France	
Europe	W. Germany	
Austria	Liechtenstein	

$1,201 and above *(includes 7.7% of the world's population)*

	Average per-capita output		*Average per-capita output*
America		*Asia*	
United States		Kuwait *	
and Canada	$2,521	Qatar *	$2,722
Europe			
Luxemburg	$1,399	*Oceania*	$1,315
Sweden		Australia	
Switzerland		and New Zealand	

* These small countries are major oil-producers.

Source: Everett E. Hagen: "Some Facts about Income Levels and Economic Growth," *Review of Economics and Statistics,* XLII, No. 1 (Feb., 1960).

called Decade of Development. The poor countries of the world are unanimous on this issue if no other: they want to share in the material progress that they have seen so bountifully distributed in the West. How can they achieve this goal? What problems do they face?

Now to a certain degree the problems that the modern under-developed country faces today are the same as those faced by the economically advanced countries a century or two ago. One partial way of looking at the problem is to say that these countries are now trying to achieve the same kind of industrial revolution that Britain achieved in the late eighteenth century, the United States in the early nineteenth century, Russia and Japan in the late nineteenth century, and so on. To the degree that this is true, one can look to past history for clues to steps that these underdeveloped countries must undertake today.

This, however, is only a partial and incomplete approach to the problem, because there are a number of important respects in which these countries face difficulties that are *different* from those of countries that achieved their industrial revolutions in the past. These differences, indeed, affect virtually every aspect of the development process, making recommendations from past experience somewhat questionable.

Let us take up a few of these differences with respect to the three major variables we have discussed in connection with modern economic growth: technological progress, capital accumulation, and population growth. Then, since the subject is of special interest to citizens of this country, let us say a few words about the role of foreign aid in promoting economic development.

Applying Western Technology

One respect in which modern underdeveloped countries appear to have a clear advantage over their predecessors is in the area of technological progress. Since technological progress is such an important feature of modern growth, this advantage constitutes the main reason for optimism about their ultimate prospects.

The advantage derives from the fact that although these countries have been technologically stagnant during the past century, the world as a whole has not been. When England started her industrial revolution, she had to invent the steam engine, but for the underdeveloped country of today, the steam engine already exists. So also does electricity, the railroad, the telephone, the airplane, even atomic energy and electronic computers. There has been developed during this period an enormous store of new technology that is potentially available even to the poorest and most backward countries. Instead of having to start from scratch, they have open to them all the major scientific achievements of the industrial world, and this gives them a running start, compared to the "early developers."

This advantage, however, is qualified by a number of important drawbacks.

1. The advanced technology of the West is, in most cases, unsuited to the economic conditions prevalent in most underdeveloped countries. Many of these countries are characterized by (*a*) an abundance of unskilled, semi-literate laborers and (*b*) a shortage of trained workers and managers and also of machinery and other capital goods. The advanced technology of the West, however, requires both skilled labor and a great deal of capital. The large-scale adoption of this technology in unmodified form would create enormous strains on an underdeveloped country and would also provide little employment for the vast numbers of unskilled laborers in the economy. Consequently, modification of Western technology (to make it more suitable to conditions in the underdeveloped country) is highly desirable. But such modification is difficult and, in many cases, is tantamount to the development of "new" technology.

2. Many underdeveloped countries, particularly at an early stage of their efforts, do not have the productive capacity to produce the kinds of machinery, tools, and other equipment that the installation of Western technology requires. This means that they will often have to sustain large imports of industrial goods in the early stages of their development effort. But how are they to pay for these imports? In a country like India, where exports have been sluggish and where there is a need to import not only capital goods but also food and raw materials, the problem of a balance of payments crisis may be a serious one, severely limiting the country's development potentialities.

3. Not all Western technology is unequivocally helpful in promoting economic development. The clearest instance in this respect is public health and medical technology. As we shall see when we come to the problem of population growth, the importation of Western public health and medical technology has contributed to a sharp fall in the death rate in many underdeveloped countries. This is a desirable achievement in its own right, but it has contributed to the population explosion in these countries which may pose grave obstacles to successful development.

These qualifications do not mean that the technological advantage of the modern underdeveloped country is completely nullified. It is still a major asset to have the storehouse of the industrial world to draw upon. Still, they make it clear that the advantage is somewhat less than might appear at first glance. Also, they make it clear that the effort simply to copy the latest and most advanced examples of Western technology may be an unwise and even foolhardy approach for many of these countries.

Capital accumulation is always important for economic growth, but it may be especially important in the case of the modern under-developed country because, as we have just seen, much of the new technology available to them from the economically advanced countries is *capital-intensive.*[2]

But if the need for more capital is great in these countries, the problems of supplying it may be even greater than it was in times past. There are several reasons for this. One is that many of these countries are so very poor, even poorer than England and the United States were when they were starting out. Capital accumulation requires saving, but if output per capita is very low, people may wish to consume all or nearly all of their very meager incomes. Indeed, some economists believe that there is a kind of vicious circle of poverty here:

Such a vicious circle will arise if saving depends upon output while output depends upon the rate of capital accumulation. Thus, in its simplest form, it would go: People are poor, therefore they do not save much. Since savings are small, capital accumulation will be slow. Since there is little capital accumulation, output will remain low. When output is low, people are poor. In other words, people remain poor because they are poor.

Other economists believe that these circles are not so vicious as might appear. They point out that historically even the poorest societies have been able to summon "surpluses" above consumption; for example, for waging wars. They also note that in many underdeveloped countries there are extremely wealthy individuals—large landowners, merchants, the governing classes—who form a potential supply of savings and investment if the surplus can be tapped.

Still, no one would argue that general poverty is a condition that favors capital accumulation. Furthermore, there are other factors that may complicate the situation. The rapid development of communications in modern times has meant that poor nations are often keenly aware of the luxurious living standards present in the West. This increases their desire for growth, but it may also stimulate their desire for higher levels of consumption (and hence less saving and capital accumulation) in the immediate present. Also, the social structure of the underdeveloped country may not be favorable to the utilization of

---

[2] A term sometimes used in this connection is "labor-saving." If the costs of hiring a unit of capital and a unit of labor are unchanged, then a "labor-saving" innovation is roughly one which will lead to an increased employment of capital relative to labor. This is what is meant by an increase in the capital-intensity of production.

such economic surpluses as are potentially available. In the West, energetic private individuals developed the habit of frugality and thrift at an early stage, virtually as a matter of religious principle.[3] But the wealthy Latin-American landowner or the oil-rich potentate in the Middle East may prefer to live in luxury and ostentation and devote relatively little of the available surplus to growth-generating purposes.

All this is not to say that the modern underdeveloped country will not be able to summon the capital it so desperately needs. But it does mean that the effort to do so may impose a very great strain on the society and may possibly require a major reorganization of its structure. Communist China represents something of an extreme case in this regard. China has gone at the problem of raising the rate of capital accumulation with a vengeance. In this one respect, furthermore, she appears to have been quite successful. Although accurate figures are virtually impossible to come by, it appears that China raised her rate of gross investment as a percentage of GNP from something less than 10 per cent in 1950 to 25 per cent or more in 1959. This is an extremely high rate for a very poor country such as China (output per capita measured at below $100 per year). But if the Chinese experience makes it clear that poor countries can increase their rate of capital accumulation, it also makes it clear that this effort may be accompanied by (a) a massive reorganization of the society and (b) deep and sometimes shattering economic strains. The increase in China's investment has been virtually wholly due to the dominating role of the state in her economy since the early 1950's. By 1957, for example, over 96 per cent of all industrial investment in China was undertaken by the government. The state has also promoted various forms of collectivization in agriculture to increase the available surplus in the rural areas. The strains of this effort have shown in a number of ways, most dramatically in the breakdown of both industrial and agricultural production that took place after the beginning of the "Great Leap Forward" in 1958. Although recovery from that collapse has now taken place, Chinese society continues to be riven by turmoil as every day's newspapers clearly indicate.

The point, then, is that although capital accumulation problems are not insurmountable in today's underdeveloped country, they are very severe, owing to the combination of a large need and a relatively inadequate means of supplying that need. The great question—from the point of view of the public interest of the world as a whole—is whether less violent means than those employed by China can be found to solve this particular problem.

[3] Indeed, some economic historians have argued that it *was* a matter of religious principle. See, for example, the classic work: Max Weber, *The Protestant Ethic and the Spirit of Capitalism* (New York: Charles Scribner's Sons, 1952).

The Population Problem

We come now to the last of the three major factors in economic growth: population growth. And here we must linger a moment, since this problem looms so large for many underdeveloped countries, especially in Asia, but also in somewhat different form in Latin America.

In the last chapter, we noted that many of the leading early nineteenth century British economists, especially Malthus and Ricardo, took a pessimistic view about the future possibilities of economic progress. The main reason they did so was that they believed in the so-called *Malthusian theory of population.* This theory, in essence, states the following:

The consequence of a rising standard of living will be that the birth rate will rise and the death rate will fall and there will be a massive increase in population. Because of the law of diminishing returns (population pressing against the "fixed" natural resources of the society), this rise in population will force the average standard of living back down to the subsistence level. Thus, although societies may progress for a time, the ultimate future is dismal. Population growth will inevitably expand to the limits of the economy's means of providing for that population, reducing the mass of mankind to the barest of subsistence.[4]

We noticed that the predictions of these writers failed notably for the countries to which they were applied (economically advancing countries like Britain), for the fundamental reason that technological progress and capital accumulation in both agriculture and industry enabled total output to advance much more rapidly than they had anticipated. Also, as living standards in these countries rose, it turned out that birth rates, far from continuing to rise, began to fall. The role of the family became altered in an increasingly urbanized society. More women wanted careers. Parents began to want more education and other spiritual and material benefits for their offspring. In consequence, families in these advancing economies began to have not more but fewer children. The rate of population increase in all these countries fell far below the "biological maximum" that Malthus seemed to fear.

When we come to the modern underdeveloped countries, however, we find a very different situation. The population problem here

[4] In his famous *Essay on the Principle of Population* (1798), Malthus put the problem in the dramatic form of two "ratios." He saw population growth as tending to occur at a "geometric ratio" (i.e., 1,2,4,8,16,32 . . .) while he believed that food production could increase only at an "arithmetic ratio" (i.e., 1,2,3,4,5,6 . . .). Ultimately, food supplies would run out, population growth would be brought to a halt, and everyone would live in a state of misery.

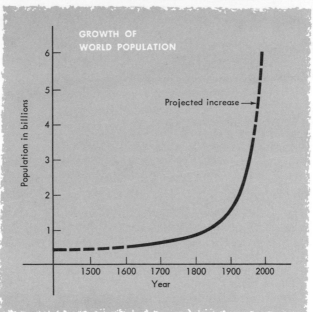

GROWTH OF
WORLD POPULATION

Population in billions

Projected increase →

1500 1600 1700 1800 1900 2000
Year

FIG. 15-1

The striking acceleration of population growth in modern times is made apparent in this curve. It should be noted that population figures for the world as a whole are only estimates, even today. For earlier centuries, they are very rough approximations.

is quite similar to the one Malthus posed, although for somewhat different reasons.

Where Malthus was right was in foreseeing the enormous potentialities for rapid population growth once certain constraints were removed. Figures 15-1 and 15-2 tell something of the basic story of what is happening in the world at the present time. They show the great acceleration of world population growth in modern times, and they show, further, that it is in the underdeveloped world as a whole that this rate of increase is highest. Thus, if present trends are maintained, the share of Asia, Africa, and Latin America in world population will go up from 71 per cent to 81 per cent over the next 40 years.

Now if we were to compare the rates of population growth in the underdeveloped countries of today with those of the economically advancing countries of a century or two ago (i.e., when *they* were

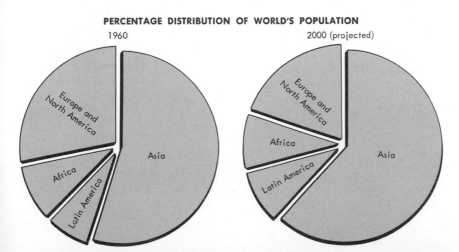

PERCENTAGE DISTRIBUTION OF WORLD'S POPULATION

1960   2000 (projected)

Europe and North America

Asia

Africa

Latin America

Europe and North America

Africa

Asia

Latin America

FIG. 15-2

beginning to industrialize), we should find that whereas most of the advanced countries had rates of increase of 1 per cent or less per year, the modern underdeveloped countries have characteristic rates of increase of 2 per cent, 2½ per cent, or even above 3 per cent per year.[5] These are very respectable rates, even by Malthusian standards.

Actually, the reasons for these high rates of increase are not exactly those Malthus anticipated. After all, standards of living are much higher in the economically advanced countries, whereas these high rates of population growth are occurring in countries that are still desperately poor. Many factors have played a role in this phenomenon, though the main single fact, as we indicated earlier, is that it has been possible to apply even in very poor countries many of the techniques of modern medicine, disease prevention, malaria control, public health, sanitation, and the like. This aspect of Western technological progress has been fairly easily transferable even to quite backward societies. The result has been very sharp declines in death rates in these countries. In some extreme cases, like Ceylon, the death rate fell to *one-third* its previous level in a matter of 30-odd years. At the same time, birth rates have remained very high—often twice the level of birth rates in the more developed countries. The result: the population explosion we have heard so much about in recent years.

The consequences of these very rapid rates of population growth are many. The general problem is that, with rapid population growth, a much higher rate of growth of output must be sustained if output per capita is to be raised at all significantly. With an annual 3 per cent rate of growth of population, a country must maintain at 3 per cent rate of growth of GNP just to stay even. (Remember that in the United States, our historic rate of growth of GNP has been about 3½ per cent.) With a 4 per cent growth rate, output per capita will rise only at roughly 1 per cent per year. At such a rate of increase, a country that today has an output per capita of, say, $100 per year would still be well below $200 a year at the end of the twentieth century. Given the rising expectations of most poor countries in the 1960's, such a rate of progress would be regarded as quite unsatisfactory. Yet with population growing at 3 per cent, or even 2 per cent or 2½ per cent, these countries will be greatly strained to achieve much more than perhaps 1 per cent or 1½ per cent per capita increases per year.

The problem is intensified, moreover, when we consider certain other aspects of population growth. For one thing, there is the struc-

[5] There were, of course, some advanced countries that had high rates of population growth in the nineteenth century (the United States, we know, was one), but these countries were in the so-called regions of recent settlement, where there was a superabundance of land and other natural resources. Population growth in this context was, as we have indicated, probably advantageous.

ture of the population to consider. Countries with high birth rates will typically have a large proportion of children in their populations. Figure 15-3 contrasts the population structure of a rapid-population-growth, underdeveloped country (Costa Rica) with a slow-population-growth, developed country (Sweden). A large proportion of children in the population means that there are more dependents and fewer productive workers in the society, creating a drain on the productive capabilities of the economy. Even more serious, perhaps, is the pressure that population growth creates in already densely populated areas.

Not all underdeveloped countries are overpopulated. There are regions in Africa, Latin America, and even in a few small countries in Asia that are relatively underpopulated. But the bulk of the world's poor live in countries where overpopulation is already a serious problem. (India with 500 million people and China with 750 million people comprise half or more of the underdeveloped world.) And in these

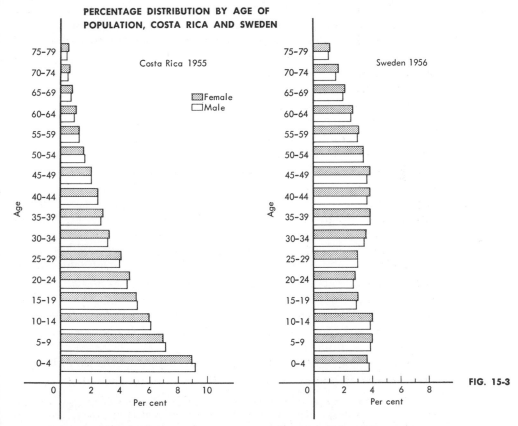

Source: Harold F. Dorn, "World Population Growth," in Philip M. Hauser, ed., *The Population Dilemma* (Englewood Cliffs, N.J.: Prentice-Hall, Inc., 1963), p. 24.

countries additional numbers pose at least two extremely serious problems:

1. *Pressure on the land in agriculture.* Population growth in these countries where land is already scarce means that the law of diminishing returns makes further increases in agricultural output, and especially food supplies, very hard to come by. Many economists think that some of these nations have already reached the stage of "absolutely diminishing returns"—i.e., where the further application of labor to the land brings no increase in agricultural output at all. (In Fig. 14-5, this would mean that the total output curve had reached a point where it stopped rising, no matter what the increase in population was.) [6] If overcrowding on the land leads to less efficient methods of production, then food production might actually decrease as population increases. This does *not* mean that these countries will not be able to expand their food production in the future. The law of diminishing returns states what happens when only one element in the picture changes. But other elements may change. There may be capital accumulation in agriculture. New techniques of agricultural production may be employed. The effects of overcrowding *do* mean, however, that favorable improvements will have to be very strong to raise total food production as rapidly as population growth. To increase food production *more* rapidly than population growth (in order to raise food output per capita) will be extremely difficult. Nor is there any real evidence that this goal has yet been achieved by the underdeveloped world as a whole.

2. *The unemployment problem.* Equally serious is the unemployment problem to which rapid population growth in densely populated areas may give rise. There is no further room for employment in agriculture, because of the heavy rural overpopulation that already exists. On the other hand, the ability of the industrial sector to employ more workers is seriously limited by the nature of the technology employed. We have already mentioned that modern technology makes great demands on capital goods and on skilled labor but relatively smaller demands on massive infusions of unskilled labor. But if the agricultural sector cannot take them and if the rate of expansion of the industrial sector is insufficient to take them, where will these increasing numbers of unskilled laborers find employment? To understand just how serious a problem this is, one has to have some idea of the magnitudes involved. India, for example, in the course of a 15-year

---

[6] Economists use the term *marginal product* to refer to *additions* to total output as we add more of a particular factor of production, *cet. par.* The *marginal product of labor* would be "the addition to total product as we added one more unit of labor to the productive process, everything else unchanged." Another way of saying that the total output curve is no longer rising as we add more laborers to the land is to say that the marginal product of labor has fallen to zero.

period adds to her labor force about 70 million workers, or, roughly, the equivalent of the total labor force of the present-day United States. Moreover, India adds this extraordinary number of workers to an economy that is already suffering from serious unemployment. For example, at the end of India's Second Five-Year Plan (1962), it was estimated that there were 9 million unemployed Indian workers and another 15 to 18 million partially unemployed or underemployed workers. The problem of finding jobs for such huge numbers of laborers is one of the great costs of rapid population growth in densely populated areas. Nor, as in the case of food supplies, is it clear that this problem has as yet been generally solved by these countries.

When we add together all the various difficulties that rapid population growth entails for these poor countries, when we remember, further, the problems of capital accumulation and the difficulties of adapting Western technology to the drastically different conditions of the modern underdeveloped country—when we put all this together, we may begin to understand why many economists feel that the poor countries today face much greater obstacles to their successful development than did their predecessors. Indeed, we may feel more than sympathy. We may want to know in what ways, if any, we can be of help.

The Role of Foreign Aid

The United States has been of help. One of the brighter chapters in human history is the story in the past two decades of American attempts to provide economic assistance to less fortunate nations. At the beginning of this period, our foreign aid was heavily focused on European reconstruction through the Marshall Plan. Beginning in 1949 with President Truman's Point Four program of technical assistance and continuing on to the present time, however, the United States has been giving regular and substantial economic assistance to the underdeveloped countries of the world. We are currently giving such assistance both unilaterally (through our Agency for International Development or our "Food for Peace" program, for example) and multilaterally, as in our contributions to the World Bank. Although Cold War motives and strategic considerations have played a part in these programs, simple humanitarianism has never been completely absent, either. There is no need for any American to be ashamed of his country's record in this regard.

Still, foreign aid is controversial, and it has become increasingly so in the mid-1960's. Why?

Some of the criticism of aid derives primarily from noneconomic considerations. There is, for example, the sometimes expressed view that by aiding foreign countries we are likely to find ourselves entering into military commitments which may in turn lead us into ever more costly limited (or not so limited) wars. The economist is not the one to judge this kind of criticism, since it is basically a political or foreign policy criticism. Still, one may wonder in passing whether it is foreign aid that is leading us into these further commitments or whether it is simply that these commitments provide part of the motive for the foreign aid. If the latter is the case, we should ask if there are other grounds that justify aid even if further commitments are not to be entered into.

There are, however, at least two criticisms of foreign aid that deal fairly directly with economic questions. The first has to do with the *cost* of the aid program to this country and whether or not it is sustainable over time. Foreign aid clearly does cost this country something, both directly and in terms of the balance of payments problem we discussed in Chapter 13. Without belittling these costs, it is only accurate to state the following facts: (*a*) our economic assistance to underdeveloped countries constitutes a very small percentage of the expenditures of the federal government and a minuscule percentage (about ½ of 1 per cent) [7] of our gross national product; (*b*) the percentage of our national income going into foreign aid has been declining in recent years and, indeed, is very substantially below the percentage of national income we devoted to the economic assistance of Europe under the Marshall Plan; (*c*) the practice of tying aid expenditures to purchases of American goods has drastically curtailed the net cost to the American balance of payments of aid expenditures. This cost (with respect to AID expenditures) has dropped from a $1 billion addition to our deficit in 1961 to an estimated $205 million addition in 1966. The cost is clearly there, but it is not so heavy as some critics would suggest, and furthermore it has been declining over time.

The other central criticism from an economic point of view has to do with the effect of aid on the prospects of the recipient countries. Does aid really help? Or does it simply encourage dependence on the United States, with the consequence that the aid program may go on forever?

[7] It is actually fairly difficult to calculate the true "cost" of aid to us as a percentage of our national income. This is because aid comes in different forms: grants, loans, commodity aid under the "Food for Peace" program, etc. One estimate for the year 1963 is that our total aid program cost somewhere between 0.48 per cent and 0.74 percent of our national income. (Source: I. M. D. Little and J. M. Clifford, *International Aid*. Chicago: Aldine Publishing Company, 1966.)

These questions are very difficult to answer, the main reason being that time is still too short to tell. Some Americans have been disappointed because the aid program has not brought quick results. Such expectations were encouraged perhaps by the outstanding success of the Marshall Plan in Europe. Some of it may have been due to the overzealous advocacy of aid by its supporters in the early days. In any event, in the mid-1960's it does begin to look to many citizens that the aid program is going on forever, and they begin to wonder if it is really having any useful effect at all.

Here the analysis of this chapter may be helpful in putting the problem in some perspective. For one thing, this analysis should make it clear *why* the development process in these poor countries takes so much time. The analogy with the Marshall Plan is virtually irrelevant, for there we were dealing with countries that had already mastered the tricks of modern technology and growth, had a literate, technically skilled labor force and abundant managerial talent, and needed only a modest infusion of resources to put them on the path again. What we have shown in the case of the underdeveloped countries, however, is that the problems they face are extremely difficult and that their poverty is so acute that, even under the best of circumstances, the achievement of a decent living standard will be accomplished only by the end of the century. To demand quick results under these circumstances is simply to misconceive the nature of the problem.

The other way in which the analysis of this chapter should help us is in understanding more specifically the potential impact of aid on an underdeveloped country. Some economists have described these countries as facing two fundamental *gaps* as they try to make their way to self-sustaining growth.[8] The first is a gap between domestic savings and the rate of investment required for a desired rate of growth: the *investment gap*. The second is the gap between the country's exports and the imports required for a desired rate of growth: the *trade gap*. The investment gap arises, as we have seen, because the need for capital is so great and the ability of the poor country to provide the capital is so limited. The trade gap arises because the export capabilities of the poor country may be limited, and yet it may need imports to survive (as in the case of food shortages) and also to grow (as in the case of capital and other industrial goods that must be imported from abroad).

Now the fundamental *economic* case for foreign aid (assuming, of course, that it is our goal to assist these countries develop) rests on three propositions.

[8] See, for example, Hollis Chenery and A. M. Strout, "Foreign Assistance and Economic Development," *American Economic Review*, LVI, No. 4, Part 1 (Sept., 1966).

1. If these various gaps are not filled, the countries involved will not be able to achieve modern development, or at least not in an acceptable length of time.
2. Foreign aid is an effective means for filling these gaps.
3. There is reason to believe that these gaps will diminish and ultimately disappear as development proceeds over time.

This third proposition is particularly relevant for those who ask whether foreign aid must go on forever. It is based on the belief that as a country develops, various forces will emerge that will reduce its dependence on foreign assistance. In the ideal case, this will happen because: (a) development will raise total output and output per capita, and it will be possible to channel a large fraction of these increases in output into added saving and investment; (b) development will provide the country with a greater export capacity and, at the same time, with a greater ability to produce domestically the capital and other industrial goods needed for further development; (c) development will bring improvements in the agricultural sphere and also, hopefully, an improved environment for solving the population problem. If such trends occur, then, although aid may still be required for a substantial length of time, an eventual end will be in sight.

Now these propositions cannot guarantee us that aid will do the job. (Guarantees are seldom to be found in any area dealing with complex economic, social, and political problems.) Nor can they tell us that foreign aid is the only route to these ends. China, we know, is receiving no foreign assistance at the present time; she is attempting to fill her gaps by an extraordinary reorganization of her national life. Perhaps the most that can be said is that foreign aid seems to be one possibly effective alternative to other alternatives, and these other alternatives are likely to be very harsh on the people of the countries involved, and they may have disruptive international consequences.

Nothing is certain. There is no ironclad case for foreign aid. But there is a case for it, and the reader himself will have to decide whether it is strong enough to merit the sustainable but nevertheless real costs aid involves.

Summary

The process of modern growth, so vigorous in certain industrial countries, has as yet had little impact in raising living standards in the underdeveloped countries that constitute somewhere between one-half and two-thirds of the world's population. Although output per capita figures are somewhat suspect, the depth of poverty in these countries shows up clearly in any measure we might use. Their average family incomes are perhaps one-tenth or less of what we enjoy today in the United States. These countries are trying to achieve now what the economically advanced countries achieved a century or two ago—an industrial revolution that will put them on the path of modern economic growth—but the circumstances they face are quite different from those that faced the "early developers" of Europe and North America:

1. *Technology.* The underdeveloped countries have the entire storehouse of modern technology to draw upon. This is a clear advantage, but it is qualified by the fact that this technology is not well-suited to conditions in these countries, that it may require costly imports from abroad, and that, in certain cases (notably public health and medical technology) it may raise certain new problems (the population explosion).

2. *Capital accumulation.* The need for capital goods in these countries is great, especially in view of the capital-intensive nature of much modern technology, but the ability to raise domestic savings and investment is limited by the general poverty of the countries, the desire for increased consumption now, and, in many cases, the absence of a social structure that promotes the productive use of economic "surpluses" that may exist. In the case of China, the rate of capital accumulation has been raised considerably but at the cost of a drastic reorganization of the society and with severe strains on the economy.

3. *Population growth.* Falling death rates (largely due to improved public health and medical technology) and very high birth rates have caused a population expansion that raises the specter of Malthusian problems for many underdeveloped countries. The rates of population growth in these countries are, on the average, much higher than they were in the economically advanced countries when they were setting out on the path of modern growth. The consequences are: the difficulty of raising total output fast enough to achieve increases in output per capita; the heavy burden of large numbers of dependent children on the productive workers of the society; and, especially in heavily populated regions, the problem of increasing agricultural output rapidly enough to feed the growing population and the difficulty of finding employment for these massive additions to the labor force. India, who faces all of these problems, affords an example of the difficulty of finding jobs for the growing labor force when agriculture is already overcrowded and industry cannot use such large numbers of unskilled laborers.

Foreign aid has been an important instrument of American national purpose in coping with the problems of the underdeveloped countries. The main economic criticisms of aid are directed against its cost and its effectiveness. The cost of aid, though real, is not extraordinarily heavy, amounting to about ½ of 1 per cent of our GNP. The effectiveness of aid, however, is very difficult to judge. The basic economic case for aid rests on the belief that the underdeveloped countries face certain "gaps" (the *investment* gap and the *trade* gap) which, if unmet, will slow their economic development but which, if filled by foreign aid, will begin to diminish and ultimately disappear as development proceeds. This is not an airtight case for aid, but it does at least suggest the possibility that aid may be an alternative to other paths of action on the part of the underdeveloped countries, paths that might be painful to them and disruptive of the community of nations.

Questions for Discussion

1 • Discuss the advantages and disadvantages for an underdeveloped country of borrowing the latest Western technological ideas and methods.

2 • It is sometimes argued that the poor countries of today will be able to achieve modern growth only if they begin with rather drastic and rapid changes in their social and economic structures. This has given rise to what are sometimes called the "big push" theories of economic development. Do any of the factors discussed in this chapter seem to you to support such a view? What reasons might be offered for the hypothesis that slow, step-by-step growth is generally insufficient for today's underdeveloped countries?

3 • "Population growth was not always a problem for the countries that developed economically in the nineteenth century, but it is public enemy number one for the underdeveloped countries of today." Discuss.

4 • Is the kind of unemployment or underemployment one finds in a country like India today the same as the kind of unemployment we were discussing in Part II of this book? What differences, if any, do you see? Would the application of modern fiscal and monetary policy measures be likely to cure the kind of unemployment that exists in many of today's underdeveloped countries?

5 • Write an essay giving what you consider to be the main economic arguments for and against an extensive program of U.S. foreign aid to the underdeveloped world.

Suggested Reading

HARBISON, FREDERICK and CHARLES A. MYERS, *Education, Manpower, and Economic Growth*. New York: McGraw-Hill, Inc., 1964.

HAUSER, PHILIP M., ed., *The Population Dilemma*. Englewood Cliffs, N.J.: Prentice-Hall, Inc., 1963.

HIRSCHMAN, ALBERT O., *The Strategy of Economic Development*. New Haven: Yale University Press, 1958.

LEWIS, W. ARTHUR, *Development Planning*. New York: Harper & Row, 1966.

LITTLE, I. M. D. and J. M. CLIFFORD, *International Aid*. Chicago: Aldine Publishing Co., 1966.

NURKSE, RAGNAR, *Problems of Capital Formation in Underdeveloped Areas*. New York: Oxford University Press, 1953.

The problems
of affluence

16

In this final chapter, we turn to the problems
of what Professor John Kenneth Galbraith
has called the "affluent society." Such problems, of course, have little or no meaning
for the underdeveloped countries we were
discussing in the last chapter. For them,
ancient poverty is still the curse, and large-
scale economic development is the only serious answer. But if, as one may optimistically
expect, these poor countries do solve their
basic difficulties, then, in due course, they
will confront a set of problems similar to
those confronting the United States today.
What we are here discussing then is the
economic present of a few countries and the
economic future of the world at large.

The Issues

In a poor society, the nature of the economic problem is fairly clear, though the means of solving it may be hard to come by. In the affluent society, the means for solving economic problems are abundant, but the determination of the nature of the relevant problems is more difficult. Modern economic growth has created a range of choice about the objectives and purposes of society that was unknown two centuries ago. The consequence is that reasonable men can differ sharply about the direction in which society should proceed.

Taking the United States as the most dramatic example of modern affluence, we find at least four major issues at the present time, some of them involving quite different perceptions of the desirable future direction of our society.

1. How do we maintain or further enrich our "affluence"? That is to say, what are the problems involved in insuring a continuation of the process of modern economic growth into the future? Indeed, should we be satisfied with the historic rate, or should we try to improve upon it?

2. Are there groups in our society who either absolutely or relatively fail to benefit from the growth process? Do we in fact have both "affluence" and "poverty"? If so, what should be done about it?

3. Are there ways in which the process of modern growth actually *creates* problems for our society? What about our cities? What about the quality of our life in general? Is the great stress on increasing GNP really relevant only to an earlier historic stage of our development? Should it be abandoned as too costly to our humanity now that the bread-and-butter problems of economic scarcity have been solved?

4. What of the role of the State in the affluent society? Do we face a number of public needs that only the State can handle? Or is the greater danger in the increasing bureaucratization of life? Should the benefits of affluence be used to permit a more private or a more public pattern of society?

These issues obviously require more than the judgment of an economist; they touch on great questions of social purpose. Should we have more growth or less growth? more state intervention or less state intervention? Even deciding which are the truly important questions requires a certain philosophic insight that is difficult to achieve when one is looking not at some other country or some past episode but at one's own society at this very moment.

Still, economics has something to say on each of these questions, and, hopefully, we can provide a useful groundwork for further discussion beyond the confines of this book. Let us, therefore, make just a few comments on these four major issues.

The late John F. Kennedy was elected President in 1960 on a platform including the slogan: "Let's get the country moving again." For most public officials and for a majority of our citizenry, a prime issue, despite our affluence, remains that of maintaining a high rate of economic growth. There are many possible reasons for this. A high rate of growth is seen as a guarantee of high levels of employment in the economy, providing jobs for our increasing labor force. It is seen as an instrument of national purpose in our competitive peaceful coexistence with the Soviet Union. Furthermore, it is viewed as a necessary complement to our expectation, reinforced by a century-and-a-half of experience, of a continually rising living standard. For a variety of such reasons, the news that our growth rate has gone up in a given period is usually greeted with applause; that it has gone down, with alarm.

If this objective is taken (provisionally) to be a major goal of our society, then the economist can make a number of useful comments incorporating the information and analysis we have developed in earlier chapters of this book.

1. *There is no intrinsic reason for expecting modern economic growth to slow down in the foreseeable future.* Our survey of the growth experience of the American economy from 1839 to 1959 [1] showed no evidence of a decline in the rate of growth of output per capita during this period; furthermore, our rate of growth since 1960 has been well above our historic average. More generally, our analysis of the factors of population growth, capital accumulation, and technological progress showed that diminishing returns to land (as feared by the Classical Economists) can be regularly offset by more capital and improved methods of production, and that diminishing returns to capital (as we increase the amount of capital relative to labor) can be regularly offset by a continuing process of technological change. Even if no special steps are taken to stimulate the growth process, there is every reason to expect that output per capita in the United States will continue to rise at something like its historic rate.

2. *Full employment policies will also usually be growth-promoting policies.* In Part II, we showed the various ways in which the government could contribute to full employment in the economy. Although these policies face problems (particularly the problem of inflationary price increases), insofar as they are successful in bringing the economy closer to its full employment potential, they will have some

[1] See p. 229.

favorable effect on growth. They will do this in the short run by speeding up the rate of growth as the economy moves from a below-full employment to a near-full employment level of output, and in the longer run by the presumably larger amount of investment that will occur at the higher levels of national output.

3. *Fiscal and monetary policies to secure full employment can also be specifically adapted to growth promotion.* The point is that there is not simply one, but a variety of different fiscal and monetary policies to raise the level of aggregate demand and that, among these various alternatives, the nation can try to select measures that will be most favorable to future growth. Fundamentally, there are two approaches that may be used to achieve this end:

a) Follow a relatively expansionary monetary policy ("easy money"), to encourage as much business investment as possible, and if this threatens to create too much aggregate demand, follow a relatively contractionary fiscal policy; and

b) Select the instruments of fiscal policy so that the burdens fall more heavily on consumption while, simultaneously, attempts are being made to stimulate investment activity.

In other words, keep interest rates low; and if it is necessary to increase taxes (to prevent inflation from developing), make sure that the tax burdens fall as much as possible on the consumer and as little as possible on investment.

Now, of course, such policies may sometimes conflict with other economic objectives. This is clearly the case in the matter of monetary policy. If we look at growth and full employment only, we can say: Follow easy money and a contractionary (as needed) fiscal policy. But if we look at full employment and our *balance of payments deficit* (as we did in Chapter 12), we are likely to get the reverse answer: Follow a high interest rate policy, to attract international capital to this country, and cure unemployment by an expansionary fiscal policy. Which of these two prescriptions is to take precedence?[2] Moreover, there also are possible conflicts when we come to selecting taxes that fall heavily on consumption and lightly on investment. For such taxes are likely to increase rather than decrease the inequality of income

[2] The effort to avoid this conflict has given rise to what is sometimes called "Operation Twist." The Federal Reserve Board and the Treasury have attempted to change the *structure* of interest rates, raising the short-term rate and lowering the long-term rate. The idea is that a high short-term rate will attract international capital, while a low long-term rate will make possible continued high levels of domestic investment. Such a policy may partially, but certainly not completely, remove the conflict we have been discussing.

distribution in our society. Will the man-in-the-street put up with such treatment? Should he be required to?

What this means is that there are limits to the degree that we can use full employment monetary and fiscal policies as a specific stimulant to economic growth. However, there is at least some flexibility in this area; and if a government continually has its eye on the goal of growth, in the long run it will doubtless produce a more rapidly growing economy than would otherwise be the case. This general conclusion is very much strengthened, moreover, when we come to our last point.

4. *Technological progress can be strengthened by giving greater emphasis to education and research.* We know from our earlier discussion that technological change has been a major factor in American economic growth, especially in recent years. We also know that such change involves new methods of production, new products, new skills in the labor force, new managerial talents, and so on. The most direct ways of encouraging this process are through increased basic and applied scientific research (the wellspring of technological progress) and through the increased education and training of our citizens (contributing both to the creation of new knowledge and to the introduction of new techniques into actual practice). What the role of the government should be in this particular area, we defer for a moment. But that the increased attention both private individuals and the government are giving to education and allied fields is the surest guarantee of a continuing high rate of growth (if that is our objective), there should be little doubt.

Growth and "Poverty"

Modern growth solves many economic issues, but not all of them. In the 1960's, economists and public-spirited citizens generally became aware that there may be persistent "poverty" in the affluent society. Affluence gives us the potential resources to handle this problem. Should we, and can we, do something about it?

I have put the term "poverty" in quotes to indicate (1) that it is to be distinguished from other kinds of poverty we have discussed, such as that in the very poor underdeveloped countries or in the United States in the Great Depression, and (2) that the term involves a problem of definition. The second difficulty can be made clear by contrasting two empirical descriptions of "poverty" in the United States, both of them factually accurate.

The first comes from the report of the President's Council of

Economic Advisers in 1964. Defining "poverty" in terms of families of four with an annual before-tax income of $3,000 (in 1962 prices), the Council gave the following description of the American scene:

One-fifth of our families and nearly one-fifth of our total population are poor.

Of the poor, 22 per cent are nonwhite; and nearly one-half of all nonwhites live in poverty.

The heads of over 60 per cent of all poor families have only grade-school educations.

Even for those denied opportunity by discrimination, education significantly raises the chance to escape from poverty.

But education does not remove the effects of discrimination: when nonwhites are compared with whites at the same level of education, the nonwhites are poor about twice as often.

One-third of all poor families are headed by a person over sixty-five, and almost one-half of families headed by such a person are poor.

Of the poor, 54 per cent live in cities, 16 per cent on farms, 30 per cent as rural nonfarm residents.

Over 40 per cent of all farm families are poor. More than 80 per cent of nonwhite farmers live in poverty.

Less than half of the poor are in the South; yet a southerner's chance of being poor is roughly twice that of a person living in the rest of the country.

One-quarter of poor families are headed by a woman; but nearly one-half of all families headed by a woman are poor.

When a family and its head have several characteristics frequently associated with poverty, the chances of being poor are particularly high: a family headed by a young woman who is nonwhite and has less than an eighth-grade education is poor in 94 out of 100 cases. Even if she is white, the chances are 85 out of 100 that she and her children will be poor.

This description emphasizes both the extent of "poverty" in the United States today and how it falls with a particularly cruel burden on certain groups in American society—the Negroes, the relatively uneducated, the elderly, the poor southern farmer, the fatherless household, and so on.

A second description, completely consistent with the first, but giving a different sense of the rate of progress toward solving the "poverty" problem, is indicated by the last two columns of Table 16-1. Here we find that the percentage of American families with incomes below $3,000 a year has fallen sharply from 1947 to 1965—from 30.0 per cent to 16.5 per cent, or by nearly half in a period of 18 years. The figures for families with incomes of less than $2,000 show the same sharp percentage drop. Furthermore, if we went back a few years earlier, we should find that there was a fairly considerable reduction of income inequality in the United States between the mid-1930's and 1947. Over the last three decades then, the percentage of American families with incomes below the $3,000 mark has probably fallen from 60 per cent or 65 per cent of all families to its present 16 per cent or 17 per cent. On this view, the striking thing is not the

TABLE 16–1 / PERCENTAGE OF U.S. FAMILIES CLASSIFIED POOR BY CHANGING AND FIXED STANDARDS, 1947 TO 1965 (IN 1965 DOLLARS)

		Percentage of families with income		
Year (1)	Median income (2)	Less than one-half the median [1] (3)	Less than $3,000 (4)	Less than $2,000 (5)
1947	$4,275	18.9	30.0	17.2
1948	4,178	19.1	31.2	18.1
1949	4,116	20.2	32.3	19.5
1950	4,351	20.0	29.9	18.1
1951	4,507	18.9	27.8	16.3
1952	4,625	18.9	26.3	15.8
1953	5,002	19.8	24.6	15.4
1954	4,889	20.9	26.2	16.7
1955	5,223	20.0	23.6	14.6
1956	5,561	19.6	21.5	13.0
1957	5,554	19.7	21.7	13.0
1958	5,543	19.8	21.8	12.8
1959	5,856	20.0	20.6	12.1
1960	5,991	20.3	20.3	12.1
1961	6,054	20.3	20.1	11.9
1962	6,220	19.8	18.9	10.9
1963	6,444	19.9	18.0	10.2
1964	6,676	19.9	17.1	9.2
1965	6,882	20.0	16.5	9.1

[1] Estimated by interpolation.

Source: U. S. Bureau of the Census, Current Population Reports Series P-60, No. 51, "Income in 1965 of Families and Persons in the United States," January, 1967. Reprinted here from Victor Fuchs, "Redefining Poverty and Redistributing Income," Public Interest, No. 8 (Summer, 1967), 90.

enormous extent of "poverty" in the United States, but how quickly it is being reduced.

These two views of the generally agreed upon facts bring out the important definitional question: Should "poverty" be considered in *absolute* terms, i.e., existing when a family or an individual has an income below some minimum necessary to guarantee him a certain fixed standard of life? Or should it be defined in *relative* terms, i.e., existing when a family or an individual has an income below some given fraction of the average or median level of income of American society at that time?

Actually, for our purposes, there is no need to exclude either kind of "poverty." [3] The more serious clearly is *absolute* poverty, where the families in question may face acute problems of inadequate clothing and shelter and, in some cases, even malnutrition. But *relative* poverty is also a significant social phenomenon. When a family is notably poorer than its neighbors with respect to housing, consumer appliances, education, entertainment, and all the tangible and intangible comforts that people in the affluent society have come to expect, then its sense of its own poverty can be as acute and demeaning as a much lower standard of absolute income (but a higher relative position) would have been in an earlier day. Think of it in terms of a political analogy: the medieval serf had no vote to determine how his society should be governed, and it probably never occurred to him to miss the privilege. By contrast, in a society accustomed to universal suffrage, the denial of the vote to a group of its citizens would rightly be considered outrageous. It is very much the same with regard to relative poverty: when every one around is well-to-do, the disparity of a much lower living standard creates a serious social and psychological problem.

Now insofar as the question is one of relative poverty, then it is clear that modern economic growth does not automatically solve the problem, or it may do so only very slowly, over the course of decades or perhaps centuries. What is at issue here is the *distribution of income* in the society. The general pattern of income distribution in a society can be illustrated as in Fig. 16-1 by what is called a Lorenz curve. If there were a perfectly equal distribution of income in the society, then income distribution could be represented by the straight line, *OA*. Twenty per cent of the households have 20 per cent of the income; 60 per cent of the households have 60 per cent of the income, and so on. The degree of *in*equality of the income distribution can then be measured by the extent to which the curve departs from this straight line. Curve I represents a greater, curve II a lesser, inequality of income distribution.

There is some evidence to suggest that in the very long run, economic growth does move a society in the direction of a somewhat greater equality of income distribution (i.e., moves the economy

---

[3] Of course, for other purposes—say, framing specific anti-poverty legislation—it may be necessary to have a precise definition in mind. In this case, however, it is also possible to revise the definition over time, as circumstances change.

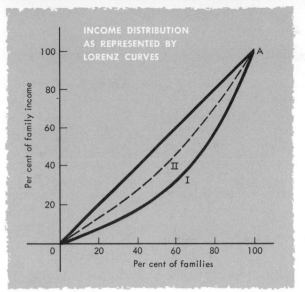

INCOME DISTRIBUTION
AS REPRESENTED BY
LORENZ CURVES

Per cent of family income

Per cent of families

Curves I and II
each show an income
distribution that
departs from
complete equality.
Many people feel
that in view of the
problem of relative
poverty, our society
should attempt to
move toward a more
equal income distribution;
e.g., from a distribution
like that of Curve I to a
distribution like that of
Curve II.

FIG. 16-1

from curve I toward curve II).[4] However, this process is uncertain, and it may be slow. Indeed, if we look back at Table 16-1, we can see that in the period 1947 to 1965, low-income families in the United States did not do particularly well in a relative sense. Using the criterion of a family income of less than one-half the median American family income,[5] we see in column 3 that the percentage of families that were poor in this relative way did not decline over these 18 years (in fact, it increased slightly from 18.9 per cent to 20.0 per cent). Thus, although modern growth can be counted on to raise the average family income absolutely in a fairly dramatic way even in short periods of time, it may have no effect or only very slow long-run effects on the position of the relatively poor. Insofar as our society is concerned to alter its general income distribution in favor of the poorer members, then it may have to take specific measures to do so.

Furthermore, we must not assume that even *absolute* poverty is completely a thing of the past. The fact that in 1965 nearly one-tenth of all American families had annual incomes of less than $2,000 a year (in 1965 prices) must be a matter of concern to all of us. The families in this very low income range are often cast aside from the more general development of the economy as a whole. Professor Galbraith, in his *Affluent Society*, described two kinds of poverty that he felt were fundamentally different from the kind of general poverty

[4] See S. Kuznets, *Six Lectures on Economic Growth* (New York: The Free Press, 1959).

[5] Victor Fuchs, in his article "Redefining Poverty and Redistributing Income," *Public Interest*, No. 8 (Summer, 1967), uses this criterion as a definition of "poverty" more suitable than those deriving from an absolute income level (e.g., $3,000, $2,000, etc.).

known to us in the historic past (or to underdeveloped countries today). These are: (1) *case poverty*—resulting from individual deficiencies, whether poor health, mental inadequacy, lack of education, inability to adapt to the discipline of modern life, etc.; and (2) *insular poverty*—resulting when a region, whether urban or rural, becomes isolated from the general stream of economic progress and a kind of vicious circle is set up: slum living, lack of health and educational facilities, ignorance of opportunities elsewhere, and an inability or unwillingness to take advantage of them if known. This vicious circle guarantees further isolation and further poverty in the future.

Once again, modern economic growth, although it may ameliorate this hard-core poverty, is unlikely to remove it altogether. For the characteristic feature of both *case* and *insular poverty* is that those who suffer from them have somehow been removed from or proved inadequate to the processes that create affluence in the society at large. They are outside the mainstream and have little economic or educational base for finding their way back.

The question of what to do about poverty in the modern American economy, either absolute or relative or both, is a hotly debated political issue. Questions of income distribution almost invariably involve some social conflict, since any redistribution of income is precisely that—taking away one person's income and giving it to another. The one who receives is likely to feel that this is only proper; the one who loses may take a different view. There are, however, at least two fairly noncontroversial points that are useful to have in the back of one's mind when thinking of this problem in the future.

The first is that although it will not cure the whole problem, the achievement of a continuing high level of employment in the economy as a whole is certainly a desirable first step in approaching the "poverty" problem. To put it negatively, the burdens of unemployment are likely to fall with particular severity on the nation's poor and consequently to worsen the poverty problem both in a relative and absolute sense. What this means is that there is no conflict of purpose —indeed there is a unity of purpose—between solving the unemployment problem and solving the poverty problem. The various measures of fiscal, monetary, and other policies we have discussed earlier in terms of maintaining adequate levels of aggregate demand will make a definite contribution toward limiting the growth of poverty in the United States; and if this is not the whole solution, it is at least an important part of it.

The second point is that many of the more specific measures that may be taken to reduce poverty may have social benefits that outweigh their costs to the rest of society. This is likely to be particularly true of all measures that are concerned with improving the health, education, training, and skills of the underprivileged. For in improving their capacities and their ability to take part in the modern economic process, the society is also increasing their productivity and their general contribution to the nation's output of goods and services. Thus, what in some degree may involve income redistribution among the members of the society may also involve the addition of more highly productive workers and consequently greater income for the society as a whole. And this is quite apart from what many would consider the *political* desirability of allowing no substantial group of individuals in a democracy to lag educationally and culturally far behind the rest.

These two points make it clear that quite substantial advances can be made even if no major frontal assault on the present pattern of income distribution in the United States is contemplated.

Growth and the Quality of Life

We move now to what, philosophically speaking, is an even more complex question: Is growth desirable? Or to put it only slightly less grandly: When a society has reached a stage of wealth where all the necessities of life and a high (by historical standards) degree of comfort have been assured to the overwhelming number of its citizens, does it thereby reach a stage when the costs of growth begin to exceed its benefits, when its energies should properly be turned in other directions?

This is not an altogether new question. Even in the nineteenth century, the great philosopher-economist John Stuart Mill yearned for the day when mankind would look for "better things" than a continuation of the constant "struggle for riches." Mill wrote:

I confess I am not charmed with an ideal of life held out by those who think that the normal state of human beings is that of struggling to get on; that the trampling, crushing, elbowing, and treading on each other's heels, which form the existing type of social life, are the most desirable lot of human kind, or anything but the disagreeable symptoms of one of the phases of industrial progress.

Mill actually looked forward to the coming of a "stationary state," providing, of course, that the population problem (that had worried his predecessors Malthus and Ricardo) could be handled and a decent standard of life guaranteed the working classes.

In the United States in the mid-twentieth century, we have achieved a standard of life for the average man that far exceeds anything that Mill had hoped for. In consequence, there are those who argue that the time has now come to reconsider the pivotal role of economic growth in our social life. The argument has many variants, but it is built around two fundamental themes.

The first theme stresses the *declining benefits* of modern growth in the affluent society. Why do we want more goods, the critics ask. Certainly not out of economic necessity. Not even for added material comfort; historically, men have been content with far less abundance than we now enjoy. Essentially, they answer, we want more goods because a growing society creates the very wants that it in turn supplies. These wants may be created by other consumers in the manner of "keeping up with the Joneses": my neighbor has a new and fancy automobile and thus I, too, must have a new and fancy automobile. Or they may be created by the industrial producers through advertising and other means of public persuasion: if you do not buy such-and-such a product, your personal and social life will be jeopardized if not ruined. In either case, a kind of self-cancelling process of want-creation and want-satisfaction is established. If I buy more because my neighbor buys more, and if he buys more because I buy more, then we can both keep on accumulating purchases indefinitely without either being any better off than if we had remained content with less in the beginning. Similarly, in the case of producer-induced demand: business firms advertise to convince the consumer that they need the goods that they would not have missed had the advertising and the additional production never occurred.

Few critics would claim that these are the *only* motives that make consumers wish additional goods—one may want to buy more records or books, for example, simply because one likes to listen to music or to read—but such motives clearly do enter into many of our purchases and, to this degree, the benefits that accrue from still additional economic growth are far less than they appear in the statistics. As the society becomes ever more affluent, these benefits can be expected continually to decline.

The second theme of this argument has to do with the *costs* of economic growth. Growth has always had associated costs. In our discussion of the English industrial revolution (Chapter 14), we pointed out the tremendous dislocation in the traditional pattern of life that the birth of the industrial system involved. Indeed, even the *measurement* of growth is made difficult by the fact that many of the products that we include in our GNP may actually be nothing but costs of an industrial-urban society. Suppose we lay tracks and set up a commuter train service from the suburbs to the city. Should we consider this act of production an addition to GNP, or should we argue that commuter services are simply a required cost of having an industrial-urban society and would have no value were our society organized differently? More generally, there may be important *external diseconomies* connected with the growth process. By this we mean that private acts of production may lead to costs that fall not upon the individual producer but upon society as a whole.[6] Here the critics can point to a number of effects that amount to a virtual catalog of the weaknesses of our industrial-urban society. Our air is becoming befouled with chemicals and smog. Our streams and rivers are being polluted with industrial wastes and detergents. Our fields, meadows, and forests are being defaced by highways and billboards. Our highways themselves are being menaced by the ever-increasing stream of automobiles, buses, and trucks that add to the pollution of the air and require still further roads and highways to encroach upon our natural beauties. It is now generally agreed that our cities have reached a point of crisis. It is a crisis of transportation (as more and more vehicles cram themselves into a limited space), of finance (as the need for social services grows and the middle and upper income groups move out to the suburbs), of race, culture, and education (as Negroes, Puerto Ricans, and other minority groups are left in economic deprivation in the inner city) and, ultimately, of the quality of life (as the cities, once centers of civilization and art, become ever more tarnished and tawdry).

The critics of the continuing emphasis on economic growth stress these deficiencies deriving from the growth process while at the same time pointing to the declining benefits that the process brings. They ask: Is it not a paradox that the richest society in history should be creating not great works of art and beauty and culture but the megalopolis, the freeway, and the slum?

We have put the case sharply, not to try to persuade the reader of its validity, but to make sure that the question is not overlooked. An increasing GNP has many benefits that we have mentioned in earlier pages. For one thing, it provides added resources to meet many of the very problems that we have just been discussing. But it is important at this stage of our social life to remember that this is not simply a one-way street. Growth confers, but it also can corrode. One must inspect the balance with some care.

[6] There may also be *external economies* in the growth process. Our example of the dam whose benefits accrued to other businesses besides the firm building the dam (Chap. 4) is an example of an *external economy*. The significance of "external effects" in general, as we shall see in a moment, is that they create a divergence between private and social interest and thus form an argument for collective or governmental intervention in the economy. It should be said that the measurement of these "externalities" is often extremely difficult in practice.

The State, the Private
Individual, and the Public Interest

Our discussion in the last section leads inevitably to a question that has been running like a central theme throughout this book: the relationship of the State and the private individual to the public interest. In terms of this final stage of our analysis, we can put the problem this way: Has the achievement of affluence in any way affected the desirable balance between the public and the private sector in the American economy? Do we face a situation today that requires new approaches as contrasted with those that have guided us throughout our historic past?

Here, perhaps more than in any other area of our field, the intermingling of economics and politics and of empirical description and value-judgments are inextricably intertwined. Basically, the reader must reach his conclusions on this matter himself, hopefully using some of the tools of economics he has mastered in the preceding pages to clarify the range of possibilities open.

The author will confine himself to what amounts to a personal comment on two trends that seem fairly fundamental in the American economy of the present time. These trends are in many ways in spiritual conflict, and it is at least arguable that the resolution of this conflict stands as the most important piece of outstanding business confronting our society.

One of these trends manifests itself in an awareness of the increasing need for governmental intervention in many areas of our economic life. If we consider any of the major problems that we have taken up in this chapter, we are likely to find that the solution involves a more active role of the government than it would have in times past. Whether it is promoting a higher rate of growth, or eliminating "poverty," or improving the state of our cities or the general quality of our life, public intervention of one sort or another seems indicated. A fundamental reason for this is that many of the present needs of our society seem to involve those "external" effects that we were just discussing, where private and social interest will generally diverge. Take education as an example. Improved education may be regarded as an indispensable aid to a higher rate of growth, as a necessity for the reduction of hard-core poverty, and as an important route to the improvement of the cultural level of our society. But education is a classic case where "external" effects are so important that private individuals or business firms will often not have the motive to provide as much of this particular service as society may require. If I train a man to become an engineer and he then works not for my firm but for some other firm or firms, then I will have suffered the costs but not enjoyed the benefits (which go "externally" to other firms or to society). Consequently, I am unlikely to undertake privately what may be in the interest of society to undertake.

Since many of our current problems involve various externalities —whether they have to do with education or purer air or water or protection of our natural heritage—and since such problems generally require more than private management, the case can be made that our society has reached a point where the private versus public balance must be shifted in the direction of the latter. This is one of the main themes of Galbraith's *Affluent Society*.

At the same time, however, there is another current in our society that seems to cut across this apparent need for more governmental intervention. This second current involves a criticism of the increasing bigness, impersonality, standardization, and bureaucratization of our national life. In its extreme form, this criticism manifests itself in a thoroughgoing distrust of "the establishment." "The establishment" may be conceived to consist of any large, impersonal institution, whether the giant corporation, the huge labor union, the large university or—the biggest of all institutions in contemporary American life—the federal government. In a more moderate form, the criticism emerges as a desire for more decentralization in governmental action through increasing reliance on state and local governments and through more stress on voluntarism at the personal and community levels. In either case, there is evident a mood of disenchantment with the results achieveable by always turning to Washington for solving problems. There is a desire to return to a less managed, less conformist, more personal way of life.

The issues here are deep and difficult. Take, for example, an issue that is likely to become increasingly important in the affluent society: the financing of the arts. In a certain sense, the arts are the most private and personal products of our society. The artist must remain individual, human; he must be free to criticize the society in which he lives. All this is in accord with the mood of disenchantment with the bureaucracy that we have just mentioned. But how is art to be encouraged economically? Almost immediately, we begin to think in terms of foundation grants or state subsidies—reliance on the very mechanisms of the establishment that we are at pains to disavow.

It should not be thought that all this is new. What we are witnessing today is simply another chapter in a very long story that involves the relationship of the individual to the collective society of which he is a part. Indeed, in one sense, it is a less agonizing chapter than earlier ones that history has recorded. For the debate now can be carried on within a general context of wealth and prosperity, whereas, historically, it was often the economic survival of groups within the society that was at stake. At the same time, it is an intellectually fascinating debate and one of no little social importance. For the first time in history we are asked to decide how a massively rich society should use its riches. What kind of life should we attempt to create for ourselves and for our descendants?

Faced with such global questions, economics alone will not provide all the decisive answers. Hopefully, however, it will form an indispensable background for their intelligent discussion.

Suggestions for
further reading in economics

We have listed a number of readings after each chapter in this book, but some of you may also wish general guidance in pursuing the study of economics in the future. Probably the most important next step to take is the further study of the fundamentals of economic *analysis*. As you will have observed in the course of this book, economics has a systematic structure that underlies most of the conclusions economists draw about issues of public interest. To advance in the understanding of the field, one should proceed to master this basic structure.

In the case of *microeconomics*, there are a number of textbooks ranging from the elementary to the advanced that present the essentials of modern theory. A short list, proceeding roughly from less to greater difficulty, is: Peter C. Dooley, *Elementary Price Theory* (New York: Appleton-Century-Crofts, 1967); Robert Dorfman, *Prices and Markets* (Englewood Cliffs, N.J.: Prentice-Hall, Inc., 1967); Richard H. Leftwich, *The Price System and Resource Allocation*, 3rd ed. (New York: Holt, Rinehart and Winston, 1966); Kenneth E. Boulding, *Economic Analysis*, 3rd ed. (New York: Harper & Row, 1955), Parts I, III.

In the case of *macroeconomic* analysis, there is the excellent short treatment we have referred to several times: Charles L. Schultze, *National Income Analysis*, 2nd ed. (Englewood Cliffs, N.J.: Prentice-Hall, Inc., 1967). Two more extensive treatments at the intermediate level are Martin Bailey, *National Income and the Price Level* (New York: McGraw-Hill, Inc., 1962) and Maurice W. Lee, *Macroeconomics: Fluctuations, Growth, and Stability*, 3rd ed. (Homewood, Ill.: Richard D. Irwin, Inc., 1963). In the specific area of monetary theory, an intermediate text is Lester Chandler, *The Economics of Money and Banking*, 3rd ed. (New York: Harper & Row, 1959). In international trade theory, there is the clear but not easy treatment of Richard E. Caves, *Trade and Economic Structure* (Cambridge: Harvard University Press, 1960).

The theory of economic growth has not yet reached the point where it can be summarized in any standard and easily accessible way. For the serious reader (who also has a taste for some mathematics), there is a general summary of growth theories in John Hicks, *Capital and Growth* (Oxford: Oxford University Press, 1965), and also in the long review article by Hahn and Matthews, "The Theory of Economic Growth: A Survey," in the *Economic Journal*, December, 1964.

The above suggestions have to do with economic theory only; the interested student will also want to acquaint himself more extensively with some of the outstanding problems of our present-day economy. Among the more provocative books are: John Kenneth Galbraith, *The New Industrial State* (Boston: Houghton Mifflin Co., 1967) and also by Galbraith, *The Affluent Society* (Boston: Houghton Mifflin Co., 1958); Milton Friedman, *Capitalism and Freedom* (Chicago: Chicago University Press, 1962); Michael Harrington, *The Other America* (New York: The Macmillan Company, 1962); Joseph A. Schumpeter, *Capitalism, Socialism, and Democracy*, 3rd ed. (New York: Harper & Row, 1950) especially Part II: "Can Capitalism Survive?"; Gunnar Myrdal, *The Challenge to Affluence* (New York: Pantheon Books, 1963); and Henry C. Wallich, *The Cost of Freedom* (New York: Harper & Row, 1960).

Finally, the interested student will want to become acquainted with some of the professional journals which carry forward the work of the practicing economists of the United States and other countries on a current basis. Among the more important journals are: *The American Economic Review, The Quarterly Journal of Economics, The Economic Journal, The Review of Economics and Statistics, Economica, Econometrica, The Journal of Economic History,* and *The Journal of Political Economy.*

INDEX

Index

A

Advertising, 73-74, 119
Affluence, problems of, 265-80
  growth of:
    and "poverty," 269-75
    and the quality of life, 275-77
  issues, 266
  maintaining high rate of growth, 267-69
  the State, the private individual, and the public interest, 278-80
Affluent Society (Galbraith), 273, 279
AFL-CIO, 76
Africa, 16, 17
  annual per capita output, 246, 247
  economic growth process, 243, 244
  population problem, 253, 255
Agency for International Development (AID), 257, 258

Aggregate demand:
  and economic growth, 220
  and GNP (national income), 105, 111-13, 115, 118, 119-23, 126-30
  fiscal policy and, 134-49, 153, 162
  monetary policy and, 167, 181
  government expenditures and, 134ff.
  and inflation, 189-97
  and international trade, 208-10, 211, 213
  Keynes on role of, 94, 95-96
Aggregate economic systems analysis, 87-97, 113, 118-30, 129-30 (see *also* Macroeconomics; Microeconomics; specific subjects, e.g., Fiscal policy; Gross national product; Monetary policy)
  suggested reading, 281
Agriculture; agricultural production, 60-65 (see *also* Farmers; Food production)

B

G

H

I

M

O

P

S

T

U

Underdeveloped countries, 243-62 (see also specific countries)
  agricultural pressures, 256
  applying Western technology, 248-49, 261
  capital accumulation, 250-51, 261
  economic growth process and, 243-62
  historical vs. modern development, 245-48
  inflation and, 186, 188
  meaning of economic underdevelopment, 244-45
  population problem, 252-57, 261
  role of foreign aid, 257-60, 261
  unemployment problem, 256-57
Underemployment (undercapacity) production, 15, 34, 129-30, 145, 149
Uneducated, the. See Education and the educated
Unemployment. See Employment-unemployment
Unemployment equilibrium, 95, 129-30
Unemployment in the United Kingdom (chart), 90
Unemployment in the United States, per cent of the labor force, 1900-1965 (chart), 89
Unemployment problem (chart), 15
Unions. See Labor
United Kingdom (see also Great Britain and the British)
  annual per capita income, 247
  unemployment, 89, 91
United States, 40
  agriculture, 60-65
  antitrust legislation, 79-80
  and corporations, 68-69, 70-75, 79-82
  depressions and panics in, 4-7, 17, 89 (see also Great Depression)
  fiscal policy and national debt, 151-63
  foreign aid programs, 212, 213, 257-60, 261-62
  GNP of, 56, 57, 65, 67, 102-15, 254
  growth of government, 54-65, 67
    causes, 58-60
    example of, 60-65

United States (Cont.)
  expansion of expenditures, 54-58, 65, 67
  high rate of economic growth (problems of affluence), 265-80
  inflation (1955-65), 186-97
  and international trade, 199-213
    balance of payments difficulties, 210-12, 213
  Keynes and "new economics" and, 96-97, 98
  and labor unions, 57, 75-78, 79-82
  and market economy, 19, 20
  and mixed economy, 54-65, 67-82
    private sector, 67-82
    public sector, 54-65
  modern economic growth, 220-40
    annual per capita output, 247, 254
    capital accumulation, 234-36, 240
    growth trends, 224-34, 239
    history of, 221
    population growth, 234ff., 239
    technological progress, 236-39, 240
    urbanization, 225, 226
  monetary policy and money, 166-82
    and inflation, 194-97
  "poverty" and poverty in, 269-75
  poverty in, 6-7, 17 (see also Poverty)
  and public interest, 79-82
  rate of economic growth, compared to Soviet, 46, 48
U. S. balance of payments, 1947-1965 (chart), 211
U. S. gross national product, 1910-1965 (chart), 102
United States' population, 1800-1966 (chart), 225
U. S. Steel, 71
Universities. See Higher education
Upward-sloping supply curve, 28-29
Urbanization, 225-26 (see also Cities)

V

Value added method of calculating GNP, 109, 110, 114